Recovery Sucks
An Extraordinarily Imperfect Journey of Recovery

Amy Hart

NEWMAN SPRINGS PUBLISHING
320 Broad Street
Red Bank, NJ 07701

First originally published by Newman Springs Publishing 2023

ISBN 979-8-88763-490-6 (Paperback)
ISBN 979-8-88763-491-3 (Digital)

Printed in the United States of America

This book is dedicated to Jenny and Donna, whose therapeutic help saved my life from misery. Jenny taught me to be a good mother to myself and my children. Donna helped me take it to a professional level. Jenny and Donna, your services changed the course of my life in a perfectly positive direction. I will be forever grateful.

Contents

Introduction ix

Homecoming Queen 1
How Being Crowned Homecoming Queen Ruined My
    Life Then Set Me Free 3
The Logistics 6
Adults Are Dumb 9
My Inner Philosopher Surfacing 11
Truth Teller 13
Researcher 17
My People 22
My Brother 26
My Sister 28
My Uncles 31
My Mom 33
My Dad 38
My Stepdad 43
My Journey through Shame 48
Weight Management 53
Keeping Up Appearances 61
My Divorce 67
Divorce—It's Not the Answer You Think It Is 70
Jeff 79
I Can't Follow a Recipe to Save My Life 80
Motorcycles 82
Emotional Abuse 83
Who's the Manipulator? 86
Deconstruction 89

Conscious Recovery 92
How I Became a Mediator..94
Mediation 96
High-Conflict People 102
Island of Misfits 104
I Was in My Addiction 108
Steve...111
I'm an Alcoholic...121
Alcoholics...128
Healthy People (Drinking or Nondrinking) 131
Alcoholics Not in Recovery (Drinking or Nondrinking)...............133
Alcoholics in Recovery (Drinking or Nondrinking) 135
Were You Raised by Wolves?..137
Addiction 140
Daily Poisoning..143
Single and Not Looking 147
Fucking Narcissism 149
Heavy..153
My Garage 156
The Beginning of the Transformation...161
Resentment 165
Who's to Blame?...171
Therapy Was a Means to Align My Self-Concept with Reality....173
Healthy Relationships 174
Unconditional Love—The Holy Grail..177
I Must Be a Mermaid 181
Problem-Solving Team 187
Therapy...189
Therapy and Re-parenting..192
Doing Therapy Right 195
What You Allow Is What Will Continue 197
Admitting That I Don't Have My Shit Together Even
        Though It Looks Like I Do 199
Getting My Shit Together..204
What Is Recovery?...206
Recovery from My Perspective..209

My Recovery 212
The Biology and Reality of Recovery..216
The Grief Process 220
Search and Rescue 225
Step 1: I Admitted I Had a Problem 227
Steps 2 and 3: I Surrendered...239
Live Your Life on Purpose 244
Steps 4 through 12 247
I Am God—God Is Me 250

Introduction

Recovery is not restricted only to addicts and alcoholics. Often, we think of addicts and alcoholics as the people with "the real problems." These are the people who have a problem with substances. If addicts and alcoholics would just get treatment and recover, their life would be just fine. If they would just get some control over these substances, they wouldn't have all the problems they have.

This is absolutely not true. First, we *all* have some level of addiction to something. In fact, most of us have what we call co-addictions in addition to our addictions. For instance, I'm addicted to unhealthy relationships with men, and I'm addicted to alcohol to numb the pain of the unhealthy relationships.

Something often overlooked is that people can be addicted to healthy and life-sustaining activities too, such as exercise, food, and sex. We cannot separate alcoholics and addicts into "them" and "us." We are all addicts struggling to manage our drug of choice.

Second, recovery is not about "getting control over" something. In fact, it is exactly the opposite. It is letting go of the illusion of control. Recovery is about acceptance and balance and aligning with a higher purpose. It is about growing up and taking responsibility for the choices you have made as an adult, even if those choices (especially if those choices) didn't turn out like you hoped.

Thirdly, we all have problems. Not all problems are solved by quitting an addiction. Not all problems are solved by living a healthy, balanced life. Life is full of problems, and recovery is about becoming a good problem solver.

Hi, my name is Amy, and I am an alcoholic. I'm also an overeater, a codependent, an adult child of an alcoholic, and I'm cursed with loving addicts and alcoholics that refuse to take responsibility in relationships. There are recovery groups for all of my "defects of character."

Overeaters Anonymous (OA) welcomes all that want to stop eating compulsively. There's Co-dependents Anonymous (CoDA), where the only requirement for membership is the desire for healthy and loving relationships. Adult Children of Alcoholics (ACOA or ACA) is where men and women meet to share their common experiences of growing up in dysfunctional homes where neglect, abuse, and trauma infected us. There's Al-Anon for those of us that love and worry about the people in our lives with drinking problems.

Of course, there is Alcoholics Anonymous (AA), where I am not welcome. AA welcomes those with a desire to stop drinking. The very first step is to admit that you are powerless over alcohol. I can't take this first step. I don't believe it to be true. I do believe I am powerless over the effect alcohol has on my body and mind, but I don't believe I am powerless over alcohol. I don't want to stop drinking.

I'm also addicted to Mexican food, hot sauce, jalapeños, and coffee. In the past, I was addicted to cigarettes and low self-esteem. There are no recovery groups for these addictions. These are the addictions I have to learn to manage on my own without a support group.

I do believe, however, that I am powerless over the laws of the universe. The universe will carry on however it carries on—with or without me. We live on a blue planet that circles a ball of fire next to a moon that moves the sea. Do you believe you understand how it all works? Nah. No one does. It's ludicrous to even consider that there is any one person that understands it all, including "God."

The most important part of twelve-step recovery groups is admitting you are powerless. This is the first step in any twelve-step program. Powerless over what, though? Some people are powerless over alcohol. I am not one of those types of alcoholics. I am, however, powerless over the laws of the universe.

Knowledge is power. However, knowing the laws of the universe does not give me power over them. Knowing and understanding the laws of the universe allows me to work effectively within the confines of those laws.

The greatest gift that is born from admitting you are powerless is access to humility. Access to an understanding that you are not in control of that which you have an illusion of control. Access to understanding that which is in your control and that which is not.

God, grant me the serenity to accept the things I cannot change, the courage to change the things I can, and the wisdom to know the difference.

I am a huge fan of twelve-step programs. Twelve-step programs were there for me when I was at rock bottom. My rock bottom was the moment I realized I could not control the man that I thought was the love of my life. My rock bottom was when I had nowhere to go except to admit that I was powerless over his choices. My rock bottom was when I pursued "recovery" consciously and with the intent to never feel rock bottom again.

There is a reason AA and all its subsidiary twelve-step groups are the largest, most successful worldwide organization. These groups have no formal leadership and no marketing department. They are required to be self-sustaining and are not permitted to accept outside contributions. Their public relations policy is "based on attraction rather than promotion." "Anonymity is the spiritual foundation" of these traditional groups, "ever reminding us to place principles before personalities." Twelve-step programs "work if you work it and you are worth it."

I have never experienced any hard drugs. I have always been terrified of cocaine, heroin, and LSD. I never understood why I was so terrified of these drugs when my peers were not. I've determined that, deep down, I knew I would inadvertently kill myself.

Today, I am prideful that I heeded Nancy Reagan's "say no to drugs" campaign. Although I really should credit my fear more than that slogan. Also, credit goes to those who died to prove my fear accurate. I am talking about the lives of John Belushi, Chris Farley, and my heartthrob, River Phoenix (less than a year older than me). These deaths reinforced my conviction that accidental overdose would be too easy.

There was a stirring deep inside me that knew just how self-destructive I could be. I believe this is where perfectionism saved me.

Perfectionism is one of the most common addictions in our culture today, from my cursory measure.

My perfect persona allowed my self-destructiveness to come out in less deadly ways. Compulsive eating, compulsive drinking, and compulsively engaging in unhealthy relationships are my heaviest hitters. Overthinking, overanalyzing, and overdoing are my backup hitters.

Over the course of my life, I have gone through periods of heavy drinking, usually when the workload was heavy. The heavy drinking leads to overeating. The weight gain leads to less exercise, which then leads to more weight gain. I've spent the last twenty years in therapy analyzing this pattern.

One of the first questions I entered individual therapy to resolve was "Why does my weight fluctuate by sixty pounds? Why not five or ten pounds? Why, when I'm gaining weight, do I not resolve it when the problem is smaller? Why do I wait for the problem to be sixty pounds?" Twenty years later, I have the answer. Which is why I am writing this book.

I began this book years ago when I lost all the weight for the fifth and final time. However, I have never gone back to see what I wrote. My guess is it was all bullshit. I was thinking I had "it all fig-ured out" because I had lost the weight for the fifth and final time. Fast-forward to today and the evidence shows that I didn't have any-thing figured out. I'm sixty pounds overweight as I write this, with a full belly of a Chipotle Mexican Grill burrito.

Today, I can look back and assess what I did well and what went wrong. I have gone through periods in my life where I took excellent care of myself. I would lose the weight and get to a place of satis-faction with my health and fitness. Then, slowly, I would fall back into compulsive drinking, eating, and toughing out an unhealthy relationship. The weight would come back on, which is where I find myself today. Same pattern, same results.

I am sixty pounds heavier than I have been for the last six years. This is the sixth time in my life that I have been this heavy. The sixth time! It will be the seventh time that I get my weight back down to a healthy weight around 135. At forty-nine years old, I'm running out of years to live in balance.

Something I've learned is to look at patterns, not people. The pattern has become entirely evident. It's not me. There is nothing wrong with me. The pattern is to blame. I've got to change the pattern if I want to change the result. This time, I'm doing things differently.

First, I am not forcibly requiring myself into the daily practices required to maintain a healthy weight. Right now, my workload is heavy with assembling this book, managing a new career, and providing my children with the attention they need during COVID-19. Once I get these words out of my body and into this book, my self-image will be in greater alignment with the healthy image I desire. I'm cutting myself some slack and allowing myself to be overweight without the intense insistence that I lose the weight now.

Maintaining a healthy weight requires a level of discipline that I know I possess. I've done it before, and I will do it again.

Discipline is not to be confused with willpower. Discipline is about organizing your life in such a way that supports healthy weight management without the power struggle over your drug or drugs of choice. Considering my drugs of choice are food, alcohol, and unhealthy relationships, what I'm doing differently is not engaging in the power struggle.

The other thing I am doing differently is that I have recovered completely from my addiction to unhealthy relationships. I do not have the chaos in my life that an unhealthy relationship brings. The stress and pressure have been entirely eliminated from my life. It's almost like living life in a vacuum—living in an environment void of the context by which it was established, becoming comfortable with the absence of something that has always been present. Therefore, the part of the pattern I'm changing is the "toughing out an unhealthy relationship."

I'm not in a relationship, and I'm not pursuing one. I have always preferred being in a relationship to being alone. So much so, I would heavily pursue an unhealthy relationship rather than remain alone. An unhealthy relationship was better than no relationship. This, I would eventually realize, is the root of my addiction to unhealthy relationships.

You know how you sometimes drink too much, and the next morning, you say "I'm never drinking again"? You know, how that overdose of a substance catalyzes abstinence from that substance, at least for a while? Well, that happened to me with unhealthy relationships. I overdosed and now I'm abstaining.

I've finally realized that if I'm going to be alone, I prefer to be by myself than alone in a relationship. It took me my entire adult life to develop this genuine preference of being alone by myself. I have done the work of recovery, and I consider myself recovered from my addiction to unhealthy relationships. My preference to be alone by myself is indicated by my lack of desire to pursue my addiction.

I do not have to convince myself or try very hard. I'm just not interested. I'm not interested in an unhealthy relationship, and I'm definitely not interested in the chaos an unhealthy relationship brings to a family. I'm satisfied and I'm not in pursuit of the thing I am addicted to. I feel recovered because I have organized my life in such a way that I am not in a power struggle with my drug of choice.

Being alone by myself is extraordinarily lonely. This feeling of profound loneliness was the feeling I was suppressing with bad relationships, alcohol, and food. And it worked too. That feeling of profound loneliness was neutralized with chaos and interminable hustling for my worthiness. I was so busy attending to and trying to organize chaos that I had no time to feel lonely.

The thing about recovering from unhealthy stuff is that the rewards are built in. Not feeling miserable is the reward. "Feeling good" has not been reason enough for me to endure recovery, but not feeling miserable has given me plenty of reasons. Removing the things from my life that were injecting me with misery brought the measureless reward of feeling "not miserable."

I will never be fully recovered from all my addictions. The best I can hope is that my life continues heading in the right direction. With each day that my life brings me, I learn, grow, and contribute. I will always have my addictions. This is a truth-telling exercise about how I learned to snuggle up to my addictions rather than fight them. It begins with recovery (a.k.a. growing up).

The purpose of this book is to give me the forum that I can't find in my everyday life. I can't find a recovery group for alcoholics that don't have a desire to stop drinking. I don't work with a group of people who understand me. My clients come to me to be understood, not to understand me. I don't have a family that understands me outside of the context of their fucked-up functioning. I don't have a forum to feel truly heard and understood. This is why I write to you.

I want to connect with like-minded people. I have a pragmatic, no-nonsense approach to life. I have a good sense of humor and a great attitude. I stand for connection. This book is my reach for connection. This book is me stepping into the arena in a meaningful way by sharing who I am with you.

I want to share what I believe to be a common experience. I believe I have lived a "normal" life. I had an awful childhood, but it balanced out with an exceptional adulthood. I don't think my experience is all that unique from yours when you obscure the details. If I had to do it over again, I wouldn't change a thing. That's how I know I am in recovery and recovering well.

I will always be in recovery, and I am proud of that accomplishment. I accept my "defects of character," and I hope to encourage you to accept yours too. "Defects of character" are what recovery groups call our "shortcomings," such as our addictions. I have learned to live a productive life despite my shortcomings. I have learned to allow my defects of character to exist without my needing to extinguish them.

Everyone needs recovery, not just those of us that actively admit that we have addictions. Recovery is an instrumental period of growth in an adult's life. It is necessary in order to be a healthy, well-adjusted adult.

Not everyone moves easily through this period of growth. Many people resist and deny its necessity. Many people never acknowledge recovery as a natural growth milestone. This is entirely understandable. Recovery sucks.

Homecoming Queen

Never in a million years did I think I would be crowned homecoming queen. It was the start to my senior year of high school. Almost done. Almost there. My life was going to start as soon as high school was over.

I had been a cheerleader every year in high school. When the high schoolers came to the middle school to teach us the cheer for tryouts, I knew I had found my calling. Loud? I can be loud. Louder? No problem.

To this day, thirty-six years later, I still remember that cheer and most of the moves. I am sure if I really tried, I could remember the cheer in its entirety. That is how much I practiced before tryouts. Enough to never forget it and more than enough to not make a mistake.

This must have been the start to my personal constitution that anything worth doing is worth overdoing. This is a blessing and a curse. It makes projects take way longer and use way more energy than they need to. Yet the results produced are extraordinary. I can't underdo anything. It's not in my constitution. "Good enough" is not an achievement; it is a starting point.

Apparently, I was popular enough to be on the homecoming court. This came as a surprise to me given that all the "popular girls" were on the homecoming court. Wait. You mean I'm one of them? Does not compute.

You know that message you get on your computer when there has been a "fatal error"? You know how your stomach sinks and you wished you'd backed everything up? You know how crushing and deflating and infuriating that message is? That is how I felt.

Of course, at the time, I didn't know that's how I felt. I can only tell this truth in retrospect. I did not have the emotional intelligence back then that I have today. The one truth I can tell you is that everything that followed from that moment only makes sense when you hear the entire truth.

To this day, I wonder if the system was rigged. I have had enough experience in life, which tells me it is entirely possible that it could have been rigged. But what was to be gained by rigging the system? It would make sense if I wanted to win and rigged the system so I could win, but it doesn't make any sense that advisors would rig the system. I guess this probably speaks to my distrust of authority.

Although I was crowned, I still didn't belong. This may not make sense to you because, as far as appearances go, I fit the image perfectly: blond, big tits, head cheerleader, popular with the boys, and loud. I was really loud, both vocally and metaphorically.

I felt like it was a scene from the movie *Carrie*, like the crowning was a joke to make a mockery of me. My suspicion was high, and reality was low. Looking back, the crown sent me into a personal crisis that no one understood. I wouldn't understand until at least fifteen years later.

How Being Crowned Homecoming Queen Ruined My Life Then Set Me Free

The term *cognitive dissonance* refers to the confusion that you experience when you have two competing concepts in your thoughts. For instance, "I hate camping" and "I've agreed to go camping." Logic and reasoning would say that if you hate camping, you wouldn't go camping. I'm going to use this extremely real dissonant concept for me to explain the concept of cognitive dissonance.

Our brains don't like cognitive dissonance. Our brains like cognitive consonance, which is congruency between our thoughts. When there is dissonance in our thoughts or behaviors, a feeling of discomfort is created by our brains. That discomfort is relieved when the dissonance is resolved. Our brains have all kinds of mechanisms by which they resolve cognitive dissonance, not all of which are helpful.

This is not intended as a lesson in cognitive dissonance. It is a simplified explanation of what happens psychologically for us when actual reality and the reality we construct in our heads bump up against each other. This camping example is an easy one.

I truly hate camping. I don't understand why people work so hard to provide a home and the comforts of home for themselves and then purposefully use vacation time to pretend they are homeless and sleep on the hard ground, exposed to insects and wildlife and the elements. It is even more dissonant when people try to bring the comforts of home to the campsite. That's a lot of work when you could just stay home and relax instead of rebuilding your home somewhere else temporarily and using vacation time to do it.

Cognitive dissonance is something our brains don't like, so our brains have all kinds of tactics to reduce cognitive dissonance. Self-justification is born of cognitive dissonance. We use self-justification to convince ourselves of one concept or the other. That way, the uncomfortable feeling of dissonance is reduced.

If I've agreed to go camping, I promise you there is a *very* good reason that has convinced me to brave the elements and pretend I'm homeless. This *very* good reason would be congruent with my other values, such as it is a desirable activity for someone important to me or a level of amenities will be provided so that I don't feel the pain of being homeless when I am not. Otherwise, I side with the concept of "I hate camping" and say no to every opportunity where camping is involved. Either way, the cognitive dissonance is resolved, and I am at peace with the camping issue.

A more serious version of cognitive dissonance occurs when our self-concept bumps up against data that proves our self-concept wrong. For instance, my self-concept is that I believe cheating is wrong, and I will never cheat. When I am offered an opportunity to cheat, most of the time, I decline. For instance, a cashier might give me too much change back. Most of the time, I would correct the error and return the excess change. However, there have been times when I have not done so.

This point is to illustrate how "real data" bumps up against "self-concept." I'm not trying to open a debate about whether or not I should return excess change or whether this example is technically "cheating" or not. My self-concept is that I am an honest, kind, and generous person. Knowingly keeping excess change is "data" that bumps up against my self-concept. An honest, kind, and generous person would return the excess change with grace.

If there is ever a time that I don't return the excess change, it causes somewhat of a personal crisis. Maybe I didn't notice the excess change until I got home, or the next time, I spent cash and wondered where that $10 came from when I thought I only had $1. Should I drive back to the store and return the change before they close the tills for the night? Or maybe I noticed, but the cashier irritated me, so I didn't mention her mistake since it was in my favor. Is this something an honest, kind, and generous person would do? Cognitive dissonance creates a personal crisis when it bumps up against self-concept.

When I was crowned homecoming queen, the cognitive dissonance I experienced caused a severe personal crisis. The data that I was well-liked bumped up against a self-concept of not deserving the honor. It bumped up against a self-concept of "I'm not one of them." My self-concept of "I don't belong up here, and I certainly won't be crowned" bumped up against my name being called over the echoing stadium speakers and a crown being placed on my head.

"Severe personal crisis" is not an understatement. Severe crisis was exactly what my body was experiencing. In an effort to reduce the cognitive dissonance, return my crisis-induced state to an equilibrium balanced with my negative self-concept, I was compelled to disclose the eight years of sexual abuse that was happening at home.

The Logistics

I disclosed the abuse to a school counselor. I hadn't told anyone about the abuse in the preceding eight years because I didn't know there was anything to tell. Additionally, I didn't know who to tell. The sexual abuse was so disorienting and confusing that I didn't know if it was good or bad or right or wrong.

I always wondered if what I was experiencing as a young girl was what every girl experienced. I wondered if this was how we were "supposed to be taught" the sexual stuff. That's what he told me, so why would I question it?

I wondered if my mom knew about it. If she knew about it and allowed it to happen, then it must be okay. If she didn't know about it, I knew I wasn't supposed to tell her. He made sure I knew that much, that this was our secret because I was so beautiful and special and "your mother wouldn't understand."

Understand what? I don't understand! What is happening? I don't like this! This is not my secret. This is not my doing. How is this our secret? No one understands. This doesn't make any sense. My brain can't handle this!

When a brain develops from the age of nine to seventeen with this type of stress induced by cognitive dissonance, shit gets a little wonky. Neuroscientists say "What fires together, wires together." This level of confusion branded my self-proclaimed "researcher" status. I obsessively researched sexual abuse until I discovered the answer, that sexual abuse is not a "normal" part of growing up for every girl.

Finally, by the time I was seventeen, I knew that what I was experiencing was not "right." I knew that I was keeping a secret that was harmful to me and the wrongdoer. I knew that I didn't want to be a part of this secret anymore. I didn't want to suffer any more than I already had. That was all I knew. The evidence that I made the choice to disclose the secret is proof of my not wanting to hold the secret by myself anymore.

I certainly didn't know anything about "mandatory reporting." I learned very quickly. As soon as I told the school counselor, these head-spinning words came out of her mouth: "I have to tell your mother and report this to the authorities."

The next thing I knew, the counselor told my mother, and we were being visited by Child Protective Services. Talk about cognitive dissonance being resolved. This was serious. I had no idea. This secret was my "normal." Why was such evasive action being taken? I guess someone has done something wrong. Who? More cognitive dissonance.

I really don't remember much of the details of Child Protective Services (CPS). I remember very minimal contact with CPS. I remember having to go to a "victims" group while my mom and stepdad had to go to a "perpetrators" group. The three of us drove together to these groups. I have no idea where my brother and sister were during this time. My parents dropped me off at my group then went to their group. They picked me up after, and we continued with life as though nothing out of the ordinary had happened.

I remember driving myself to these group meetings at some point. I don't recall how many weeks we had to go, but it was weeks, not months. Talk about bureaucratic protocol bullshit. We did what was required of us and then continued on with our lives as though nothing had happened. Undoubtedly, this was where I developed my perfection for keeping up appearances. Apparently, someone did something "wrong enough" that we were all required to endure this punishment, but who and what? More cognitive dissonance.

The "authorities" told us what we needed to do, and we did it. We checked the boxes and moved on. We had to do some kind of minimum for the State's ass to be covered, and that was it. I believe this was where the seed was planted in me regarding my belief that "the legal system is not designed to support family issues."

What didn't help matters was that my stepfather was a very successful attorney and powerful personality. There was a lot at stake for him to keep this under wraps, and he knew how to do it. Never mind what was best for me or the other children in our family. The only people in our family that mattered were the adults. Let's just all pretend that there are no problems here.

So our family kept living together to keep up appearances as though nothing was wrong. We were so convincing that even I was convinced. I finished the first semester of high school at an alternative school that allowed me to work from home instead of attending school. For whatever reason, I couldn't show my face in school. This was the first time I remember using food for pain relief.

I would drive myself somewhere to study and eat delicious food. I love food so much. I also remember procrastinating completing work by playing Nintendo. I didn't like this feeling of avoiding responsibility, but I loved the feeling of accomplishment from a game well played. I was grooving my path to addiction.

The beginning of my addictive personality began kicking into high gear. There were no illegal drugs, but there were drugs I could choose easily and that were extremely accessible, including my boyfriend at the time. Matt was the sacrificial lamb that I offered to my addiction god.

To this day, I love Matt more than anyone that has come after him, which is why I shoved him away at nineteen years old. I knew I was poison and needed to find my own way. I was going to poison our lives together. I truly wonder about that. I did that to save him. Martyrdom is a symptom of addiction.

Adults Are Dumb

I returned to school at the beginning of the second semester of my senior year. In those three months, I tried to pull myself together. I got a job as a hostess at a local restaurant. I went back to school with a renewed vigor to maintain good grades and graduate with the people I had spent the last four to seven years with. I was convinced that I was going to be okay. I just needed to pretend nothing was wrong, and everything was going to be okay.

When I returned to school, I returned to a lot of questions and a lot of rumors. What broke my heart was the rumors started by parents—rumors started by parents and perpetuated by kids. I didn't care that kids were talking shit. I cared that the parents were talking shit. Another mark against "authority." Parents suck.

The rumors I remember were these:

1. "She's in rehab for cocaine."
2. "She is pregnant."
3. "She is goat herding in Montana."

Obviously, these rumors could not be further from the truth. Goat herding in Montana? I'm sure some drunk parent was joking around when that one came up. That parents' kid either overheard that stupidity or that stupidity was spoken directly to the kid, who then brought it to Torrey Pines High School. TPHS—oh yes, we are the best!

This was another cognitive dissonance issue where my self-image bumped up against the image others had of me. I took a lot of pride in "saying no to drugs" (although drugs were not offered to me nearly as much as Nancy Reagan told me they would). I took a lot of pride in being a "good girl" and being responsible and getting good grades. To have all that taken away from me because I left school to hide incest from their knowledge was a sucker punch I didn't expect.

Who knows? Generally, people need a way to justify their dissonance when they see "the girl who has it all" leave school when she is crowned homecoming queen. It makes no sense to people who have always wanted some kind of notoriety. What else would justify her parents allowing her to leave school? A drug addiction would justify leaving school temporarily. A pregnancy also would. Goat herding in Montana? That just makes no sense.

My Inner Philosopher
Surfacing

It may seem ludicrous that I didn't know if the sexual abuse was right or wrong. Adult brains seem to draw a clear distinction that sexual activity between an adult and a nine-year-old is wrong. To explain my confusion, perhaps you have to remember what you "knew" at nine years old.

At nine years old, I ate my SpaghettiOs because my mother fed them to me. I went to school because my mother told me to. I played in the street because my mother told me to "go outside and play," and we lived in a cul-de-sac. Bottom line: we do what our parents tell us to do. We don't "know" anything at nine years old, especially the complexity of relationships and sex.

Is sexual abuse right or wrong? The complexity of this answer might surprise you. To be honest, I don't think there is a universally "correct" answer that categorizes sexual abuse as "right" or "wrong."

This is my inner philosopher coming out. I majored in neuro-science at the University of California at San Diego until I found out I could graduate sooner with a general biology degree. Most of my classes were focused on neuroscience, and I realized, while the subject fascinated me, I didn't want to nerd out on a micro science. I wanted to graduate sooner than later and get on with my life.

Little did I know that I would not work in a field that exercised my science degree. However, my degree in science provided the foundation for the PhD in life that I have self-accredited. My minor in philosophy and minor in exercise physiology also contributed credits to my self-accredited PhD in life program. I am fascinated by the science behind how our bodies and minds work.

As far as the sexual abuse, I will let you decide if it was right or wrong. You will have to read to the end to understand why I take an ambivalent position on this. In most cases, I would say sexual abuse is wrong. In my case, I would say it was what saved my life.

Truth Teller

I am not a storyteller. I am a truth teller. This does not make me very popular in my relationships. In my profession, it is the most difficult part of my job: telling people what they don't want to hear and convincing them to hear it.

My sister came over the other day. She's really my stepsister. We weren't raised together, but right now, we have the same set of parents. As adults, we have become friends, and I am always happy to expand my family.

As she was leaving, she said, "Thanks a lot. I thought my life was fine until I came over here. Now I have a problem I didn't know I had."

Denial can be a powerful force in our lives.

What she and I talked about was wedding invites. People get really weird about invitations. Whether it be a wedding, a funeral, a party, a barbecue, or whatever, there are some people who get personally offended if they have not been invited to something they wanted to be invited to. Some still get personally offended even if they didn't want to be invited anyway.

People become very judgy about invites. I recall one friend being upset that she never got invited to her neighbor's. "They always have a ton of cars in their driveway, and I can hear them having a good time!" She was being quite judgy that these people were partying, and she was taking it personally that she wasn't invited.

This is where keeping an open mind can be helpful. Instead of assuming that the neighbors are partying and don't want to party with you, you are entirely capable of assuming something else. If you are going to assume anything without obtaining the data, why would you assume they don't want to party with you?

Maybe they have a large family and host a lot of obligatory family gatherings. Maybe they are hosting a specific group meeting such as a book club or recovery group or divorce group. Maybe they are not partying at all. Maybe they are hosting an evangelical cult meeting.

Judging is a way that we separate ourselves and keep our distance from others. It is easier to judge than it is to connect and understand. Understanding requires connection, and connection requires subjecting yourself to criticism and judgment. In a word, connection requires vulnerability.

Life is about connection, and in so many ways, we prevent connection unwittingly. We protect ourselves from criticism and judgment by not reaching out. We justify our decision to not reach out with stories that we tell ourselves about the other people.

In a world where denial is your platform, truth telling can be very confusing. Some people like truth telling, but most people don't. Some people don't like that I can see through the image they project to the world. Some people are oblivious to my ability to do just that.

Some people are unable to see their own depth; therefore, they have no idea of the depth that I see. Some people are astounded at the depth I see, but they don't want what I see to be true. Not many people like hearing the truth. The truth means you've got work to do instead of blaming someone or something else.

You can only be as honest with other people as you are with yourself. Showing up to relationships in "good faith" is hard work. Good faith is a genuine interest to listen with an intent to understand. It is keeping an open mind. It is authentically sharing information openly and honestly. Good faith is a willingness to work together to find a satisfying resolution to issues in the relationship.

If information is not shared openly and honestly, I call this "lying by omission." It is important to provide relevant details and be transparent. If not, the truth is obscured by lack of information. For instance, someone is, technically, not lying if he didn't tell you he has a girlfriend. However, not sharing this information openly and honestly and then proceeding to make out with you is "lying by omission" in my book.

In order to be honest with me, this guy must be honest with himself. He must first admit to himself that the woman he is dating is his "girlfriend." (Watch out, boys. This is called commitment.) Then he also has to be willing to close the door to the possibility of a relationship with me if he is already in a relationship and values monogamy (more commitment). If he is unwilling to accept these two truths and then chooses to not share openly and honestly with me that he has a girlfriend prior to making out with me, that's on him. That is "lying by omission."

I can see it all clearly, and I'm not judgmental about it. I don't judge people; I truth-tell. It may feel like judgment, but it is not me doing the judging. It is the listener judging himself to the truth I tell.

Judging is what people do instead of looking at themselves. Judgment is easier to access than understanding. I don't judge people for lying or being dishonest. Instead, I use my critical awareness to keep a safe distance.

My critical awareness tells me that someone who has lied or been dishonest does not deserve my unearned trust. This person can only be as honest with me as he is with himself. If he can't be honest with himself about the truth, then I can't depend on this person to be open and honest with me about the truth. Truth is in the details.

I don't judge. I use critical thinking to understand. Critical thinking is a skill that is developed as we mature. As humans, we have some proclivity toward critical thinking, but most of our critical thinking is developed through exercising the parts of the brain that do the critical thinking. This part of the brain is called the prefrontal cortex. It is the home of "executive functioning" versus "primitive functioning."

When a signal comes into the body that tells our body to fight, flight, freeze, or faint, our executive functioning uses critical thinking to assess danger. In order to engage the executive functioning, time and practice are needed. Our fight, flight, freeze, or faint response happens neurochemically in our body in a fraction of a second. It then takes the body a few seconds to catch up to those neurochemical signals. It takes practice and a few more seconds to bring the prefrontal cortex online to assess danger and alter the response.

My critical awareness and critical thinking tell me that I can count on rigid, closed-minded thinking from judgmental people. This is why judgmental people feel like I am judging them. Rigid, closed-minded thinking does not allow for the possibility that I am not judging. I am truth-telling.

As a truth teller, I call it like I see it. You might not like the call, and that does not mean I'm wrong. It does not mean I'm right either. It just means I tell my truth, and my truth is mine.

Researcher

In writing this book, I reviewed years and years of journaling. I've cataloged it and coded it for my own purposes. My research is not a formalized process. It is my process.

As far back as I can remember, I have been research-focused. I have heard Brené Brown say that she is a "qualitative researcher," where she uses a "process of inquiry" conducting long interviews. Then she and her team "code them by hand." When I heard her say this recently, I realized, *Oh my god. That's what I do.*

I suspect I do not do it like she does it, but that is the best description I can give of my process. Writing this book has been an exercise in examining the qualitative research I have gathered over the last twenty-five years about myself. I reviewed years and years of my own growth through my journaling and various other sources of research. I have read hundreds of books and done a shit ton of therapy.

I have bookshelves full of four-inch binders filled with my research and journaling. I have bookshelves filled with hard copies of books and virtual bookshelves filled with audio and Kindle books. I literally have more than a million words in digital journaling. I have them cataloged in an Excel spreadsheet. I suspect my decade of hand-written journaling matches my decade of digital journaling.

My "research" was not a curriculum imposed upon me. I researched feelings, relationships, parenting, and science. I watched movies, read books, listened to songs, *and* took notes. My research was my effort to understand me.

I used the website www.helpyourselftherapy.com to understand my feelings. The site owner is "Tony." In my journaling or when discussing situations with people, I would say, "My friend Tony says..."

I started with his book *The Basics*. This gave me a basic translation of what my feelings were telling me. I would research specific feelings too.

There were times when I would feel unjustifiably embarrassed about something I said or didn't say. It has always been extraordinarily difficult for me to ask someone to remind me of their name, for instance. Or sometimes I would say something and feel like an outrageous idiot for saying it. Later, upon reflection, I would question that feeling of embarrassment and ask whether the situation warranted that level of embarrassment.

Why was forgetting someone's name—who was hardly an acquaintance, someone I've only met once—such an embarrassing error? Why was asking a question, which I honestly wanted the answer to, excruciatingly embarrassing? I would then pull up the trusty internet and research *embarrassment.*

I would often start with www.helpyourselftherapy.com and then branch my research off from there. When I researched *embarrassment* on Tony's site, this led to deeper research on shame and guilt, which eventually led to Brené Brown, and I continued to branch off from there. My own research, combined with a lot of therapy, changed my relationship with my feelings. I stumbled into therapy inadvertently.

My mother always told me I was going to need a lot of therapy to overcome all my problems. Don't you all wish you had a mother that would monitor your progress like that? While she ended up being right, even a broken clock is right twice a day.

Therapy is not useful if you don't know why you are there. My therapy journey began with my eldest daughter, Madison.

While Madison was actually my stepdaughter, it was not evident to those around me that she was not my biological child. Daughter or stepdaughter, there is no difference to me. I mean no disrespect to her mother by calling her my daughter. My contribution to the raising of Madison absolutely constitutes my right to call her my daughter from my perspective.

I was the primary care provider for Madison through all her formative years. I became a stay-at-home parent on the alternating weeks we had her. She attended our neighborhood school because

I was home to provide before- and after-school care, even on her mother's weeks.

I was the one who took her to the doctor when she was sick. When I told her pediatrician at four years old that no one could understand Madison's speech, even the doctor looked at me skeptically. When I said "not even her mother" can understand her, the doctor then gave me a referral to a speech therapist. I took her to the speech therapist. I paid for the speech therapist. I got her into the early learning program provided through our amazing school district to get her speech to an adequate level to be understood in kindergarten. When social issues began to arise in third grade, I was the person who searched for resources and attended with her.

After attending some therapy with Madison in an effort to understand what was happening in her world, I began to understand that I was part of the problem. While Madison did have some issues, how we, as parents, managed those issues was critical to Madison's well-being. I don't remember the specific question that prompted my question, but here was my question: "How do I do that?"

The therapist answered, "You start talking about what happened to you."

At that point, I asked her if she could be my therapist. This was where much of my journaling started in 2007. While I attended individual therapy, I also attended therapy with my daughter. I also began a short-term trauma group therapy and participated in couples counseling. Throughout the course of the last twenty years, I have had some form of therapy consistently two to three times per week. In the fall of 2019, that was the first time in twenty years that I didn't have regularly scheduled weekly therapy and group therapy. I wanted to fly solo and see how I would manage.

The conclusion of my therapy, along with the hard hit of isolation caused by the coronavirus, collided to open the gateway to this book. I have talked about writing a book for the last five years. I started it many times and got absolutely nowhere. I have written chapters in my head. I have written chapters to the men in my life. I've written novels of unstructured journaling.

Bringing structure to my writing was the greatest challenge I faced in this process. While I can write for others like nobody's business, I can't write for myself. I constantly obstruct my own process by saying, "No one is going to care. What I have to say doesn't matter to anyone."

I've convinced myself to test that theory rather than let it deter me from writing. I know that my friends and family reach to me for support. So maybe, just maybe, what I have to say does matter.

Because my research is not formalized education, I have a hard time legitimizing it. I have a difficult time feeling worthy of your attention. I struggle with staying focused and centered on myself for a constructive purpose.

That being said, one of my greatest qualities is that I try anyway. How will I ever know if what I have to say matters if I don't ever say it? How will I ever know if my story is a shared experience if I don't ever tell it?

I decided to try. Every time the voice in my head said "you don't matter," I would say back to myself, "I want to see for myself."

Some people call it bravery or courage. I call it effort. For whatever reason, effort comes naturally to me. In fact, I work tirelessly, relentlessly, and probably obsessively. This is how the motto "anything worth doing is worth overdoing" became associated with me.

It's not that I'm not afraid. I am. I am fearful that the critics will reinforce my fears with their criticism. I am afraid that the answer is "you don't matter" and that no one cares what I have to say. That doesn't deter me from stepping into the arena. Brené Brown said, "If you are not in the arena getting your ass kicked, then I don't care what you have to say."

I have never been afraid of being in the arena in my small life. I will share almost anything with almost anybody. I'm kind of a slut like that. I've been known to call myself an "emotional slut" in that I will spill exactly how I feel with a detailed explanation on why I feel that way. I'm not talking about opinions. I'm talking about a deep and meaningful discussion of actual feelings.

This book is a meaningful effort to step into the arena. To speak my truth in a forum heard by more than my immediate surroundings. To compile my research in a meaningful way and make comprehensive sense of it. It is to pass what I've learned on to you and to share myself in a way I have never done before.

As I've compiled my research and overcome my self-defeating thoughts, I've awarded myself a "lifetime achievement award." I am giving myself a PhD in life. I have given myself a master's degree in dealing with narcissistic and other difficult personalities. Somehow, even though it's self-administered, I feel like it legitimizes my research.

Just as Brené Brown did with her research, I looked for patterns and themes until I reached saturation. This is where the pattern or theme is represented across all the research. I did not do this in any formalized way. I only knew it was what I did once I heard Brené Brown say it's what she does. This is how I know that while my research was not a formalized curriculum, it shaped my perspective irrevocably.

After all my therapy and getting all my words out on paper in my journaling, I was able to reflect objectively on the data. I was able to review all my "research" and reach valuable conclusions. Sharing my research with you is sharing my deepest thoughts and feelings in a semipermanent way. Putting things in writing puts it into the universe in a way that can't be taken back. You can't unbake a cake.

My People

In this truth-telling exercise of writing this book, I will tell the truth about the people in my life. You may have the impulse to condemn or criticize my people. You also may have the impulse to think that I am showcasing bad behavior for the purpose of exposing the toxic secrets that have plagued my life and theirs. I humbly and sincerely ask that you reserve judgment until you have read everything.

While the truth may be messy, distasteful, and unappealing, this is my truth. This is my book about me. This is about my experience from birth in 1971 to the coronavirus in 2020. This book is not about my people. It is about me.

Ironically and paradoxically, this book is actually a thank-you letter to all my people. All of them. Without them, I would not have so much to write about. Without them, I might be living a mediocre life. Without them, I would not be me.

I believe my experience has both been unique and universal at the same time. I believe one of the God-given gifts that has either come from my life experience or has allowed me to tolerate my life experience is my ability to connect. I connect deeply with people, which is both a blessing and a curse.

You can only understand the curse part if you too are able to connect deeply. The curse part is about our culture's surface-level connection to each other and the universe. I am a five-page love letter in a world of Facebook posts and Snapchat messages. I'm a complex mystery in a world of highlight reels. I connect deeply with people, and not everyone likes it.

Connecting deeply means I understand more about you than you want me to. I see things you don't think people can see. This is fine as long as I only see your good stuff. As soon as I start poking around the parts you don't want me to see, things get uncomfortable. My people don't connect deeply. I'm looking for people who do.

Connection requires vulnerability. A person needs to be willing to be criticized and judged in order to obtain connection. Connection can occur easily and pleasantly if there is no judgment or criticism. Connection is more difficult when judgment and criticism are present.

This is where the curse comes in. I connect to you whether you want me to or not. Whether you are mean to me or not. Whether you judge, criticize, and condemn me or not. The curse part is that I don't find many people who connect in loving ways, and I don't get a choice about the connection I feel.

They say that people who have managed the level of trauma that I have managed have at least one adult that kept their compass pointed true north. I have struggled my entire life wondering who my one person was. It certainly has not been obvious to me. I often wonder if I didn't have one person and instead had lots of terrible people with "one-off good qualities" that contributed to my true north.

However, in writing this book, I discovered who that one person was. The answer is going to surprise you. I promise that.

In many ways, I was accurate that my people were not great people. In many ways, I did learn from their good qualities and rejected their bad qualities in building my "self." In many ways, I learned that there were things that were in my control and things that I could not control.

I have always wondered what it was about me that allowed me to keep a good attitude and be successful despite the odds. I remember feeling as though the odds were gravely stacked against me. I have truly wondered why I didn't end up dead in a ditch with a heroin needle in my arm.

I am not saying that for dramatic effect. I truly have wondered what was different about me that has allowed me to be moderately successful rather than dead in a ditch. The dissonance created between my trauma and my success has been a compelling force that prevented death by self-destruction.

I remember being fourteen and sitting on the floor of my bedroom, doing research about sexual abuse. Remember, back then we didn't have the internet. I had library books and *Seventeen* magazine. I had public service announcements, after-school specials, and pamphlets handed out at school. Two pieces of data drove my life's research.

First, sexual abuse is wrong. I learned this in an after-school special called "Something Special About Amy." Crazy, right? My name was in the title, and it was about sexual abuse not being a universal experience but a "special" experience.

In a world full of confusing information, this information piqued my curiosity. If it's wrong and it's happening, how do I make sense of my world? When I was a child and learning about my world, how was I to manage this information? Is "special" good or bad?

It took many years just to figure out that what was happening in my world was not a universal experience of all young girls. If not everyone, why me? If what is happening in my world is "wrong," what can I do with this information?

Let me introduce you once again to my inner philosopher. Judgments of "right" and "wrong" are extremely complex. We all want "justice," and "justice" is different for different people. This is the purpose of a jury of peers—to determine justice by a measure of majority.

I don't want to get into a deep philosophical discussion here. My purpose is to demonstrate how my mind works. My mind does not work on a scale of right and wrong. It does not work on a scale of black and white. I do not judge, and I do not criticize. My mind works in gray scale.

The second piece of data that drove my life's research was a staggering statistic. This piece of data falls more in the "fact" category. It is something that is provable or disprovable. That statistic was this: the vast majority of child abusers were abused themselves.

Keep in mind that I was a child with limited resources. This data compelled me for two reasons. First, the horrible pain that I felt as a victim of childhood sexual abuse was something I *never* wanted to cause someone else to feel. I didn't want to become a child abuser, so I needed to understand how to *not* become one. Second, this statistic laid the groundwork for compassion. It was highly likely that the person abusing me had been abused himself. It was highly likely that the "reason" I was being abused was because my perpetrator had been abused too.

Lots of people talk about their "people." They talk about their "tribe," their trusted advisors. They talk about their "help you hide the body" friends. I don't have these kinds of people.

My people are distrusted advisors. They are people from whom I learned "what *not* to do." I wouldn't hide a body, and I wouldn't help someone hide a body. I don't have a tribe. I have me, my two kids, and my two chocolate Labs.

I've never had a "person." I've only had people trying to fuck my life up—not purposefully and not consciously, but fuck it up all the same. Again, I thank them for that. I'm not being sarcastic or facetious. Without my people, I would have nothing to tell you. Nothing to write about. Nothing to rebel against.

As you read about my life and my experience, you will read a lot about my people. Please remember, this is my experience, not theirs. I tell you these truths not to condemn them but to express my "self" and my experience. It is not about them. If they want to tell their experiences, they can write their own books. This is my book. This is about me and how I became the person I am today.

My Brother

I remember me and my brother catching tadpoles in a nearby pond and putting them in a fish tank. We were living in a house in Clairmont Mesa, California. We would go to the pond with cups and catch the tadpoles. We brought them home and asked our mom, "Can we keep them?" We put them in a fish tank and watched them develop into frogs. I think they all escaped once they could jump.

I adored my older brother and tagged along with him wherever he went. He took good care of me. One time, we walked to a nearby Burger King. Apparently, we terrified our mother because she had no idea where we were. I remember my uncle Scott finding us as we were walking home, and he let us know we were in big trouble. I had no idea what we had done wrong. I was just following my brother.

As we grew together in those early years, I really looked up to my brother. I wanted to wear his clothes and hang out with him. I became a tomboy because I wanted to be just like him.

When we moved to another house in Clairmont Mesa, we lived on a cul-de-sac. We had lots of kids in the neighborhood, and my brother and I would play with them. We would play hide-and-seek, kick-the-can, and ride bikes. I remember my brother being my best friend until we grew older and grew apart.

My brother never caught the overachieving bug. Instead, he caught the underachieving bug along with poor social skills. In high school, people were always shocked to find out I had a brother. They would follow it up with disbelief: "He's your brother?" We were so extremely different. I was social, high achieving, and had lots of friends. He remained that same little boy that I used to play with in the cul-de-sac.

I always wanted to protect my brother. I wish I could have been stronger. I remember fantasizing about beating up the people who teased him. I was a total tomboy until I realized the seductive power of breasts.

I love my brother deeply. He and I share the same genetics. We have the same mother and the same father. My genetics align with my mother, and my brother's genetics align with my dad. We are authentically brother and sister. Our bond is unbreakable, and sadly, it is emotionally disconnected.

I will love my brother more than any person here on earth until the day I die. I couldn't save him, and he couldn't save me. We had to save ourselves. That was where the emotional connection got lost.

I don't know if I will ever be able to forgive myself for not preserving our emotional connection. We still try, and we are pretty good at it. There is just so much emotional disparity that I don't know if our authentic bond is recoverable.

My Sister

My little sister, Shannon, might as well have been my daughter. She was born when I was nine years old. My best friend, Renee, and I couldn't wait for her to be born! We had all our fingers and toes crossed, hoping she would be the New Year baby. She was a few days late but was my favorite person all the same.

To this day, I feel like I raised her until I moved out. I'm sure I didn't actually do much, but I was her person, and she was mine. To be perfectly candid, I disclosed the abuse when she was "getting to be that age." What age is that? She was approaching the age I had been when the abuse started.

I recall the very first time when things were very clear that the touching was not appropriate. My mom was able to look back at photographs and determine that I was nine at that time. My sister was eight and would be nine in January. I disclosed the abuse in November, just before her ninth birthday.

Coincidence? I don't think so. This was my mothering instinct kicking in at seventeen years old. The *only* reason I disclosed the abuse was because I wanted her safe. I was worried that he would start abusing her if he hadn't already.

Shannon is the product of my mother and stepfather. She is my half sister. When my sister was born, the emotional separation began with my brother. I didn't know how to take care of a child, but my mom taught me.

She showed me how to microwave bottles and put my sister to bed in her crib. I remember one time when my mom left Shannon in my care. I couldn't get her to go to sleep, so I told her we would go to Disneyland tomorrow if she went to sleep now. It worked.

My sister was probably one or two at the time. I remember my mom not being pleased with me that I promised Disneyland. I also remember thinking, *What difference does it make? She won't remember and doesn't understand English yet.* Again with my inner philosopher.

My sister and I were always close in a mother-and-daughter kind of way. I would take her to her soccer games and practices. I would pick her up from school. I would play with her and take her places. My boyfriend Matt and I took her and her friends to Family Fun Center for her eighth birthday.

Throughout the years, my sister and I have had times of closeness and times of distance, both due to physical distance as well as emotional distance. Our age difference creates a maturity differential, as does our lifestyles.

I was in college while she was in elementary school. I moved out of Southern California to Vegas, where my mom had opened a bagel store. My soon-to-be first husband was going to run that store for her, so we moved there, creating a physical distance from my sister.

Eventually, I ended up in Washington State. My family is originally from Walla Walla, Washington. My mom and dad were born there and became high school sweethearts. My soon-to-be first husband also had family in Washington State. We decided to move to Washington when things did not work out with the bagel store.

I went on to work for The Bon, which would eventually be bought out by Macy's. At the end of my time with The Bon, the store was converting to Macy's. My sister was in high school and struggling with her identity. Our mom and her dad were going through their divorce.

My sister went on to get her PhD in child psychology while I went on to get my self-accredited PhD in life. I married and had kids. She attempted to follow in my footsteps, but it didn't feel right to her. She continued with school and has developed a successful career counseling families.

Since her dad was my abuser, there was potential for us to have a conflict. However, my sister and I had our own bond that was not contaminated by her dad. I adore my sister and expect that our emotional distance will lessen over time as she catches up in our nine-year maturity difference. I love Washington, and she loves Southern California. I don't expect our physical distance to lessen.

My Uncles

My uncle Scott and my uncle Rich were around a lot more than my uncle Jim. These are my mom's brothers, who all grew up in Walla Walla. My mom and my uncle Jim are somewhat competitive with each other, while my uncles Scott and Rich are both my mom's younger brothers. My uncle Jim has never left Walla Walla. My uncle Scott came to live with us in Southern California. My uncle Rich went on to be very successful in Las Vegas, Nevada.

I have always talked about my uncle Scott being my favorite uncle. I don't really mean to play favorites here, but if they are mentioned in this book, they are my favorites. My favorite brother, my favorite sister, my favorite mom, my favorite dad, and my favorite uncles.

My uncle Scott had moved back to Walla Walla after living with us in Southern California. He married my aunt Mary shortly after returning to their hometown, where they knew each other from high school. Eventually, they would give me my cousins David and Amanda, whom I adore as much as I adore them!

My uncle Scott was always there for me, both by being a caregiver as I was growing up and as an emotionally supportive person in an emotionally disconnected family. To this day, he is the most "available" adult in my family. He has given me trusted advice and counsel over the years.

My uncle Scott and my aunt Mary even sent my cousin to me. Amanda, who is eighteen years younger than me, was supposed to head to Colorado for college. Mary called me and asked if she could come stay with me in Seattle instead of moving so far away. I agreed, enthusiastically!

Amanda lived with me for a year. I was raising three kids at the time, and she needed to start college. She gave me the needed relief from child-rearing, and I gave her the adult support that she needed while learning to live away from home. I cooked and expanded her culinary horizon while she got me addicted to *Gossip Girl*. We developed a strong bond and loved each other's company. Amanda is definitely a product of my uncle Scott, with the same diplomacy and good heart that I always adored about my uncle.

Tragically, my uncle Rich died at the tender age of sixty-two four years ago. He had been living a very successful life in Las Vegas as an enthusiastic salesperson and public speaker. He had always been the star athlete of the family and went on to coach at UNLV. His funeral service filled a stadium—literally.

My uncle Rich, from my perspective, is the outward expression of an emotionally disconnected family. He is the platinum standard of "keeping up appearances." Everything looked exceptional on the outside. He was the fittest sixty-two-year-old you had ever seen. I promise that. Yet he died of an unexplainable heart attack in his sleep. Fucking tragic.

My Mom

I am finding it extremely difficult to write about my mom. There is something sacred about motherhood that prevents me from speaking my truth. This is partly why recovery sucks.

Sometimes you have to speak your truth even if it goes against popular opinion or social norms. Exposing my mother's failure at motherhood almost seems like sacrilege. Here's the paradox. Did she really fail?

I'm here today writing this book. I've survived a lot. Who's to say that her failure is not responsible for my success? Who's to say that her type of motherhood wasn't exactly what I needed to prepare me for a hostile and difficult world?

Here's the thing about my mother. I believe she is a diagnosable narcissist. I do not say this to disparage her. I say it as an explanation as to why she conducted motherhood the way she did.

It is *always* best practice to *never* tell a narcissist that they are a narcissist. *Ever!* However, to tell my truth, I must disclose this fact. I believe her narcissism fucked me up more than the sexual abuse I endured. I have to "out" her. She's not going to like it.

Here's the thing about narcissism. Narcissists raise narcissists. So if you are going to accuse my mother of being a narcissist, then put your accusations where they belong—on her parents. Then put their narcissism on their parents and so on. There is not one person to blame here, and that is not a comfortable concept for many. If you feel the need to blame something, blame the pattern, not the people.

You don't know what you don't know. Narcissists do not know they are narcissists. They are not trying to piss you off and argue irrationally with everything you say. The very root of narcissism is lack of self-awareness.

I am not accusing my mother of being a narcissist. I am explaining why I have had such a difficult time developing healthy relationships. I am not going to do a deep dive on this one. You are just going to have to take my word for it. My mother is a "don't confuse me with the facts" kind of person. Logical, rational thinking is not her strong suit when it comes to relationships.

The mother-daughter relationship is one of the most complex relationships on this planet. For the purposes of my truth, what I can tell you is this. It is entirely possible to love someone deeply and hate them at the same time.

It is this relationship that patterned my love-hate relationships with every adult in my life. I'll tell you how this developed. It started with my mom divorcing my dad. She has always explained to me that my dad would never show public displays of affection. That was a big problem for her, so she divorced him.

Then she interfered with my dad's visitation. Back then, before fathers' rights needed a boost, it was called "visitation." In my profession, I absolutely hate this word. Only parents that are extraordinarily inadequate should be allowed to "visit" their children. All other parents have a "residential schedule" or "parenting schedule" with their children.

When I say she interfered, this was not purposeful, nor was it intentionally malicious. However, subconsciously, it served to punish my dad. Mothers, think twice about interfering with your children's father's desire to have parenting time with his children. You may get blamed in the end by your children.

In my mom's defense, my dad didn't fight very hard. She said no. He said okay. It is no wonder I have developed a passion for mediation. People, "no" is the start of the conversation, not the end. I work with my clients on following up the "no" with an alternative solution.

Then my mother married a man who sexually abused me from the time I was nine until I was eighteen and moved out of the house. Yes, Mom, he still attempted after I disclosed the abuse and we stayed in the same household for the remainder of my senior year. Also, you did go on a girl's trip and leave me in his care after my disclosure too.

In my senior year of high school, after being crowned home-coming queen, the dissonance between how things appeared on the outside and how things felt on the inside became so great that I disclosed the abuse at seventeen years old to a high school counselor. The first thing my mother did was confirm with him that I spoke the truth.

Motherhood lesson number 1. When your child reveals sexual abuse to you, don't reserve judgment until you have confirmed with the person that committed the crime. Go ahead and judge the crime committer right away. This is your child, for crying out loud! Why would your child lie to you about something so shameful? If later, you determine that your child was lying, deal with that then.

Also, what would she have done if he denied it? What would have happened then? Probably nothing different from what happened. Here's a tip. If your daughter tells you that your husband has been molesting her for ten years, don't trust a single word that comes out of that man's mouth. Confirm? Deny? Who the fuck cares? Would you really trust a child molester over your own child? This is the type of nonsense my developing brain incorporated.

Motherhood lesson number 2. A child's behavior is purposeful. If your child is lying to you, there is a reason for that. Children are not inherently naughty. Parents make them that way. So if your child is naughty, it is your fault, not your child's.

Motherhood lesson number 3. Your job is to protect your children. In cavewoman days, a mother's job was to protect her children from harmful animals, nourish them, and model for them how to be an adult. Today, a mother's job is not much different. Instead of harmful animals, we have harmful people. Instead of nourishment, we have fast food. Instead of good role models, we have children in adult costumes.

Motherhood lesson number 4. Don't keep your children in the environment just determined to be unsafe. Do what you have to do to get your children safe. They are depending on you.

I don't know if this next part makes my mother a bad mother or just an idiot, but how do you *not* know the secret behavior of your husband of ten years! I mean, if you didn't live together, that might make sense. I mean, on some level, she had to know that he was getting sex somewhere. Maybe she assumed he was having affairs. Maybe she assumed that better anyone else than her. Either way. As a mother, this is one I cannot excuse. Ladies, if you don't know what your husbands are up to, you are not In a healthy marriage.

If you are so clueless about what a healthy relationship looks like versus finding out that your husband has been molesting your daughter for ten years, you deserve that kind of bomb dropped on you. Your daughter doesn't deserve it, but you do. Your daughter took the hit for you.

In an effort to keep up appearances, the family all stayed together except my brother, who had been shipped off to the army, where he became addicted to drugs.

Motherhood lesson number 5. Shipping your sons off to the army because you don't' know what else to do with them is not a good reason to send them into hostile territory. I couldn't protect my brother in high school, and I definitely couldn't protect him across the country in boot camp.

Luckily? To my mother's relief? My stepfather did not deny the abuse. I believe he minimized it, but he didn't deny it. "It only happened a few times."

Oh. Well. Okay. That makes it so much better. You are an infrequent child molester, not a frequent one? Seriously?

Well, let's see. The child molester's measure was "a few times." The child's measure was "it's been happening for ten years." No matter how you slice that shit up, it's still shit.

My mother also confirmed with my stepfather that he had not been molesting his daughter—my half sister, Shannon. I believe what he said was "That is ludicrous! I would never touch my own daughter. That is sick!"

Please tell me you see the nonsense here too. So much fucking nonsense in my life.

Today, our world is not as physically hostile as it is emotionally hostile. Our emotional infrastructure is relatively underdeveloped compared to the physical infrastructure built to protect us from the environment. Biologically, the females are built for the emotional nurturing, and the males are built for the physical demands. In today's world, biology gets completely obscured by our social infrastructure promoting equality.

As for the physical infrastructure, to prevent the nightly waking, I would lock my door. Weirdly, he would knock on my door. Ugh, sure, hang on a second. No. Not really. I would pretend to sleep and not answer the door.

When my mother found out I was locking my door, she disallowed it. She explained that if there was a fire, she wanted to be able to get me out. This made sense at the time, but now my adult brain processes that completely differently.

One time, our fire alarms went off unexpectedly in the middle of the night. There was no sleeping through that. My head throbbed from the terror. Also, I had four windows in my room. Would I be incapable of saving myself? Lastly, how likely would it be that not only would we have a fire, but that the fire alarms wouldn't wake me, I would be trapped or unconscious, *and* my locked door was somehow a problem?

It did not occur to my mother to be curious as to why I wanted my door locked. It did not occur to her that it is natural for children to require privacy. It did not occur to my mother that I was trying to protect myself from something and did not give a single fuck about fire.

It falls on the mothers to raise emotionally intelligent children. If the mother is not emotionally intelligent herself, her children are already at a disadvantage. Combine this disadvantage with the homogenization of middle-class America, and you get mediocrity at its best.

I don't believe my mother was "the worst" by any standard. I don't think my mother was "the best" by any standard. There is no way to measure motherhood with any kind of accuracy. However, I believe I am an honorable, compassionate, useful adult, so she must have done something right.

My Dad

My mom divorced my dad when I was five. My brother was six. My brother and me are eighteen months apart. We lived in a great house in Clairmont Mesa. I will refer to this house as "the tadpole house." This was the house where my brother and I caught the tadpoles at and grew them into frogs.

I remember my brother and I shared a bedroom. We had a little bump out with a window that overlooked the driveway. We had bunk beds. He had the priority top bunk.

My parents' bedroom was downstairs, and our bedroom was upstairs. My uncle Scott's room was upstairs too, and it had access to an attic.

The kitchen was a typical seventies kitchen. It was downstairs along with a living room and my parents' bedroom. We had a patio out back and a large driveway. I think we had a two-car garage right below our shared bedroom.

I remember getting chicken pox when my brother had chicken pox. I remember our preschool, Chapel Knowles. I remember my best friend, Ronnie. I think Ronnie got chicken pox too. I remember catching the tadpoles and growing them into frogs, and I remember our miniature dachshund named Pepsi.

I remember my uncle Scott living in this house more than I remember my dad living in it. Maybe it's because we continued living there after my dad moved out, or maybe my dad wasn't around much. I'm not sure. I do remember my mom and dad telling us they were getting divorced while we were all lying in their bed downstairs.

I honestly have no idea how accurate my memory is. Our memory plays nasty tricks on us, including the comforting notion that it doesn't play nasty tricks. I guess my memory also speaks to how young I was.

I remember visiting my dad once in an apartment. I don't think he was cut out to be a good dad at this juncture in his life, especially a good dad in a separate household. I remember him snapping at me in a no-nonsense kind of way at my childish behavior. Earth to Dad, I was a child. That's why I had childish behavior. The next memory I have is visiting him in his Rancho Peñasquitos condo, where we went to a mall to visit his soon-to-be wife.

She turned out to be a lovely lady. Perfect for my dad. They went on to build a life together and have two children. I don't remember seeing them much except for Christmas and occasional get-togethers. I think my dad was working hard and building a separate life.

There were about four summers where we would go to Lake Tahoe and spend a week there. This is my strongest memory of being with my dad and Roxanne. Some years, we would meet up with aunts, uncles, and cousins from my dad's side of the family. I don't remember much other than going to Circus Circus and hanging out in the arcade while my dad went to the casino.

My dad was a smart dude. He was an engineer and quality control manager for Sony. I remember one conversation with my dad where he was explaining the odds in blackjack to me. He explained to me that people who have a problem with gambling don't know when to stop. He told me that he always leaves Tahoe "ahead." I don't know if that was true or whether he was justifying his addiction.

During my younger years, I only remember seeing my dad infrequently. I don't think it was an every-other-weekend situation. I think maybe I saw him once a month or so for a weekend. We would spend Christmas Eve with my dad and Christmas with my mom. We would spend the week in Tahoe every other year. Over the course of eight or nine years, that was not very much time together.

This left my dad a lot of time to build a separate life. He built a beautiful Christian family complete with marriage to a beautiful blond Christian woman and two beautiful blond children. These children were raised in the same household as my dad and stepmom, so they grew into responsible, conservative adults who thought the world of my dad.

Once my biological brother and I hit our teenage years, my dad and Rox had their kids. I was a busy teenager and cared a great deal about my grades and cheer squad. I got a lot of validation for my overachieving, so I kept doing it. Once my brother and I hit our teenage years, I don't recall seeing our dad much at all. He was building a separate life, and so was I.

I talked to my dad on the phone occasionally, and I would scan the conversation for relevant and useful information. I remember him telling me that he didn't think anyone should get married before the age of twenty-five. Check. Don't get married before twenty-five. When that bit of advice didn't work in his favor, I began questioning the value of his advice.

I married my first husband because I had been with him for five years. I was twenty-four at the time, which, logistically, could save my dad's accuracy. The problem, however, was not my age. The problem was my disposition. I married this man because I didn't see any other option. My vision had narrowed from "The world is your oyster" to "You have no choice but to marry this man because you have been with him for so long." The age factor was irrelevant, according to my inner philosopher.

I believe my dad held to that theory because he felt like he and my mom were "too young" to get married. While my inner philosopher agrees with that argument, there were more significant problems than age. For instance, the fact that my mom would divorce him because he refused to show affection.

Notice how both of them wouldn't accept responsibility. For my mom, it was my dad's fault. For my dad, it was age's fault. To my dad's dying day, this was the best explanation he could give me. As for my mom, she reminds me nearly every time I see her that my dad was not affectionate; therefore, she had to divorce him.

According to my dad's argument, all I needed to do was be wary of my age, not the relationship. According to my mom, all I needed was someone affectionate. Both of them were contributing their failed marriage to outside factors. I can tell you right now, their marriage didn't work because they had entirely different values.

This is evident when you look at how their families turned out once they separated and built new families. My dad's family grew into a typical, ideal Christian family. My mom's family turned into a disconnected upper-middle-class family with a nasty secret. Definitely different values driving those buses.

My dad went on to live a successful life with his beautifully built Christian family. To this day, his other daughter adores him. He was the best dad any little girl could ask for. It's so strange how two daughters can have entirely different experiences with the same dad.

My dad wasn't a bad guy. He was just completely disconnected from his first family and children. My brother and I were marginalized in his scope of family. We were all but forgotten.

My dad was diagnosed with amyotrophic lateral sclerosis (ALS) in 2013. Almost to his dying day, he fought the diagnosis and tried many alternative treatments. He believed he had Lyme disease because the symptoms mimic those of ALS. He lived about two years after his diagnosis. His Christian family was right by his bedside the entire time.

In 2014, my dad's daughter was making plans to marry her longtime boyfriend. I offered to make her wedding invitations for her. I made 150 custom, handmade invitations for her. I worked with her to create a custom design with her colors and taste. I'm sixteen years older than her, and this was the one way I felt I could contribute to her life.

She had moved her wedding up because my dad's condition was worsening, and she wanted him to be able to participate in her wedding. She got married in March of 2014, just as I began considering my second divorce. My dad ended up dying a year later after being in an assisted-living arrangement for that year.

As a result of not feeling connected to that side of my family, I wanted to attend the wedding to see my dad and try to connect more deeply to his family. I would visit my dad two more times in his assisted-living arrangement. The connection wasn't there.

My dad called me from his deathbed to tell me that he wasn't leaving me anything in his will. He felt as though I was well enough off that any contribution he made would be insignificant. I think he was calling to ask my permission to leave me nothing. I told him that it was his life, and he had to choose what was right for him. He left me absolutely nothing.

I find it interesting that my name is in the disease that killed my dad. I also find it interesting that he rejected the diagnosis despite the evidence. I struggled with whether or not to attend the funeral.

I was struggling with the dissonance between him doing very little for me throughout my life and the complicated travel arrangements for a family of four to travel to Southern California. If emotional connection were there, I would not have thought twice about it. However, our relationship was emotionally bankrupt.

In the end, I chose not to go. I think attending the funeral would have added insult to injury. Suffering through a celebration of life for a man that was wonderful to other people wouldn't be so bad if he had also been wonderful to me. However, he seemed to feel indifferent about me. In the end, I guess my mom was right. My dad was unable to show affection.

I once asked my dad why he didn't fight harder to see us when we were kids. He blamed my mom. He said she was difficult to deal with.

He was preaching to the choir. I understood. However, that was not an excuse. Again, "no" is the start of the conversation, not the end.

Now that I had my own kids, nothing on this planet could keep me from raising them. He didn't try harder because his priority was his new family. Meanwhile, my brother and I suffered through being raised by my mom and stepdad.

My Stepdad

My mom met my stepdad when we were living at the tadpole house in Clairmont Mesa. She was working as a court reporter to try to make a living despite having two young children at home. My stepdad had moved out to San Diego from Pittsburg to open a West Coast branch of the law firm he was working for.

I remember meeting him at the tadpole house. I was very young, so my memory is likely distorted. I have one memory of my stepdad being at the tadpole house. I have two memories of my dad being at the tadpole house. I have at least fifty memories of my uncle Scott being at the tadpole house.

The next thing I remember is moving to the cul-de-sac house in Clairmont Mesa. My mom, stepdad, uncle Scott, brother, and I all moved into this house to begin our new life as a family. I began kindergarten, and we lived in this house until I completed fifth grade.

I remember asking my mom if I should call my stepdad "Daddy." She decided to shove me directly in front of him and have me ask him. "Go ahead, ask him. Ask him what you just asked me. Go on." I don't remember anything else about this other than how intensely awkward and confusing it was. I felt forced into a level of intimacy I wasn't comfortable with. Then I was forced to follow through with my question because I had asked the wrong person. Oh my gawd. This is all starting to make sense.

I think I was only trying to understand the logistics. I had a family photo of my dad, mom, me, and my brother. I labeled it "Dad, Mom, Amy, John." I don't know if I labeled it that way or crossed "Dad" out later, but either way, my brain knew my dad was not a part of our family. Therefore, I was wondering if the person I call "Dad" now is my stepdad. Everyone has a dad, so I just wanted to know who to assign that role to.

Instead, I was forced into an incredibly awkward situation where I was expected to have the maturity and courage of an adult. I was to ask an intimate question of a man I just met. I was to have a dialogue with him as though I had the agency of an adult. This is what is called "grooming." This is the type of gateway activity that leads to sexual abuse.

Not too long after that awful incident, my mom and stepdad decided to get married. They wed at our cul-de-sac house on New Year's Eve 1978. We had a huge party. My mom insisted that I wear this awful maroon-colored velour dress.

Remember, I was a tomboy. I hated dolls and dresses, and I especially hated saddle shoes. I don't know why, but I just did. Most likely because my mom wanted me to like those things so badly that I resisted them as a properly rebellious child would. She wanted me to be exactly like her and did not tolerate any indication that I was different from her or had autonomous preferences that were different from hers.

Either way, she made me wear this ugly-ass dress, *and* she made me be the flower girl. Again, I have no idea why I didn't want to do it, but I didn't! I had to be all by myself, on parade, in front of this huge group of people, walking down our stairs by myself! No thank you!

I remember throwing a fit and not wanting to do it. I honestly can't remember if I had to do it or I got away with not doing it. I suspect I finally did it just to put an end to the power struggle. Again, this is more grooming. Don't do what you want to do; do what I want you to do.

My stepdad was becoming a very successful attorney. This was evidenced by my mom's Porsche 911sc and our need to move to a big home in Del Mar. I don't mean to sound unappreciative, but at the same time, this was where my personal values began diverting from my family's values.

It was extremely important for them to move to this beautiful home, and it was extremely important for me to stay with the friends I had made over the last six years. Additionally, I had one more year of elementary school. We moved right as fifth grade ended. I would go to sixth grade in an unfamiliar environment.

It was an awkward time as I was heading into puberty. That's a pretty shitty time to destabilize my support network and home. Additionally, all the kids I was going to school with had grown up with each other and attended school together since kindergarten. I was an outsider with an identity crisis.

It was this experience that convinced me that I would never move my kids unless I absolutely had to. This explains why I have lived in my home for twenty-one years. I value community, and I know how hard it is to create a new community.

Eventually, my stepdad would go on to become very successful professionally. People loved him, and people hated him. Most people loved him because he made them a lot of money. The people who hated him did so because he played dirty. He was dirty, and he took their money.

He was, literally, one of the best in the business.

The other day, I came across this book that someone wrote about him. My first thought was *Oh, fuck no. This motherfucker has a book out! All the more reason to get my story on paper. If he's going to have a public perspective, so am I.*

My mom and stepdad were together for about fifteen years, from about the time that I was five until I was about twenty. He maintained a sexual relationship with me from the time that I was nine until I moved out of the house at eighteen. I graduated high school and moved out. Less access, no more abuse.

The confusing part about the "abuse" was that it didn't feel like abuse. It didn't physically hurt. In fact, our bodies, being biological, would respond whether you wanted them to or not. Therefore, my body developed biologically properly and responded to unwanted sexual touch.

It wasn't painful. Abuse is painful. This is one reason it was so confusing. Additionally, he would tell me how beautiful I am and how special I am. He was always very gentle and very loving. He explained to me that he was going to teach me everything to be a good lover. Combine this presence with the physical and emotional absence of my biological father, and you have a petri dish to grow confusion.

Never mind that these lessons were in the middle of the night, disrupting my much-needed sleep. I felt like I was constantly being woken up every day of my life to learn sexual lessons that I didn't want to learn. Not to mention that even if I did want to learn sexual lessons, this was the last person on Earth I would choose to teach them to me.

At any rate, the lessons were not optional. The lessons did not cause physical pain. They caused the much more obscure emotional pain. Emotional pain is much more difficult to detect and much more difficult to manage when you don't understand the emotional universe.

The grooming that was done in the early stages of our familial relationship set the stage for escalation of sexual activity. My mother insisting that I do what she tells me to do rather than what I want to do prevented me from saying no. It also prevented me from going to her when the abuse was escalating. Additionally, her shoving me into an intimate conversation with him, specifically, was her invitation for him to test just how much she was inviting him to.

For the next ten years, my stepdad would act like we had a mutually consensual romantic relationship. It's no wonder that I have patterned my current romantic relationships after this one. My partners did not need to be emotionally present, just sexually present. Had any of my partners brought in the money like him, I might not have a book to write.

After I disclosed the abuse to my school counselor, my mom and stepdad continued living together for a couple more years. They continued to act like "there are no problems here." I guess my mom didn't want to derail her plans for the mansion they were building in Rancho Santa Fe. As I have said, denial can be powerful.

They finished building the mansion and lived there together for a couple years. This was probably a pretty smart financial move for my mom. The longer she stayed with him, the more money she would have access to when they divorced. This man was a money-making machine.

When I graduated from college, he gave my mom a Montblanc pen to give to me. It was green and gold. Definitely not my taste. It was a thoughtful gesture, but really? A $600 pen?

The other thing about my stepdad is that he usually didn't do the gift shopping. His secretary did all the gift shopping for him. I knew this to be true for my mom because she would tell me that she could tell what gifts he picked out versus ones she picked out. It is entirely possible that he did the shopping for the pen, given the color and style choice.

I kept that pen for many years. I don't know why I kept it, and I don't know why I got rid of it. I don't even know when I got rid of it. I'm guessing this has some significance that I will determine later.

Fast-forward to today. His fourth marriage is to someone my age. She is very similar in personality and was more appropriately aged when they got together. He's seventy-four, she's fifty-two, and I'm forty-nine. I believe they have been married for ten to fifteen years. I don't keep tabs on them, but my sister fills me in here and there. My sister has a good relationship with her. It's just like having her sister back home!

My Journey through Shame

I've honestly always wondered what it was about me that allowed me to go on to live the beautiful life I live. I've always wondered how the hell I keep it all together. Truly. The reality is, I keep it all together on the outside, and inside is a bustling factory trying to manufacture worthiness.

I vividly remember the first time I felt the horrid feeling of shame. I could not identify it at the time. The only thing I knew was that it felt awful.

The first time I felt this feeling, I was ten years old. I was standing in our powder room, which was right off the kitchen in my childhood home. I was looking in the mirror, and I felt this awful feeling. It was a mental feeling, not a physical feeling. I was a kid and didn't make any sense of it.

At this age and until I was in my twenties, I was restricting bowel movements. It wasn't until I was in college and learning college-level health and biology that I learned that bowel movements were not only necessary but a fundamental and unavoidable part of a healthy daily routine. There was no shame in bowel movements.

In college and in life, I developed a profound appreciation for human biology. There are an astounding number of processes your body does for you without your knowledge or control. The human body is absolutely extraordinary in its ability to process autonomically (without your control). Billions of processes from macro levels (such as breathing) to micro levels (such as transferring oxygen throughout your body through the vascular system) govern your body to survive.

The human body is extraordinary. Biology is extraordinary. If this concept does not give way to humility, you have more understanding to do. You do not have autonomous control over your body. The only control you have is how you treat your body.

For whatever reason, I was denying my body this necessary movement. I was disallowing my biology to do what it naturally does for good reason. I was trying to retain waste rather than eliminate it. I was trying to control something—anything.

I honestly don't think I fully understood bodily functions until I gave birth to my son at thirty-two years old. His birth was the catalyst to understanding how to raise a little human being to be a healthy adult human being. The research began.

I read books. I researched online. I talked to friends. I cross-referenced their advice with doctors or other research. I leaned on our pediatrician. I figured shit out.

In the process, I learned what parenting I had missed out on. I honestly had some pretty terrible parenting. I truly had to figure everything out on my own. I had to figure out that bowel movements were natural and necessary. I had to figure out that sexual abuse was wrong.

From my research, a concept emerged. Restricting bowel movements is entirely normal for children being raised in an emotional environment that is out of control. Being raised in an environment that is chaotic and does not make any sense gives a child the sense of powerlessness. Powerlessness can be a discouraging feeling that leads to despair if not understood properly. Since I had to figure out everything on my own, my journey through shame has been a long-term course in understanding powerlessness.

In an effort to control what feels out of control, children may restrict bowel movements to exercise control over something or just anything. The feeling of powerlessness can be an exceptionally disorienting feeling. Without a good parent to gently explain powerlessness and the discomfort, a child must tough it out on her own. If I have no power, what is my purpose? If I have no purpose, why endure pain?

I don't know if bowel movements were painful for me or scary. I was not conscious of what I was doing or why at the time. I was staring in the mirror at myself during and after restricting a bowel movement.

A flood of yuck surged over me. Not physically but emotionally. I didn't know what the surge of yuck was, but I knew it felt awful. I didn't know it at the time, but that flood of yuck was shame. I don't think it is a coincidence that shame feels like the diarrhea of the soul.

I did what all of us do when we feel something awful. I buried it. I didn't like feeling it, so I didn't. I ignored it, and I pretended it didn't exist. I thought that was terrible, and my glorious mind put me in denial.

Our brains automatically do that for us. Denial is a very natural part of brain functioning. I believe our brains protect us in that way until we have the strength to deal with whatever we are denying. Problems arise when your brain gets stuck in denial.

This is what happened to me. My brain was stuck in denying that the horrible feeling of shame existed in me. For the last forty years, that same feeling would surge through me at times. I didn't understand it, so I denied it an opportunity to land. Just like an unidentified flying object requesting permission to land and the permission was being denied.

In my twenty years of weekly therapy (two to three times a week), the consternation of this feeling caused the elusion of it. The feeling would surface, unannounced and unwarranted, causing a flurry of confusion. What is this feeling? Why am I feeling it?

I don't half-ass anything. Therapy was no exception. Therapy helped me establish a healthy relationship with my feelings rather than ignore and deny them. However, I still could not quite identify this feeling.

Through my twenties and thirties, I identified it as "profound loneliness." It wasn't just loneliness; it was profound loneliness. Adding the word *profound* was the only way to provide a more accurate description of how intense this feeling felt.

Shame is a particularly difficult feeling to identify. It does not make sense. Shame is a manufactured feeling. It does not occur naturally. It is contrived by self-worth bumping up against data that proves you are not valued. Shame is the feeling of self-worth being squeezed through a filter of your existence being wrong. Shame is the feeling that something is so extraordinarily wrong with you that you don't deserve to exist.

Shame is not authentic in that I don't believe a person would ever feel the awful feeling of shame if another human being didn't infect us with it. Like a toxic communicable disease, passed from generation to generation, shame is passed from one person to another. Without acute detection and eradication, shame spreads like the coronavirus, where infected people unwittingly spread the disease because they don't know they are contagious.

I believe I may have been infected at the early age of potty training. I do recall feeling ashamed about bowel movements into my teens. I do wonder if this is why my shame manifested through the restriction of bowel movements.

At any rate, I was clearly infected at nine years old by someone who didn't know he was carrying the disease. People don't just wake up and decide to become child molesters. Shame has infected them and has gone untreated. Shame is a driving factor in narcissism, and narcissism is a driving factor in child abuse.

This intense feeling of shame would elude my consciousness until my forty-ninth year and the writing of this book. At sixty pounds overweight eight months into 2020 and five months into the coronavirus, the toxic feeling would flood over me when I would look in the mirror.

Without all the chaos and distraction of unhealthy relationships occupying my thoughts, I considered this feeling. Up until now, I identified the feeling as profound loneliness. As I stood looking in the mirror at my unpleasantly large body, I thought to myself, *I'm not lonely*. If I wasn't lonely—and especially not "profoundly lonely"—then what was this feeling?

Why is it here? What does it want? What is it trying to tell me?

Here's what this feeling was telling me. "Amy, you are a strong, courageous, attractive, successful person that is sixty pounds overweight. Being overweight is temporary. It is not a character flaw. You have been fit before, and you will be fit again. But first, you have to deal with me. My name is shame."

When I say the feeling of shame makes no sense, what I mean is that the feeling exists regardless of whether or not it makes sense that it exists. When I told my therapist that I had an astounding breakthrough and that I identified the elusive feeling as shame, my therapist asked me, "What do *you* have to be ashamed of?"

I could not think of a single thing. It made no sense that shame was flooding over me. I work hard, and I'm nice to people. There is nothing for me to be ashamed of except the extra weight I was carrying.

Seeing an overweight body in the mirror automatically sent a flood of shame through me. In years past, shame was lurking in the deep dark corners of my athletic and fit body, eluding detection. I didn't know it was there. Shame performed a sneak attack on my heavy body. It ambushed me when I was heavy and hid from me when I was thin.

As I write this chapter, I work through my shame. My shame is not mine. It was passed on to me through the shameful behavior of others. I have nothing to be ashamed of. I must eradicate this shame if I don't want to infect others with it.

Just like an authentic feeling, shame comes and goes as it pleases and has a mind of its own. Feelings do not require your consent. Feelings show up unannounced and stay until it is time for them to go. You can resist their presence or try to shove them out the door, and they will stay until you are ready to accept them.

When you have developed the strength and the fortitude to give feelings a place to land without letting them take up residence, you have matured. You have grown up. You have developed an emotional quotient (EQ). You have recovered your authentic self.

I'm giving shame a place to land without allowing it to take up residence. I am understanding why shame is here, and I am gently shooing shame toward the door. I understand why shame showed up like a feral animal. However, I am not going to feed it, and I am going to let it know that it doesn't belong here. This is my home.

At the end of this process, shame will have one less host in this world.

Weight Management

As a result of this weight gain, I have been able to extract shame from its hiding place. Shame was lurking, undetected, in the deep dark crevices of the rubble, hiding my authenticity from myself. The shame was in there, undermining my self-worth while masquerading as self-esteem. While wearing my athletic, fit body, shame would retreat further into the depths to escape detection. I would look in the mirror, and I liked what I saw. The shame was nowhere to be found.

Now sixty pounds heavier, I look in the mirror, and that flood of yuck surges through me. I don't like what I see. The surge is spontaneous. It is instantaneous. It just happens without my consent. However, this time, it does not escape my awareness.

What is this feeling? Why is it here? What is it trying to tell me?

Oh my gawd! It is shame! Shame! What are you doing here? Why are you bothering me? You feel awful. Why are you doing this to me? What are you trying to prove? Please leave me alone!

Interestingly, these are all questions and statements I wanted to scream at my stepfather but never did. I never understood. *Why me?* That emotional pain was so great that it created the foundation for my constitution.

Shame is the stealth shrapnel of childhood sexual abuse. Childhood sexual abuse is the hollow projectile containing the indiscernible bullets of shame that assault self-worth. Childhood sexual abuse explodes these bullets of shame over the innocent child and buries her authenticity under the rubble.

Because the violence is not obvious, the shame goes undetected. If there were blood and bruises, the massacre would be discernible.

Shame is leached out of the bullets, undetected and eroding self-worth without the host's knowledge.

Escaping detection is a survival mechanism for shame. We automatically bury shame because it feels so awful. We bury it from our conscious awareness. In order to eradicate it, we must first identify it. Then we must question it. Then we must decide what to do about it. This all requires conscious awareness that shame expertly eludes.

Existentially, I believe this is why I have put my sixty pounds back on. I believe my coronavirus sixty is here for a reason. It is purposeful.

These sixty pounds were the only way I could extract shame from its hiding place. It was the only way I could spontaneously trigger the feeling of shame. That flood of yuck only came about when I saw my overweight body in the mirror.

There is no reason to overanalyze this. There is no way I could have devised such a divine plan. It is what happened without my consent. The only consent I provided was by what I put in my mouth and the cessation of exercise.

The power struggle that I have fought with for most of my adult life is "taking care of myself." We all have a personal responsibility to take care of ourselves. I have struggled with this concept for as long as I can remember.

Remember, I entered therapy to determine why I gain and lose sixty pounds. Why not five pounds? Why don't I address the problem when I see the weight packing on?

The answer is this: because this is not a question of logistics. It is an obscure question about the subconscious and feelings. It is a deeply rooted question of authenticity and recovery.

My many years of losing sixty pounds is proof that I know, logistically, how to do it. In the beginning, I did need to learn logistics. I learned the logistics through Weight Watchers.

Weight Watchers is, without a doubt, the most effective long-standing program out there. It teaches you how to manage your food and exercise requirements to "take care of yourself." It is the most realistic, universally applied, easy-to-follow program that will teach you what you need to know to take the weight off and keep it off (if those logistics are "the problem").

I also did much of my own research through various other channels. My passion for cooking was inspired by providing healthy meals for myself and my family. I loved reading cookbooks, healthy eating magazines, healthy eating books, and tips regarding healthy foods. I developed a realistic, easy-to-maintain method for preparing and eating delicious healthy food.

One of my methods is to "get the vegetables in any way you can." If you have to dip them in ranch dressing or cover them in a delicious sauce, do it! Get the vegetables in one way or another. Either do it more pleasantly through making them taste good or less pleasantly through suffering through the ingestion without a delicious vehicle. My theory is that the more fruits and vegetables I eat, the more satisfied my biology feels. The more satisfied my biology feels, the less "craving" and "overeating" occurs.

When I'm being disciplined about my food intake, I allow myself to eat as much fruits and vegetables as I want. If I am going to overeat anything, it will be fruits or vegetables. The other thing I do is try to minimize the fattening and so delicious sauces. I do not eliminate sauces. Ever! I believe that the purpose of food is to deliver sauce to my mouth. I live for sauces! Especially those decadent and extraordinarily fattening sauces!

The most important part of my method is that I don't deprive myself. Ever! Deprivation leads to the extreme totter of overindulgence. The point is to learn to live in balance, not teeter-totter between deprivation and indulgence. My *mind* does not like extremes. My *mind* loves balance. My *mind* and *body* are in a constant battle.

Another part of my method is to eat satisfying meals. In order for a meal to be satisfying, it needs to be something I like. Also, generally, foods that are warm are far more satisfying than cold food that is supposed to be warm. Lastly, nutritious food is far more satisfying biologically than junk food or fast food.

A word about fast food. Without question, our bodies get addicted to fast food. You can tell this by the "sick" phases our bodies go through when binging on fast food. The first time, you might feel sick, but the satisfaction outweighs the illness. Then your body becomes addicted to fast food, and then you crave it. Then when you go off fast food, your body does go through withdrawal. You will feel sick in an effort for your biology to convince you to grab some fast food. It is a vicious cycle.

Stay away from fast food if you can. Otherwise, be aware of this cycle and fight getting sucked into this cycle. Fast food is very low in nutrition and very high in satisfaction. Thus, becoming addicted to fast food is easy and deprives your body of much needed nutrients. Being addicted to fast food creates a state of deprivation that your body is constantly trying to fill.

Which brings me to water. Water is the lifeblood of this universe. Earth is 80 percent water, and so are our bodies. Water is essential for every process in our bodies and out. When in doubt, drink water!

We often eat when we are thirsty. It sounds silly, but your brain can't always tell your mouth exactly what to ingest. The body sends the same signal to "consume" when it is deprived of anything. Therefore, if you are dehydrated, your body will send the signal "consume," and you might eat when you are actually thirsty.

Therefore, my number one weight-loss technique is to drink water constantly. That way, my body is never dehydrated and sending me false signals. I drink water on a very regular schedule to prevent all kinds of illnesses. Many biological problems result from dehydration. We have plenty of water around, so why would we deprive our bodies of this essential nutrient unless we were taught to do so?

I also drink plenty of water to show my gratitude for having clean water readily available to me. Not taking advantage of this glorious privilege is a slap in the face to the countries that don't have clean water readily available. Taking clean water for granted is a dangerous proposition.

Where my power struggle comes in is that I teeter and totter between "taking care of myself in healthy ways" and "taking care of myself in unhealthy ways." That is why my weight fluctuates sixty pounds. When I've teetered and I take care of myself in healthy ways, the weight comes off. When I totter and take care of myself in unhealthy ways, the weight comes back on.

Why this teeter-totter? Well, the answer is pretty simple. Taking care of ourselves in healthy ways is "responsibility." Taking care of ourselves in unhealthy ways is "playtime." I have always struggled with balance between responsibility and playtime. This struggle is all about growing up.

The Aesop fable "The Ant and the Grasshopper" has always been a metaphor for me regarding this struggle. The ant was busy working during the summer to prepare for the harshness of winter. The grasshopper wanted to play. This is where balance and compromise are necessary.

I don't want to be the ant, and I don't want to be the grasshopper. I want to be a balance between the two. Someone once told me that the opposite of "play" is not "rest." He said the opposite of "play" is "depression." We must "play" even as adults. "Playtime" is the totter from "responsibility."

I love the results of taking healthy care of my body. My body feels good and looks great! Everything in my closet looks great on me, and I feel good about myself.

However, taking healthy care of my body is a lot of responsibility! It requires daily exercise worked into my busy schedule. It requires meal planning and grocery shopping and cooking. It requires minimizing my alcohol intake. All these things require dedication, perseverance, and responsibility.

I don't love the results of taking unhealthy care of my body. I don't feel good, I don't look good, and nothing in my closet fits. Daily poisoning with alcohol is another negative feedback loop just like fast food. I avoid looking in the mirror, and my mental state is depressed.

However, I do love that taking unhealthy care of my body feels like playtime. It feels like taking a break from all the responsibility and burden of being an adult. It's my way of being childish in my adult body. It's my "I don't wanna" temper tantrum about taking care of myself in healthy ways. It is my adult "playtime."

When I'm taking unhealthy care of myself, as I've been doing for the last year and a half, I'm essentially "goofing off with my personal responsibilities." I take care of everyone else instead of taking care of me. This is what I was taught as a child of abuse.

Taking unhealthy care of my body means I'm not exercising, I'm eating fast food, and I'm drinking a lot. It is my way of not taking personal responsibility for taking care of myself, just as the adults in my life taught me. They taught me what I was "supposed" to do. I was "supposed" to lie there while I was molested. I was "supposed" to listen to my mother.

I didn't learn I was supposed to drink a lot of water. I didn't learn I was supposed to eat healthy meals. I didn't learn I was supposed to exercise regularly to maintain heart health. I didn't learn any of these basic health lessons until I was in college.

At the time, listening to my mother was all about "looking good." It had nothing to do with being healthy. It was about depriving myself of essential nutrients so I could be thin and look good. I was never any good at this. I could look good, but I couldn't successfully deprive myself. Thank God!

This is why the teeter-totter developed between deprivation and indulgence. As a grown-up, it is time to stop playing silly teeter-totter games. It is time to know that this teeter-totter can kill you.

Instead of teetering and tottering between taking healthy care and unhealthy care of myself, I need to grow up. I need to realize that no one is in charge of taking care of me except for me. Those of us who didn't have good parents to teach us how to take good care of ourselves struggle with this more than those who had good parents.

Those of us who were abused in various ways struggle to take good care of ourselves because we were taught that we weren't worthy of good care. Literally, the word is *abuse*. We were taught through abusive action. We were taught that abusive action is "how we take care of each other." We are taught that we don't take care of ourselves. Others take care of us, and this is how they do it.

Children don't learn through what we tell them. Children learn by what we show them. In fact, the intellectual brain might learn what we tell them, but the subconscious does what it was taught. If the subconscious was taught abuse, that is what it does. The worst outcome of childhood abuse is that we don't know how to take healthy care of ourselves because our parents did not know how to take healthy care of *themselves.*

What I have learned in this year and a half of taking unhealthy care of myself is that my behavior is almost identical to my stepdad's. Minus the sexual abuse. I drink like he did. I eat like he did. I don't exercise like he did. I work like he did. This is my totter.

My teeter is when I'm being perfectionistic like my mom. Over the years, my mom gained an appreciation for health over looks. She is in her seventies and walks forty miles per week. She eats well, cooks a lot, and has maintained a healthy weight over the last thirty years. She was not this way when I was growing up, but we have both become this way over the last thirty years. Except for when I totter.

If this isn't proof positive that we learn through what our parents show us, I don't know what other proof is needed. I am a perfect amalgamation of my mom, my stepdad, and my biological dad. By the way, I often find myself rather grateful that I have my dad's genetics. I believe it saved me from being exactly like my mom. Additionally, ALS is not genetic. I checked as soon as I heard my dad's diagnosis.

The only way to tap into the subconscious is to elevate problems to the executive functioning part of our brain that is responsible for our conscious thinking. Which is why I began therapy with this question: "Why sixty pounds?"

Why can't I maintain my ideal weight of 135 pounds? I can get myself there, but I can't stay there. Why?

I have an extremely high pain tolerance thanks to the abuse. Things have to get very loud for me to hear them. Pain has to be significant in order for me to feel it. I never need pain meds even after my C-sections or any surgery. I just don't feel physical pain. Except for stubbing a toe or hitting my funny bone. Those hurt like a motherfucker.

For me, sixty pounds is the outward expression of emotional pain. Five pounds is not painful. Ten pounds is not painful. Apparently, sixty pounds is my pain threshold. This is where my biology takes me when I'm acting like my stepdad (minus the sexual abuse). I had to get here, once again, to make this connection.

I have never made this connection before. Isn't it interesting that looking in the mirror causes a flood of shame? That's not my shame; it is his. I have been the carrier for his shame. It has been lurking in the deep dark corners of my subconscious. Now that I have brought it to my consciousness by gaining sixty pounds, I wonder what will happen.

Here is what I suspect, given what Brené Brown has taught me. I have exposed the shame. I am writing about it. I am placing the shame where it belongs, on the rightful owner of that shame. I have become conscious of this, and now I will be able to live my whole-hearted life, in the arena, with Brené.

I suspect that when this book is finished, the weight will come off. I will have had a sufficient overdose of being heavy, and I won't come back to this place again. I have removed the men from my life who were contributing to my emotional pain, and now I will have removed the man who caused my emotional pain to begin with. I had absolutely no idea I was carrying that shame.

Being overweight is my biology's way of keeping me in the equilibrium state of abuse. My biology was taught that abuse is "home." My biology drives to go home to the confusion and misery of "home." It is my job, as an adult, to override that biological drive to go "home." I need to create a new home that is peaceful, pleasant, and productive.

Keeping Up Appearances

Keeping up appearances became a way of life. It was not inauthentic. I was not faking it. Keeping up appearances was, genuinely, a part of my character. I didn't do it on purpose. It was all I knew.

After being sexually abused was swept under the rug by both the authorities and my parents, how could I know that keeping up appearances was not a genuine and authentic way to live? Even when my mom told my biological dad about the abuse, no one came to rescue me. In fact, my dad wouldn't even talk to me about it until years later.

Keeping up appearances would become a way of life for me. It was all I knew. My mom and stepdad kept up appearances after I disclosed my abuse. We continued on with life as though nothing important had been revealed. We lived a high-achieving, "looks pretty on the outside," "sweep everything under the rug" lifestyle. The message we sent to the world was this: "Keep moving. There's nothing except good stuff to see here. There is nothing criminal going on behind these doors."

I had no idea there was a different way to live. I developed from child to adult in this fucked-up family. I'm still a part of this fucked-up family. How could I know that putting my energy into being genuine and authentic was not only okay, it was the preferred way of life? How could I know that it was okay to be me?

I wasn't purposefully "hiding" problems. I genuinely didn't know there were problems. I married my first husband, who was thirteen years my senior, because what else was I going to do? Break up with him? I literally felt like it wasn't a choice but an obligation. Otherwise, what would that say about me?

We had been living together for three years. If we weren't building a future together, what were we doing? If I wasn't planning on staying with this guy, why did I stay so long? A loyal person would stay. So I stayed. It was about what was right for him, not what was right for me. What I didn't know at this time—which would take thirty years to learn (no exaggeration)—was how much identity and value I wrapped up in having what appeared to be a partner.

There were a lot of problems in my first marriage that I wasn't aware of. First, I was expected to be an independent earner and pay my half of the bills. I was nineteen, and he was thirty-two. He was a successful independent contractor; I was a student. We lived in Cardiff-by-the-Sea, which was not a cheap place to live in.

Instead of acknowledging the discrepancy in our earning potential, I believed in not being a financial burden. I believed in paying my way. Never mind that it was my mom and stepdad, at this point, "paying my way." Nevertheless, it was my duty. My obligation was to stay and pay my way. My worthiness was tied up in what I contributed financially.

Instead of seeing this as a problem, I saw it as a way of life. What did I know? I was nineteen. We got married and stayed together until I was twenty-eight. We bought a house together and kept finances split exactly down the middle, even though I was working a minimum wage job in retail. I paid all the bills and submitted a spreadsheet to him for his half of the bills. This should have been my first clue that I was doing more than my share.

After working my retail job for three years out of college and being promoted to management then to the administrative offices, I got laid off. I loved my nine-to-five administrative job and was not willing to go back to the grueling hours of an associate or a manager. I was scared but excited to take this opportunity to find a different industry. After all, I am smart. I graduated from college with a degree in science. I overdo everything I attempt.

Then this was the conversation that shocked me out of my make-believe world that my husband saw me the same way I saw myself:

> Me: I've been given the opportunity to be
> laid off or return to management. I think I'd like
> to find a different job.

Him: No way. You aren't qualified for anything else. You won't make as much money anywhere else. You have to take the management job.

Do you see why my worthiness was tied up in what I contributed financially? I took the management job. For one day. Then I went to my manager and said, "Can I change my mind and get laid off instead?" He obliged and the next thing I knew, I was at the unemployment office. This was back in the day of pagers and pay phones. I called Andrea, my friend who had switched from our retail management positions to an outside sales rep for a pager company. She rented me a pager, and I started looking for jobs. I gave my résumé to a staffing agency.

I landed a dream job at Nextel. It was akin to slave labor, but I loved it. I was hired by my future husband and father of my children. I worked my ass off for Nextel and received the benefits of a fast-growing industry in cell phones. I absolutely loved my job and worked extremely long hours for my salary. I was okay with that arrangement since my current husband had no faith in me or my abilities. I was proving him wrong every hour I contributed to Nextel.

Within a few months of starting my job at Nextel, I told Andrea she needed to come work with me. Pagers were going obsolete, and she could have a future here. Within a year, I asked my husband for a divorce. I saw the possibilities for a new life, and I was going to take it.

People that have worked outside sales jobs know the party lifestyle I am talking about: conventions, working with business owners, long hours with coworkers. My coworkers and I got to know each other pretty well, and there was a lot of messing around that came with that territory.

Today, I see my first marriage much more clearly than I did then. That was thirty years ago that I began that relationship. My first marriage got me away from home and created the illusion that I had a family. My second marriage is my only other marriage. The retrospective purpose of my second marriage was to get me out of my first marriage so I could build the life I wished I had as a child.

While I was at Nextel, my mother called me. I was twenty-eight. She told me that she found a friend of a friend who was an attorney. This attorney wanted to negotiate on my behalf with my abuser to obtain restitution for my lost childhood. I stood on my high moral ground and refused. For about a minute. My high moral ground was thunderstruck by the idea of not having to work as hard as I was working.

Within six months, I was financially set for life. Or so I thought. Life is expensive. However, for those of you wondering how I can afford my lifestyle, here is your answer.

I got a very large settlement to keep my mouth shut. My attorney was a very smart guy and had my settlement pay out over twenty years. That way, I couldn't blow all my money in one place. That strategy worked, and twenty-two years later, I'm still financially secure, although I spent a lot of money on building a high-end lifestyle. Not for looks but for comfort.

At any rate, all that messing around with my coworkers at Nextel led me to my next marriage. Norm came into our marriage with a pregnancy, and I came into our marriage with financial freedom. While that sounds like a recipe for disaster, it really wasn't. It was this exact dysfunction that I needed in order to align myself with my higher purpose. I mean, it was kind of a disaster, but I am grateful for it.

There was a bit of overlap and no "between marriages" for either one of us. He and I had both been with our previous spouses about the same amount of time, roughly ten years. Couple these midterm relationships with our long-term relationship and that equals two people who don't want to be alone. Add the impropriety on top of that and you get an eighteen-year relationship to prove beyond a reasonable doubt that it was true love and justifiable infidelity.

My husband and I spent seventeen fun-filled years together and one year divorcing. We co-parented well with his ex-wife, and we had two incredible children of our own. We played hard, and we lived well. Neither one of us worked outside the home for most of this time. There was plenty of time to play.

We appeared to be the ideal family. Husband, wife, beautiful home, serving the community, two point five children, and a chocolate Lab. We mastered the appearance. We looked like the ideal family, but all we did was play. No one was earning, and there were skeletons in the closet.

When I say "we co-parented well," I mean "I co-parented well." I repaired the relationship with his ex by being an overproducer in the care of their daughter, Madison. Most of our years together, I provided before and after-school care for Madison. I also paid her child support on behalf of my husband. I cared for the son that Madison's mom later had with her second husband. In honor of Madison, I emotionally supported Madison's mom and her entire family when Madison's stepdad died unexpectedly. I paid my penance.

When I say "we played hard, and we lived well," I mean my husband played hard, and I paid for the living well. I worked my ass off being the mother of his daughter and then, later, to our own children. My husband contributed very little in terms of taking responsibility. He was better at accumulating things that I needed to take care of. Houses, boats, cars, personal watercraft, fishing gear, hunting gear, tools, shops, a business—it's an enormous list.

By the way, do you see the correlation here to restricting bowel movements? Retaining waste rather than eliminating it: this applies to both the physical stuff and the emotional stuff.

At one point, we owned and operated a business out of our garage. We lost money on that business, not because the business was a failure but because we didn't manage money well. And when I say "we," I mean I managed the money, and he didn't. I was not bad at managing money. We just got so busy working that we weren't running the numbers. Plus, deep down, my husband was not passionate about working. He was much more passionate about smoking weed and playing Battle Pirates online.

At one point, there was a conversation when our youngest was approaching school age. Who was going to work and bring in some money? I was willing, but my earning potential was not nearly as great as his. We decided he would work.

About sixteen years in was when I realized that Peter Pan was not growing up. I had been growing up all along, and it was time for me to have a partner that contributed more equally. His efforts to contribute were failing on all fronts. He was a lot of fun to play with, but responsibility was not his thing.

This became evident when he began looking for a job. He could say he was "trying," which meant searching the internet for jobs. He was not willing to accept a job below his dignity. He spent a year going from résumé builder to résumé builder because no one was calling him back when he would submit a résumé. My guess is that "below his dignity" was "out of his league." So rather than problem-solve effectively, I paid for more and more résumés to be built.

Then I paid for courses in project management. Then insurance sales certification. Eventually, he was working with his uncle, aunt, and mother in an insurance business. He was "working" nine to five with no salary. He got a couple thousand dollars in commission once, but that was about it. He worked this job for a couple years for no pay. I didn't realize that when I asked him to get a job, that I needed to be more specific about it being a *paying* job.

Not only did I not have him home where he could help out, he also was not bringing in any money. Then he was in an "at fault" car accident on his way home from work. He hit a pizza delivery driver who opened a workers' comp lawsuit.

This was more destruction than I could handle. I asked him to bring home money, and instead, he brings home a lawsuit against him. We didn't seem to be headed the right direction. I was pulling hard in a positive direction, and he was inadvertently deadweight, making my job so much harder than it needed to be.

We did many years of couples therapy where I constantly asked for more contributions. Any contribution would do. Contribute time or money. Neither happened, so I asked for a divorce.

My Divorce

I was very committed to my eighteen-year marriage in 2013. Retrospectively, it turns out that 2013 was a pivotal year for our marriage. By the end of the year, I had asked my husband to enter rehab so he could learn healthy habits. Like many of us, he was raised in a household devoid of healthy habits. Raising three children cleared up for me why having healthy habits was important.

Our children absorb what we do, not what we say. I had been on a ten-year journey to establish healthy habits around alcohol, food, and exercise. I used half-marathon training goals to facilitate those healthy habits. By 2013, I had successfully completed six half-marathons since 2004. For some of them, my weight was in the 160s or 170s, and I completed the halfs in more time. And some of the halfs I completed with close to two-hour times when my weight was a healthier 135 or 140.

For many years, I tried to force myself to set a goal of under two hours. I have yet to accomplish that. My best time so far is 2:02 with a close runner-up at 2:07 during my divorce in 2014.

My husband, being the loyal and compliant person that he is, went to rehab. He spent January of 2014 in rehab and then extended for another month. In early February, they sent him home to "test the waters" and see how it felt. He would visit with family and then return for another month of rehab.

During his time in rehab, there were visiting hours only on Sundays, and only from 1:00 p.m. to 5:00 p.m. In January 2014, I hauled myself and three kids to Oregon to visit during this restrictive time frame. My kids were fifteen, ten, and seven at the time. This was the first time I traveled with my kids without another adult present. While my fifteen-year-old was always extremely helpful with the younger ones, they were also siblings and had authority issues with one another. Additionally, my fifteen-year-old was not the easiest child to raise. I can attest to that now as I watch home videos, and my kids are twenty-two, sixteen, and fourteen now.

I had been parenting on my own for a couple of weeks in January at this point. After traveling with the kids without another adult present, my stress level was charting out. When we finally got to the rehab center and visited with their dad, we played games, toured, ate snacks, and met his friends. It was very relaxing. My only thought was *I'm staying. You take the kids and go home.*

What I realized after two visits to the rehab center (or should I say relaxation-learning center) was that I had been primarily parenting on my own for fifteen years. I had no trouble managing the household at home without my husband present. I had significantly more trouble managing the household *with* him present. Add to that these trips to the relaxation-learning center where he got to lie around with no responsibilities and read Brené Brown and go to therapy and recovery circles and meet new friends, and I realized this was backassward.

If anyone deserved time in a relaxation-learning center, it was me. But I take my job too seriously as a parent to be able to relax when I am not caring for my kids. If I had someone I could depend on to take good enough care of them, I would have been able to relax. I have never had that. Even to this day.

I am not saying that my children always have to be under my care or they are not safe. I am saying I can't trust anyone to keep them safe for an extended period of time. I cannot trust any adult to put my kids first before themselves—to get them to their activities on time and pick them up from school and to care for them.

Yes, to some extent, these are my issues. These are my control issues and my superiority issues. However, to some degree, my issues have not been proven wrong. It's not like my husband was always stepping up and being a stellar parent. He would do what I asked him to do, but I would have to ask. If I didn't think of asking because I was too busy doing, I was blamed for not asking.

Anyone that has managed a busy life with three kids knows that if you are burning the candle at both ends, it requires *a lot* more energy to *remember* to ask than it does to just do it yourself. So, sure, blame me for not asking. But where does your responsibility come in to do the things you are supposed to be doing *without* being asked?

Having my husband in the relaxation-learning center and caring for the kids by myself taught me two things:

1. I can totally do this by myself.
2. It is so much easier without him interfering.

This led to acute anxiety on his visit home between relaxation-learning stays. I remember thinking about him returning home. I was making coffee, and my entire body was shaking with fear. The kind of shaking where I could not lift my coffee without it slopping out. This was not the kind of fear where I was scared for my safety. It was the kind of fear that told me I cannot do this life like this anymore. The denial was stripped away.

So began the divorcing process. If I only knew then what I know now. That was not the moment that I realized I wanted a divorce, but it was the moment I realized I needed a significant change. When he returned home from rehab in early March, I left for Southern California to visit family, friends, and run a half-marathon.

I returned from that trip and asked my husband to move out. Again, being the loyal and compliant person that he is, he did. I needed space. I couldn't do this the same way anymore, and it felt the same. I don't know where he moved, but he would come by the house and gather things for his place. That was fine, but he would also pull into the garage like he still lived here. He was desperately trying to keep everything the same, and I was desperately trying to shake everything up.

By May, I knew I wanted a divorce. Again, being the loyal and compliant person that he is, he complied. I got an attorney, so he got an attorney. God Bless America. I wish I had that to do over again. It was at that moment that the situation hit a trajectory for rock bottom.

Divorce—It's Not the Answer You Think It Is

I couldn't live this way anymore. We were blowing through money, and I didn't want to be financially responsible for him. There were a lot more reasons than this one as to why I wanted a divorce, but his lack of contribution combined with his irresponsibility were the red flags that forced a hard stop.

Come to find out, divorce is not an easy process. Becoming "not financially responsible" for your partner in marriage is not as easy as you might think. From my perspective, it was very clear that he only took and didn't give. From the State's perspective, it appeared as though that was our agreement. Because I went along with it for so long, we were in a passive agreement by what I allowed.

By the way, think back to how I said my relationships were all patterned after my love-hate relationship with my mom and the "taking" of my stepdad. My relationship with my second husband, the father of my kids, was no different. It was love and hate, and all he did was take. I mean, he gave me my children and his, but honestly, how difficult is it to have an orgasm?

To some degree, I felt very taken advantage of by the father of my children. To some degree, it was my fault for allowing it. I spent millions on our family. I'm not exaggerating. Many millions of dollars were spent building this beautiful life. I could not have done it without him. Seriously. He allowed me to build the life I wanted without too much interference.

In exchange, I gave him a lot of the toys that he wanted. I bought a second home for the primary purpose of it being a great location for his hunting hobby. This home ended up being a wonderful place where we spent a lot of time with friends and family. It was an asset that I don't regret but didn't want to keep paying for.

I bought more boats than I can count. Seriously. Offhand, there were at least four boats. I bought him a new truck then, five years later, another new truck. Again, it was for his hunting. I was driving the Yukon XL Denali that I bought used, and I drove it into the ground. As he transitioned into insurance sales, I leased a Lexus GS350 that he had done so much damage to that we bought it at the end of our lease. We had so many boats, cars, trailers, and personal watercraft that I needed a spreadsheet to keep track of the licensing and insurance. I did not want this financial and management responsibility anymore.

Here's the thing about all this. It looks great on the outside, but it sucks on the inside. Responsibly managing two homes and dozens of vehicles is a nightmare. And I was the only adult managing anything, including three growing children and all their stuff. Eventually, I felt overwhelmed by our "stuff" and keeping up appearances that everything was just right. It was not just right. It was way, way, way, way too much.

Remember too how much this sounds like retaining waste rather than eliminating it. The feeling of being overwhelmed led to the decision to begin eliminating waste. Divorce was my answer to eliminating waste.

Eliminating waste was the main reason I needed a divorce. I needed him to take his "stuff" and go. His stuff felt like 75 percent of our household and 5 percent of his responsibility. I needed to reduce the amount of stuff I was managing in order to gain my sanity back. I needed to get out from under the feeling of being overwhelmed.

People think that abundance is problem-free. It is not. I have always lived a life of abundance. I am grateful for that, but it is not problem-free.

Our general culture operates from a perspective of scarcity. That is part of the problem. We become gluttonous when we don't consider that what we have is "enough." Accumulation can be just as much of a problem as scarcity. This is what my life lessons are all about. Finding a balance of "enough" and not "too much" is where all my life lessons point.

Unfortunately, the divorce process did not go as expected. We had always been friends. I don't recall him ever being mad at me. I was the one who was always disappointed and angry, which carried over into our divorce process. I expected the divorce to be amicable and civil. Wrong. When our subconscious is making decisions for us, there is a lot of room for unexpected results.

His subconscious did not want the marriage to end. Why would he? He was living the life. He was not financially responsible for our lifestyle, so he could fuck off and still live a great life. My subconscious was angry and resentful. How could he not see how much he had taken and not reciprocated?

I was so disappointed, angry, and resentful that I always had to take care of everything. Additionally, I was constantly frustrated by his criticism of how I took care of everything. If he wasn't criticizing what I was doing, he was criticizing that I was doing it and not allowing him to do it.

Here's the deal. If you are going to do it, then do it, and do it well. Otherwise, leave it to the pros. Secondly, if you don't like how I do it, do it yourself. Otherwise, keep your mouth shut. You don't get a say if you don't lift a finger.

Our divorce was no different. Everything from deciding to get a divorce to the entire divorce process—I was in charge of everything. I did the best I could, but I didn't know what I was doing. Bringing my resentment and stored up anger into the divorce process created unexpected problems. If I knew then what I know now, I would have done everything completely different.

However, life is a process. I wouldn't know what I know now if I hadn't been through the process of doing it wrong. Today, I try to be the person that I needed back then. I try to be the emotion coach and process coach to prevent divorce from escalating out of control. If my low-conflict marriage could escalate out of control, it wasn't us. It was the system.

Fast-forward to today. I am a mediator. I help couples stay focused on the outcome of dividing a single family into a two-household family without pissing each other off too much. I facilitate the decision-making process for families to make decisions for themselves about the division. I prevent families from relying on the legal system to make decisions about their family for them.

To effectively navigate the legal system, an attorney is necessary. There are attorneys that are good at what they do and ones that are not. When you hire an attorney, you must trust that they know what they are talking about because they are navigating a system that you don't know. So I hired an attorney to manage my divorce.

Unfortunately, my husband then hired an attorney. He didn't want to get taken advantage of. Seriously? Are you fucking kidding me? He was clearly confused about who had been taking advantage of whom.

I hired a smart, effective, articulate, professional woman after I interviewed a couple of attorneys, including a collaborative law attorney. When I saw the dollar signs of the divorce process "ka-chinging" in my mind, I decided to get it over with by going as fast as I could.

He hired an inarticulate attorney who primarily did estate planning, which is nothing like separating a family into two households. His attorney had a Colombo-like (minus the intelligence) style. He was inelegant and considered himself to be charming and intelligent, none of which were evident from my perspective.

So much for a speedy process. This is where I learned about passive-aggressive behavior. Passive-aggressive behavior is what happens when someone's behavior does not match their voiced intentions. You see, behavior is primarily driven by the subconscious while vocalization is primarily conscious.

Therefore, passive-aggressive people don't know they are being passive-aggressive. They think they are being honorable because they are voicing honorable behavior. They don't see the incongruence between what they are voicing and what they are actually doing.

Norm would say, "I'm not trying to be an obstructionist." Or he would say, "I'm not trying to be oppositional." Yet his behavior was not cooperative or collaborative and definitely obstructed the process.

Passive-aggressive behavior is how someone gets what he wants by slight-of-hand or tricks of illusion. Passive-aggressive behavior is legitimately nonsense. Norm didn't want to get divorced, so he was doing everything in his power to stall, obstruct, and postpone the outcome. All the while, he was stating, "I'm not trying to obstruct the process." He believed that all he had to do was state that he was not obstructing, so therefore, he was not obstructing.

I'll let you decide if this was a gesture of cooperation and collaboration. I was busy taking care of my kids and making sure their needs were being met. I was trying to keep things as stable as possible for the kids during 2014 when their dad had been absent for two months while he was in rehab and then absent from daily activity for five months after that. Madison had just turned seventeen. I had the two younger kids at their regularly scheduled karate lessons. We would typically be at karate for a couple hours.

Madison called me and said, "Amy, Dad is moving back in. Is he allowed to do that?" I was shocked and tried to clarify with her what she meant. She explained that she tried to stop him, but he shoved past her and took up residence in the guest bedroom.

If he were being cooperative and collaborative, don't you think he would have asked me rather than performing a sneak-attack hostile takeover? He waited until he knew I had the kids at karate and wham-o! He moved back in after seven months of absence without a single word to me.

I messaged him and called him and tried to clarify what he was doing. He refused to leave. I called everyone I knew, including my divorce attorney, my attorney from my sexual abuse settlement, the police, my therapist, his therapist, my mom, and his mom. I called everyone I could think of, and not a single person was helpful.

I swung by the house and picked up Madison. I took the kids and went to stay at the Westin. I was absolutely terrified for our safety. How mentally unstable was he that he was performing this sneak attack? What were his intentions? He's a hunter. He has a lot of guns. Desperate times call for desperate measures. How desperate was he?

I couldn't sleep that night. I was 150 percent triggered, and all the safety alarms in my head were screaming. No one provided any help to me, so first thing in the morning, I went to the police station. An absolutely lovely woman explained to me that I needed to obtain a restraining order. I hauled the kids over to the courthouse. The lovely lady behind the counter said, "The judge hears these cases at 1:00 p.m. Normally, she wouldn't hear this until tomorrow, but if you fill this out fast, I'll squeeze you in." Thirty seconds later, the form was filled out.

I had Madison take the kids across the street and get them some lunch while I waited at the courthouse to have my case heard. I stood in front of the judge, shaking in terror. I stated that my husband had been in rehab and then had been moved out of the house for the last seven months. I explained that he suddenly decided, without my consent, to move back into our home. I explained that he had guns, and I was terrified for my family's safety. My terror was evident in my shaking hands and voice, and was pouring out my eyes as I explained the situation to the judge.

I was not acting, and she knew it. I was genuinely terrified. She granted me the restraining order and explained that I needed to have him served. I grabbed the kids and headed home. Norm was at his nonpaying insurance job. I got all the locks changed, unplugged the garage doors, and called the security company. I deauthorized him and changed our alarm passcode. I knocked on all my neighbors' doors and asked someone to serve him.

Thankfully, all my neighbors agreed; however, they were all very uncomfortable with the idea. We had all lived together on this street for the last fifteen years together. This was a huge disadvantage when it came to "keeping up appearances"! One neighbor, a very friendly and constructive guy, agreed to serve him.

Just before Norm got home, I tested the garage door. Ugh! It still worked! What the fuck? Backup battery. Really? How do you make these smart things *not* work? I have no idea what I did, but I made it stop working.

As Norm pulled into the driveway, he was confused as to why his garage door opener wasn't working. I called 911. Madison called our neighbor, and I gave the 911 operator the play-by-play. I wanted Norm being served "on the record" so that I had recourse if he tried moving back in again. My neighbor and Norm had a pleasant exchange, and Norm drove away to the apartment he had been renting for the last five months.

Why would Norm move back in and refuse to leave voluntarily? This, my friends, is passive-aggressive behavior. He's getting what he wants by doing what he wants but saying it is not what he is doing. When I asked him why he wouldn't leave, he stated that he was going to "continue to be the stay-at-home father that he has always been." He also explained to me that I was completely overreacting and being unreasonable.

I was like, "What the actual fuck are you talking about?" Not only has he never been a stay-at-home father, but what would "reasonable" behavior from me look like? Are you telling me to not lock my door like my mother used to tell me? Are you telling me there is nothing to be afraid of and I should trust that? It's my fault that I am "scaring the kids"? Don't do scary things, and we won't be scared. Idiot!

When my attorney asked his attorney why he did that, his attorney stated that he did not advise Norm to do that. He stated that he told Norm that dads who are "still living at home" get awarded more time with their children. Whether his idiot attorney advised him or whether his idiotic behavior was all his own, "moving back in" was not a smart move. Now he had a restraining order to deal with instead of the fake "I've always been a stay-at-home dad" defense.

Acting out of desperation is never a good idea. What did he think I was going to do? That I would say, "Oh sure, Norm. That sounds great. Why don't you just sleep in the guest bedroom. I'll make all our meals and do all of the cleanup. You just rest and gain your strength, you poor dear."

Have we met? This was not a well-thought-out plan.

His attorney frustrated my attorney so much that I had to keep explaining the language of idiots to her. I don't speak the language, but I certainly understand it. I had to keep explaining that this was all part of the passive-aggressive obstruction process.

He wants to look like he's doing the right thing, but he really doesn't want to get divorced. Subconsciously, he thinks that if he can sabotage this process like he sabotages everything else, nothing will change. Everything will stay the same, and he can go back to smoking weed all day and playing Battle Pirates six hours a day after he works for eight hours at his nonpaying job.

Since then, I've learned a lot. Through the entire miserable process of working with attorneys to get a divorce, I realized the "right" way to do it. No offense to attorneys, but all attorneys can do is get you legally divorced and charge you a small fortune to do it. Even my awesome attorney was unable to emotionally divorce us.

Emotional divorce is absolutely necessary if you are going to have to work with the other party regarding anything. Families have a lot of business to take care of, and dividing into two households adds to the complication of taking care of that business. If the business does not get taken care of well, the family suffers, especially the kids.

Dividing a single family into a two-household family is not just a legal process. It is an extraordinarily emotional process that needs to be attended to properly, or there will be a lot of collateral damage. It requires a delicate, pragmatic touch that most attorneys are not capable of. It is this delicate, pragmatic touch that I provide my clients as a mediator dividing single-household families into two-household families.

I wish I understood, at the time of my divorce, the value of mediation. In Washington State, mediation is required if you are not in agreement prior to family matters being reviewed by the court. Norm and I participated in mediation, but it was nothing like what I do. I felt bullied and coerced into agreements that didn't sit well with me. The "mediator" conducting the mediation was an attorney and did not take even a moment to understand why I had the strong feelings that I had.

That being said, he did the job he was supposed to do, which was "settle" our split into two households. To be honest, I don't know if any mediator could have been the type of mediator I needed.

Two and a half years later, I began my education to become the mediator that I needed. Sitting in the conference room at Volunteers of America Dispute Resolution Center in Everett, being introduced to the material, I knew, without a doubt, that I was in the exact right place. I felt home.

Jeff

My relationship with Jeff began at the end of 2014—at the same time my divorce was being finalized. How we met should have been my first clue that this relationship was bad news. I met his ex-girlfriend at a restaurant where I would hang out and have a glass of wine while waiting for my kids to finish karate.

She and I chatted. I told her about my dad dying of ALS and that I was finalizing my divorce. She had to leave, and she invited me to join her and her ex-boyfriend for dinner with his kids. Umm…no thanks. We made plans to meet up again a week from then.

She didn't show up. She sent Jeff as her proxy. Jeff introduced himself to me, and we exchanged numbers. From that moment forward, we did a lot of texting. He was funny and charming. He made me laugh like no other. I was that person who would be walking and staring at her phone, laughing, before she would hit a pole.

I Can't Follow a Recipe to Save My Life

Jeff and I lived together for two years. I was intensely focused on him being the "love of my life" (LOML). We referred to each other as my "LOML" (pronounced *LO-muhl*). He had two kids, and I had three. We called ourselves the Brady Bunch. I loved our life together except for when I didn't.

We loved cooking together. And when I say "we," I mean I loved cooking with Jeff. Jeff didn't love anything. He was bitter and angry about his childhood. I tried to mentor him through this, but I guess he wasn't ready.

I loved cooking with him. I was so excited to have someone in my life who at least participated in something I enjoyed. I have always loved cooking and providing healthy meals for my family. Cooking is a practice. It takes time to get good at it. I didn't have anyone teaching me. I had to learn on my own.

I practiced in my relationship with Norm and raising our children. I always hosted Thanksgiving, Christmas Eve, Christmas, New Year's Eve, and just about any holiday I could. I loved cooking for people who appreciated the service.

Norm is someone who is indifferent to "good" food versus "fast food." He loves a McDonald's Quarter Pounder with cheese as much as he loves homemade mac n' cheese from scratch. It's so much easier to grab a Quarter Pounder than it is to make and clean up after homemade meals. Plus, being indifferent made it seem like "what's the use?"

Norm was so full of nonsense that he would be "tasting" red wine and give some inexperienced evaluation of it. At some point, I just began looking at him like "What the fuck are you even talking about? You know nothing." On top of knowing nothing about wine, he tried to hide that he knew nothing about it by acting like he knew. He would just throw shit at the wall and hope it stuck with whoever was listening. We call this the "spray and pray method" of sales.

I would work extremely hard on trying new recipes or new foods. And, by the way, I can't follow a recipe to save my life. I honestly don't think I have ever followed a recipe exactly. Cooking is creative, and I use recipes only as guidelines.

His evaluation of my cooking would be "it's fine" or "I would add more blah blah blah." Are you fucking kidding me! Then why don't you get off your ass and add more blah blah blah? And do the fucking dishes while you are at it!

No shit. This might be the reason I couldn't live with him anymore. At any rate, I met Jeff, and Jeff loved cooking. So much so that all our kids would say, "Can we just get takeout and eat it?" They didn't want to wait for Jeff to doctor up the takeout!

I loved cooking with Jeff and for Jeff. Jeff was never critical. He had his tasks, and I had mine. We would create menus together and divvy up tasks. He didn't criticize my cooking, and I didn't criticize his. Also, there was not much to criticize. We cooked amazing many-course meals.

We cooked for our family, and we cooked for ourselves. We would occasionally invite a few friends over and cook for them. I welcomed these people into my home and took good care of them, and we had some amazing culinary experiences together.

However, as it turns out, these were Jeff's friends—not genuine, authentic friends. They were there for the food, liquor, wine, and experience. That was as far as their depth would go.

Motorcycles

Something Jeff woke up in me was a passion for riding motorcycles. When I met Jeff, he would take me, once in a while, on the back of his Ducati Multistrada 1200. I loved being on the back of his bike.

I didn't trust Jeff, but I had to on his bike. He knew how to ride; I didn't. If I wasn't going to trust him, I shouldn't get on his bike. Jeff was reckless, so it made sense that I didn't trust him. I needed to find a way to reduce the dissonance between riding with Jeff on his bike and not trusting him to keep me safe.

Eventually, I decided it was too scary to ride with Jeff on his bike. I signed up for an endorsement course. It took two days and two classes to learn how to ride. I was a natural since I used to ride a Honda 150 to school from the time I was fourteen until I was sixteen.

It was illegal for me to ride since I wasn't licensed at fourteen, so I had to park where the school wouldn't see my motorbike. Then when I turned sixteen, I drove a manual transmission VW Rabbit, so shifting was natural for me too. After I passed my endorsement course, I bought a 2009 Ducati Monster 696 with thirty-five miles on it in 2015.

I got a great deal on this bike, and it was perfect. We rode 250s in the endorsement course. The 250s were very small and not very powerful bikes—good to learn on but not as much fun to ride as a 696! Jeff and I rode a lot together, and this became another activity we loved doing together.

Emotional Abuse

I was head over heels in love with Jeff, who I knew was an alcoholic from the beginning. When I say I "knew" Jeff was an alcoholic, what I can tell you retrospectively is that, intellectually, I knew he was an alcoholic. But emotionally, I had no idea what it meant to be an alcoholic. This is where I would like to differentiate a "problem alcoholic" from an "alcoholic." Jeff was a problem alcoholic. I was an alcoholic. Or, as we say in recovery groups, "I am an alcoholic."

The difference between the two is a level of consciousness, a level of understanding how alcohol is impacting your life on a comprehensive level. The difference between a problem alcoholic and an alcoholic is a critical awareness of how alcohol impacts your relationship with yourself and others.

Jeff was a problem alcoholic. While we would always speak flippantly about our alcoholism, we didn't have the deep and meaningful understanding of what the problems were. We moved in together after nine months of dating. Keep in mind Cuba Gooding Jr.'s advice to Jerry Maguire that "single mothers don't date." Toward the end of our two-and-a-half-year relationship, we would each try bouts of sobriety together or separately. When we would go weeks without drinking and the "problems" were still there, that's when I started differentiating.

I read Claudia Black's *It Will Never Happen to Me*. I began becoming very clear about the insidious nature of alcoholism and dysfunctional families. It is very difficult to identify because it is all I've ever known. I've never known healthy functioning, so how could I distinguish between healthy and unhealthy?

I desperately wanted to be with this man, and that was what my feelings told me. My feelings told me that Jeff was the love of my life and that I didn't want to live without him. Those feelings conflicted with the very complicated and painful feelings of being abused by someone you love. Again, I've never known any different. So as far as I knew, abuse was an inherent part of relationships.

Jeff and I would have knock-down, drag-out verbal fights. The abuse was emotional, which was even more difficult to detect. I can only say this retrospectively because I have reviewed much of my journaling and writing to Jeff during the course of our relationship. I knew in the very beginning that he was a problem. I wrote this in my journal two months into our relationship: "This is such nonsense... and honestly, I don't know how many more evenings I am willing to have ruined as a result of this." Fast-forward two years. I allowed *a lot* of evenings to be ruined. A lot.

This emotional abuse was not enough for me to say "I'm out." I would say "I'm out" occasionally, but then I would go back on my word and fall back into my addiction of being abused. It took the emotional abuse of my son for me to realize how abusive this man was. One night, I had gone to bed, and Jeff stayed up drinking. I woke up at two thirty in the morning, and Jeff wasn't in bed. I went downstairs to get him, thinking maybe he had fallen asleep on the couch.

I walked into the kitchen, and he was standing there with my eleven-year-old son. My son was sobbing. I asked what was going on. As I write this, it is painful to recall. I could not make heads or tails of what was going on. I sent my son to bed and told him that part of the problem was how late it was. Everyone was tired, and emotions run high when we are tired. We would talk in the morning.

After my son went to bed, I talked to Jeff for a few minutes about what had happened. My son had asked Jeff for some help with a utility knife that was dull. My son wanted to sharpen it. Instead of helping my son, Jeff went on some kind of rant about how the knife was garbage and demonstrated by breaking it in half. I believe this was what upset my son, not to mention the emotional abuse of a young boy by an "all-knowing adult." My poor baby boy. I could see my son's pain. I couldn't see my own. My son's pain was exceedingly more important to me than my own.

As I write this, and every time I read this, I am despondent that I allowed my son to take this hit. I feel horrible that I wasn't there for my son. I sent him to bed, and I didn't follow up with him until the next morning. My baby boy. He was the victim, and I don't know if I handled that well.

When my son woke up in the morning, I asked him what had happened. Once we were all rested, I was able to think clearly, and I explained to my son that Jeff's behavior was unacceptable. I explained that Jeff was the adult, and he should have known better.

When Jeff woke up, he didn't say a word. He went to Home Depot and bought my son a nice set of DeWalt utility knives—a variety pack with many sizes and purposes. Jeff never said a word to me about it. Any of it.

My son was working in the shop, and I went to check on him. I asked him what occurred. He told me Jeff had bought him these knives and handed them to him. I asked him if Jeff apologized, and he said yes. Never was another word spoken about this incident between any of us.

When I discussed the incident in group therapy, my cohort reinforced that Jeff's treatment was abusive. One of my cohorts asked, "Why are you staying with him?" I explained that I was aware that it was abusive and that I could tolerate being abused, but I could not tolerate my children being abused. We were living together, and dismantling our relationship and living arrangement took time. So began the deconstruction of our lives together.

I had begun reading about alcoholism in the last six months of our relationship. I had already done a lot of reading on codependence and emotional sobriety by the time Jeff and I met. Once my research on alcoholism started, I could not overlook the problems anymore. The main problem in our relationship was that his alcoholism was truly his LOML, not me.

Who's the Manipulator?

After reading Claudia Black's book, I realized that Jeff needed some kind of treatment. We couldn't do this alone. After his continually avoiding that conversation, I put it very clearly in an email. He needed to understand that the consequence of choosing "no, we are not going to have that conversation" was that he needed to start making plans to move out of my home, where I did the providing. While he contributed, the majority of the providing was mine, both financially and emotionally.

I gave Jeff the opportunity to have a conversation about committing to treatment or choosing to exit our relationship. I even gave him the opportunity to define what treatment looks like. After he wouldn't commit to having either conversation, I gave him a deadline to choose between having the conversation or leaving. He chose to leave.

Jeff tried to "ultimatum shame" me. He said that he felt I was being manipulative by giving him an ultimatum. This is Dictionary. com's definition of *ultimatum*: "a final uncompromising demand or set of terms issued by a party to a dispute, the rejection of which may lead to severance of relations or to the use of force." So yes, I did give him an ultimatum.

Shaming is not a way to get people to change their behavior. This is something I learned ten years ago when listening to Brené Brown. Jeff trying to shame me for giving him an ultimatum didn't change my behavior. The ultimatum did lead to a "severance of relations."

Here's the thing about ultimatums. Ultimatums are a last-ditch attempt at resolution. It is one person's way of saying, "This is my bottom line. Accept it or walk away." Technically, I did give him an ultimatum, but not one that was shameful. Therefore, "ultimatum shaming" didn't work for a variety of reasons.

An ultimatum where his shaming might have at least gotten me to think about my behavior would have been if I said, "Get treatment or I will kill myself!" This ultimatum is actually the absence of choice. The second option is not the choice of the decision maker. It would be my choice. Therefore, this is more of a passive-aggressive threat disguised as an ultimatum. A person that makes a demand and threatens a consequence out of the decision maker's control is being manipulative. She is forcing the demand rather than allowing a choice.

However, what I told him was to make a choice between having a discussion about treatment or leaving our family. If a family member refuses to discuss something that is important to you, I guarantee you, that person is being manipulative. This is called stonewalling. Family members that show up in good faith to a relationship share openly, honestly, keep an open mind, and are willing to listen. A refusal to have a discussion is a gesture of bad faith.

Additionally, it was not like I put him on the spot and insisted that we have the discussion at that moment. I let him know that I wanted to have that discussion several weeks ahead of time. I was calm, cool, collected, and compassionate. I respectfully asked to have a discussion.

I was persistent, and he ignored my courteous requests to have a discussion, so I laid it out clearly. Ignoring my requests was not something I was willing to accept. Therefore, I gave a deadline a week in advance to make a decision between having a discussion or leaving my home. I even included a flowchart of the decision-making process, complete with dates.

I was very clear. However, what he didn't count on was that he would be held accountable for his decision. This is the thing that alcoholics and addicts avoid. They avoid accountability. They refuse to take responsibility for the choices they make. When an adult is avoiding responsibility, you can bet you are dealing with some level of addiction to something.

Sometimes "choosing" is so threatening to people that they see forcing a decision as a hostile move. They feel they are being manipulated when the reality is, they are being held accountable for their choices. Accountability feels like manipulation to those who are avoiding responsibility. Forcing someone to make a personal decision that impacts the future of a family is not a reprehensible gesture.

In a family system, decisions must be made. Decisions cannot be avoided. Even not deciding is a decision. In fact, not deciding is another way adults avoid responsibility. Jeff accusing me of being manipulative was his way of trying to get me to back off the accountability of his decision.

People use all kinds of techniques to get you to back off. Jeff used trying to shame me as a technique to get me to back off. He accused *me* of being manipulative so I would not hold *him* accountable to having a discussion that he didn't want to have about something that was important to me.

Norm would look at me with confusion and puppy-dog eyes. That would get me into a frenzy of overexplaining. My overexplaining common sense would confuse me, and I would back off the accountability. He would also complain that he didn't feel well. This is a tactic that would postpone the discussion, and I would likely get too busy and forget about it. These are just a few techniques adults use to avoid having discussions they don't want to have.

Jeff also tried to shame me for being controlling. Truth is, I was being controlling. I was controlling my outcome by forcing him to choose between "me" and "not me." He chose "not me" and left. The next few months were very messy as I continued to establish boundaries regarding the behaviors I was willing to accept in my life and those behaviors I was not willing to accept.

Jeff's inability to see his role in our relationship was the deal breaker. His inability to be accountable for his own behavior and change that behavior so that it wouldn't cause me pain broke us. He was very busy pointing the finger at me, and I was very busy accepting blame. Except when he blamed me for giving him an ultimatum.

Deconstruction

My shock and horror at his choice to leave leveled me. This time, I would not go back on my word. I held to my word and distinctly began deconstruction.

Living together made the deconstruction more difficult. Mid-March 2017, he chose to leave. By the end of March, we had made attempts to work through our issues but to no avail. For all intents and purposes (he hated this expression, by the way), he stonewalled me and wouldn't speak to me. This was extraordinarily painful. This was the time in my life that I came across the phrase "silence is violence."

This phrase has taken on a more social meaning of "saying nothing is just as bad as doing nothing about wrongful behavior." This was not the meaning that spoke to me. In my research regarding why Jeff's silence was so painful for me, I realized that silence is emotional abuse in an intimate relationship. Manipulators use silence to get what they want. They prey on their victim's intolerance of disconnection to get what they want from their victim.

Emotionally, silence can feel like violence in the same way that words can feel like violence. Lack of words when words are needed is emotionally abusive. When dividing a family, words are needed to make decisions and show concern and care. Being silent when the person you supposedly love is trying to talk to you is violent stonewalling.

Relationship expert John Gottman identified four characteristics that create damage in relationships. He named them the four horsemen of the apocalypse. Infrequent and trivial showings of these horsemen in a relationship is recoverable. If these four horsemen take up residence, then the relationship is doomed to fail. Gottman was able to predict, with 97 percent accuracy, which couples would divorce and which couples would stay together based on the level of involvement of the four horsemen.

The four horsemen are contempt, criticism, defensiveness, and stonewalling. Stonewalling is a refusal to communicate or cooperate. In an intimate relationship, indefinitely refusing to speak to the partner you supposedly love is emotional abuse in my book. In fact, I believe any of these four horsemen can be used in an abusive way to avoid personal responsibility in the relationship.

As a result of Jeff stonewalling me, I chose to fight fire with fire. There is some risk involved with fighting fire with fire, but I was shooting from the hip and trying to take care of myself in the face of devastation. I had already faced two weeks of exceptional pain regarding the end of this relationship and his controlling our connection and communication.

I needed to know when the pain was going to end. When would his stuff be removed from my house? I couldn't tolerate seeing his stuff around the house. His stuff was a constant reminder of the loss I was experiencing.

It was exactly like he had died. Honestly, it was worse. He was choosing to ignore me and treat me as insignificant. Supposedly, he loved me and wanted to be with me, but only if I was going to live by his rules and not have any rules of my own. Until you have given yourself so completely to someone and have them reject you, the only pain that comes close to similar is the pain of losing a loved one to death.

I had emailed Jeff asking when he would move his stuff out. I explained that seeing his things was a painful reminder, and I hoped he would be able to coordinate this process quickly. Inconsiderately and indifferently, he requested that I hold on to his things until May. When I fast-forwarded that familiar movie, I saw May rolling around and him having some reason for me to hold on to his belongings even longer.

Keep in mind, folks, he *knew* for two weeks that he was going to choose to leave when I gave him the ultimatum. He had chosen to leave a month before I requested he remove his belongings. This was his passive-aggressive attempt to get me to change my mind and live by his rules with no rules of my own. No deal.

I wanted to get on with my life. If he didn't want to be in my life, I wasn't going to force him. At this point, I decided that the only thing in life that I was going to force was my ass into my jeans. I also was not going to house his stuff for him and continue making myself miserable by seeing it every day.

I called a moving company and organized for a storage container to be delivered. I hired two movers. I lovingly, tearfully, and carefully packed all his items into boxes. I had the movers pack the storage container, and I shipped the storage container off to a storage facility. I paid for storage until May. I emailed the information to Jeff and wiped my hands of that relationship.

Of course, it wasn't quite that easy and tidy. It was messy, and I wrestled with my emotions for at least nine months. However, I knew he needed to grow up if he was ever going to be a useful and productive partner in a relationship, and I knew he couldn't do that growing up with me. I left that relationship in the rearview mirror and began my new life.

Conscious Recovery

Over those next few months, I immersed myself in recovery. I called a local rehab center and asked them for help. I said to the kind lady who answered the phone, "I'm not addicted to a substance. I am addicted to a person. Can I enroll in your program?"

We chatted for a bit, and she said, "I hope we have a program for you because it sure does sound like addiction! Let me ask my supervisor."

Her supervisor got on the phone and said, "What you need is Co-Dependents Anonymous [CoDA]. Give them a call."

So I did. And I am grateful to my alcoholic boyfriend for devastating me so much that I felt the need to enter a recovery group. Say what you will about the Twelve Steps. From my perspective, the Twelve Steps are a necessary path, and they are the only path to recovery. You don't have to do them in any particular order, in any particular time frame, or with any particular group. You just have to understand them and do them wholeheartedly. You also need to connect with others who share your experience. This is the value of recovery groups.

If you read through the Twelve Steps, you might find that you are already living the Twelve Steps. That's what I found. That's when I realized that I have always had a recovery mindset. I was already living the Twelve Steps. I just didn't know it. Having the courage to show up to a recovery group opened my understanding to the fact that I have always been in recovery.

This was an important realization for me. I've always wondered why my perspective differs from so many of the people around me. I've always wondered what it was about me that kept my attitude good despite my "issues." I always wondered why I have not ended up in a ditch with a heroin needle in my arm. The answer is that I have always been recovery-minded.

My investigation has been focused on the negative. Over the years, I was focused on my alcoholism and my weight fluctuations. My alcoholism and my weight fluctuations are not my biggest problems; they are the symptoms of my biggest problem. My addiction to bad relationships was my biggest problem.

My alcoholism and weight fluctuations obscured the real addiction. They prevented me from capturing the real addiction on my radar. My addiction to bad relationships led me to overeating and overdrinking.

My conscious recovery began when Jeff left me to pursue his alcoholism. I entered recovery groups that allowed me to anonymously bond with others who spoke the same language. I continued to pursue a more focused investigation of recovery.

How I Became a Mediator

How I became a mediator is not as complicated as you might think. I was in the throes of my breakup with Jeff. Jeff left mid-March 2017. I was on what felt like rock bottom at the time. I was not drinking. I was taking good care of myself. I was searching for a way to be purposeful.

I was at the gym, and there was a woman that I would always see. I was in my midforties, and she was probably in her midsixties. I didn't know what it was about her, but I thought to myself, *I want to be like her when I'm her age.* We all need mentors, and for whatever reason, I chose her.

She was not a particularly friendly person, but that didn't bother me. To me, she looked like she had it all figured out. Why? I have no idea. I guess I see what I want to see.

She was fit and worked out moderately. She would walk on the treadmill for a while then ride the spin bike. Since I'm a runner, I would ride the spin bike at the gym for cross-training days. I would do some weights, some stretching, and various other exercises. One day, I got up the courage to talk to her when she was on the spin bike next to me.

I said, "Hi, my name is Amy. I don't know what it is about you, but I think I want to be just like you. What is it that you do for a living?"

She seemed shocked and a little mystified, but she said, "I'm a mediator."

To which I followed up with "What is that?"

She and I chatted for quite some time while we rode those spin bikes. She mentioned that there was a strong need for family mediators and that there was a place up north that did training.

I went home and googled it. I couldn't find it. I did all kinds of research, and I couldn't find what she was talking about. I'm a strong researcher, so not being able to find it didn't sit well with me.

I gave my research a rest and decided I would ask her for specifics the next time I saw her. Weeks went by, and she was not at the gym. I was becoming flustered from not being able to get this information from her, so I googled it again. Sure enough, there it was: basic mediation training at Volunteers of America Dispute Resolution Center in Everett.

I signed up for the one-week training for May of 2017. Jeff had left in March of 2017. I was thrilled to begin a path of purpose where all my knowledge about "how fucked up families can be" would be of great use.

The next time I saw my mentor at the gym (which was many months later), I was able to tell her that story along with my having completed the training. I told her how sitting in that training felt like I was in the exact right place. I felt like I had found a healthy home.

Mediation

Mediation is not to be confused with *meditation*. Who would know that one consonant could change the entire meaning of a word? Meditation is the practice of relaxation. Mediation is a means to resolve conflict between two or more people.

Ultimately, the trauma of my divorce threw me into the arms of mediation for my profession. But not before it threw me into the arms of another bad relationship with Jeff. After dealing with Norm and Jeff, I learned a lot about working with difficult people. In the end, I found my passion in mediation.

In my forty-nine-year search for a soulmate, I ended up with what felt like a degree in mental health, personality disorders, and conflict resolution. Therefore, it makes a lot of sense that mediation would feel like home for me. I find that no matter which party I am working with, I have experienced what they are going through.

Mediation is an alternative approach to resolving conflict. I primarily work with families navigating the troubled waters of divorce, but family drama and small claims are also passions of mine. In my mediation practice, I have learned that there is nothing people are more passionate about than kids and money.

Why do I bring this up now? Well, in order to successfully navigate a conflict between two or more people to a satisfying resolution for all parties, all parties must show up in good faith. Good faith is not just showing up and saying, "I'm here in good faith." Good faith is a demonstration of the following:

- keeping an open mind
- sharing relevant information openly and honestly

- being willing to negotiate from a non-fixed position of who is right and who is wrong
- treating each other and the mediator with courtesy and respect

I am a translator of emotional language. I can speak both analytics and logistics as well as emotion and faith. These are all very different languages. I often find myself translating emotion to analytics and analytics to emotion speakers.

I don't help couples divorce. I help couples divide a family into two households using a process that works for them to keep the family intact. All too often, myself included, we have too high of a dependence on the legal system to solve our family issues for us. This is an inherently stupid move.

The general population is completely out of touch with the emotional toll of the court system. We overlook that emotional toll and believe it is the only route to complete the divorce process. The reality is, it is not the only route, and it is definitely not the advantageous route that we think it is. It does not keep a family intact. It polarizes and destructively divides a family.

Working with families through my mediation practice coupled with my own experience, I have learned enough about the legal system to know that it is not designed to handle family matters.

Remember my experience with legitimate long-term sexual abuse? The court did not force divorce. If there is ever a reason for divorce, shouldn't it be when your husband is trying to fuck your daughter?

No one forced our family to divide. Who's to say that divorce is the "right" answer in this situation? The court would only intervene if my parents *allowed* them to intervene. My parents didn't allow it; therefore, the court didn't intervene.

Because we weren't dividing, I figured my discomfort with the sexual abuse was insignificant. Because the court didn't do anything about ensuring my safety, I was not safe. The court is not in a position to decide what is best for your family. The point of the legal system is to keep people safe, especially children. Yet here is an example where the court system was powerless as to ensuring my safety.

Then there is the situation where people willingly ask the court to intervene to divorce them. The legal system will legally divorce you at an extraordinarily high emotional and financial cost. The thing is, the legal system *knows* this. The legal system does not want to intervene into your family matters. *We* are the ones who force the legal system to make our decisions for us when we don't make our decisions for ourselves!

There is direct adversity and hostility implicit in opening a court case. Even if you are mostly in agreement and have zero intention of being hostile, opening a court case is often perceived as an adversarial gesture. Even when it is a logical step in a required process. Relying on the court system to make decisions about your family is handing your decision-making power over to an authority that knows absolutely nothing about you, the other party, or your unique family. It is an inherently stupid move.

The legal system should only be used for filing your agreements, not for deciding your disagreements for you. There are some cases that *do* need someone to decide for them because one party is being completely unreasonable or criminal. But for the vast majority of family cases in the court system, the parties are depending on the court to make decisions for them. This instantly and ferociously increases the hostility between the parties.

Why? Because both parties immediately take an adversarial stance toward each other and begin "proving" their position. It's like when two professional boxers tap gloves and then begin their fight to see who is the best fighter. Your divorce case is no different.

Why do we rely so heavily on the legal system? Mostly because we don't know there are other ways to deconstruct our relationship with our spouse and begin a reconstruction of our separate selves. Also, we don't like taking responsibility for the choices we make. We would rather someone else be responsible. An authority, for instance, to tell us what is in our best interest.

Here's the thing. The court adamantly insists that you make decisions for yourself and your family. The only time the court will intervene is if you refuse to cooperate with your ex and reach an agreement. The court will decide for you if you refuse to decide for yourself. Guess what? Choosing to let the legal system decide for you is a choice. There is no way to avoid the consequence of that choice once it is made.

Divorce is not the answer you think it is because if you have kids together, you still must work together. You may hate each other, but you still must work together for the sake of the kids. Some of us have this misaligned belief that divorcing "gets rid" of that person, and reality is just the opposite.

If you want to maintain control over the other parent, you have to stay in the same home. If you want to see your kids 100 percent of the time, then stay in the same home. If you don't want to work collaboratively with the other parent or the other parent isn't capable of collaboration, stay in the same home. Otherwise, expect that these are all areas of difficulty in emotionally divorcing versus legally divorcing.

The inherent problem with separating a family into two homes is exactly that. Things get divided. You have to agree to that division or let a court tell you what the division will look like. You may not want to make those decisions, and those decisions are the consequence of deciding to divide a family into two households. The cascading decision is how you are going to divide.

Generally, people fight about this division because one party is ready to divide and the other is not. The party that is not ready to divide may or may not be aware of his desire to stay together. He may keep up appearances that he's ready, but what this leads to is passive-aggressive sabotage. Believe me, whether you know it or not, this is the single most prevalent reason for conflict and obstruction in the divorce process.

If you are in a situation where you need a mediator because two adults can't agree how to do the splitting, there is 100 percent chance that you and your soon-to-be ex have communication issues and different value systems. This is the most difficult part of emotionally divorcing. You are in the situation because you can't agree, and now you have to figure out some way to agree. Both parties have to let go of their judgments and criticisms of the other party. This is why you are divorcing.

You don't need a court to validate your experience for you. Additionally, trying to get a court to validate your experience for you is a truly humbling and demoralizing attempt. A court is not designed to validate your experience unless your experience has aspects of criminal behavior.

Here is what I've learned through the process. First of all, attorneys are unnecessary and obstruct the amicable splitting of households. I am sure there are some attorneys out there that can be an asset in this horrifyingly sensitive situation, but I have yet to meet one.

Even my attorney—who was a wonderful attorney—did not understand what I was going through. That wasn't her job. Her job was to get us legally divorced and complete all the paperwork. She did her job with excellence. More than anything, though, I needed to be heard and understood. I needed someone to help me make decisions for myself.

The reality was that I was in a high-conflict situation. It is almost like attorneys are immune to high conflict. It is their natural environment, so they don't notice it as deeply upsetting to some of us. The legal system is even less effective when you are dealing with high-conflict personalities.

The State of Washington requires mediation because the State believes that you are the best suited to make decisions about your family. The court does not want to impose decisions upon a family, but it will if you can't agree. There is a good chance that if you leave it up to the court, you will ensure that your conflict with the other person will remain in deadlock and undermine the health of your two-household family. Especially if one party is high-conflict.

I believe the courts are absolutely necessary for imminent safety, but beyond criminal matters, the court does not genuinely "resolve disputes." I believe the court, unintentionally, sustains conflict rather than resolves it with a decision. The court decides who wins based on the law. I believe that if you don't emotionally divorce during the legal divorce process, your conflict will continue to escalate even after your case is finalized.

I facilitate a conversation between two people not speaking the same language. I help my clients decide what is in their own best interest *absent* of what the courts may or may not decide is in the family's best interest. I assist two adults who can't agree to take individual responsibility for themselves and their future rather than allowing the court to intervene and decide what is in their family's best interest.

My goal with my clients is to assist both sides in reaching agreements on their own terms without involving the courts. I validate each party's experience so that they feel heard and understood. I facilitate emotionally divorcing while they are legally divorcing. I set both parties up for success in moving forward with their lives and leaving their conflict with their ex behind them.

High-Conflict People

Norm was inconspicuously high conflict. He hid behind his passive-aggressive delusion of cooperation. High-conflict personalities are not always obviously high conflict.

High conflict is not necessarily violent, although violence is definitely an outward expression of high conflict. Yelling and screaming is also obviously high conflict. However, high conflict is not always so obvious, especially to the legal system.

Someone who is less obviously high conflict could be a disagreeable person. It could be a person who only wants to "get his way" or who is unwilling to compromise. A high-conflict person could be a person that baits you into an argument to make you frustrated and angry. That way, you do the screaming and appear to be the high-conflict person.

If you are dealing with a high-conflict person, you can expect that person to try to use the legal system to his advantage. You can expect a high-conflict person to use the legal system as a threat or an intimidation factor. High-conflict people are not always obvious to judges and attorneys because, generally, if your case is in the legal system and the parties can't agree, someone is high conflict. It is difficult for a judge, in a short period of time, to determine which one of you is high conflict.

The problem is that high-conflict people are manipulative. They can be persuasive and charming and can "win" a case. If you believe you are dealing with someone who is high conflict, you want someone on your side who understands high-conflict people and how to work with them.

I study high-conflict people so I can work effectively with them. It is the nature of my business. I'm working with people in conflict who don't know how to resolve their own issues. If they did, they wouldn't need my services.

Island of Misfits

As I was finding my way in mediation and learning techniques to resolve conflict, I reconciled with the fact that Jeff made the decision he made for himself. I had to stop taking it personally that he left. I had to come to terms with my devastation and my desperation. Desperation leads to unflattering behavior.

At times, during the months following Jeff's departure, I would find myself enraged, sobbing, and in significant pain. As I managed that pain through therapy, twelve-step groups, taking good care of myself, and moving forward with my life, I found a new group of friends. This group of friends got me through the toughest time in my adult life simply by creating a distraction.

I began returning to the island restaurant where Jeff and I met. Jeff and I had spent a significant amount of time in this restaurant—at the bar. We were friends with all the employees. When Jeff left, I took a long break from showing up to the island restaurant. However, this was where I used to sit and wait for my kids to finish karate. I decided to show up one day, a couple months after Jeff left.

When I did, I had many conversations with "friends." I began rebuilding all the relationships "we had" into relationships "I have." Eventually, our group of friends became quite large.

Our restaurant and most of the members of our friend group live on "the island," so I began calling us the "Island of Misfits." Mercer Island is an island between Seattle and Bellevue. I-90, a major freeway, crosses from Southwest Bellevue, where I live, over the island to Seattle. My kids were doing karate on the island, and when you are "on island," you don't go "off island," even though going "off island" is only three miles to Bellevue.

At the time, traffic was terrible going between Seattle and Bellevue. It made a lot more sense to stay "on island" than fight traffic getting home and then fight traffic getting back again. Hence the need to stay "on island" for me.

However, I quickly learned that people who live "on island" don't *ever* leave the island. It is this weird island mentality. Before Jeff lived with me, he lived on the island. All my new friends lived on the island. We all congregated at this one restaurant because it was the only good restaurant on the island.

I was a member by proxy even though I don't live on island. This is what probably saved me from the invisible restrictions regarding not leaving the island. I literally had to leave the island to get myself and my kids home, where our dogs were.

The Misfits got to know each other very well. We developed our own vernacular that only our group understood. We talked openly and honestly and accepted each other's diverse views, opinions, and tastes. We were, basically, a group of teenage adults. We didn't take life very seriously and had a lot of fun together.

Another name for our broader group of friends was the FILD Book Club. It stands for "Fuck It, Let's Drink" Book Club, where we don't read books and do a lot of drinking. We developed the book club so we would have a reason to party at my house and force people off the island. We also had our fantasy football league. I had zero interest in playing fantasy football, but I loved hosting parties! I participated *so* I could host the parties.

This was how I got my passion for cooking back. When Jeff left, I stopped cooking. This was a sign of depression. I loved cooking before I met Jeff, and I loved cooking with Jeff. When Jeff left, I didn't have the motivation to pick up a cooking utensil. Until the FILD Book Club. Now I had a reason to cook, and I began to love cooking again.

Every member of our group had a special name. We also had names for people not in our group. A little backstory on the naming rights is that the funniest person in our group, "Ms. Kate," was mostly responsible for our individual names. I think "Jay 2" came up with my name, "the Professor." "Jay 1" was also known as "OG Jay." One guy had three names: "the Hammer," "Maui Jim," and "Captain." All our names fit our personalities. We also had "Sparkles," "the Cathys," and "One" and "Two" to differentiate two friends with the same name.

My Jeff was "Jeff 1," and there was another Jeff who was "Jeff 2." Once Jeff left, I designated the island as my territory and metaphorically peed all over it to keep Jeff away. I also recommended that Jeff 2 take the honor of being Jeff 1, which he refused. I ended up insisting that we rename Jeff 2, and we did. For anonymity purposes, I will not disclose his nickname as it was a mashup of his real name.

For over a year, our friend group had a tremendous amount of fun. I hosted many parties, we went to Seahawks games, we met up several times a week at the island restaurant. I catered parties at their places, and we played a couple years of fantasy football. We would even spend Thanksgiving and Christmas together.

Our group of misfit adults has been one of the best experiences of my adult life. It was nice to have a group of friends that I could always count on. They filled the friendship hole that was left when Jeff left me. I could count on this group to always be drinking when I wanted a drinking companion.

However, I could not count on our group of misfit adults for serious or deep and meaningful conversation. I was okay with that though. That was not their purpose in my life. Their purpose in my life was to give me the opportunity to be lighthearted, playful, and irresponsible.

I desperately needed relationships that were "just for fun." This group filled that gap. We helped each other out as needed and maintained a "light-duty" constitution. It was like a family we wanted to spend time with.

My experience in life is that it is never hard to find people to party with. There is always somebody partying. The more difficult problem, in my experience, is finding people who take life seriously while partying.

I have found myself explaining to people, on too many occasions, how the fable "The Ant and the Grasshopper" reflects my experience in life. I consistently feel like I'm the ant, taking life and responsibility seriously and preparing for a long winter. I also consistently find myself in relationships with people who are goofing off and not preparing, all the while hoping I would provide for them through the long winter.

Taking life too seriously has become a bad habit for me. This was why the Island of Misfits, the FILD Book Club, and the fantasy football league were needed in my life—so I could have a forum to goof off, not take life so seriously, and be a little irresponsible.

However, it was time to get back to work. We spent three years together, and we still hang out on occasion. Our island restaurant closed down unexpectedly a few months before the coronavirus would have had the opportunity to shut it down.

Many of us have grown up and moved on. There have been breakups, new dating arrangements, divorces, and other significant but typical life changes. Our group wasn't built to last. It wasn't sustainable, but it was fun while it lasted. We have all moved on and carried these friendships into their next stages.

I Was in My Addiction

In recovery groups, we call it "being in your addiction" when you are doing stuff from a place of compulsivity or letting your addiction make your decisions for you. I was fully in my addiction between my divorce in 2014 and the end of 2019. But 2020 has been an education in getting out of my addiction.

At the end of 2017 and into the beginning of 2018, I had decided to be purposefully sexually abstinent. I wanted to break my addiction to an obviously unhealthy man. I found this man incredibly attractive and very difficult to resist even though my rational brain told me he was a bad idea. This man was not honest. My rational brain knew this, but my addicted brain knew the sex was hot. I needed a fail-safe to prevent me from engaging with this snake with blue eyes.

I decided to be purposefully abstinent so that I could learn what I needed to learn. I needed to learn to live without sex. I needed to tolerate the impulse to want to have sex and resist the impulse to do so. Sex is a way that we hot-wire intimacy. It's not true emotional intimacy. It's an intimate act that masquerades as emotional intimacy. This is why I was addicted.

I craved sex for the fake emotional connection. Sex convinced me that I had the emotional connection that I was looking for. However, that emotional connection was my constructed reality rather than true reality. The snake with blue eyes was incapable of emotional connection, and my rational brain knew that.

In January of 2018, I met up with the Misfits to do some day drinking. I asked them for their help in finding me someone to date. When I was done with my sexual abstinence, I wanted to attempt to find a healthy relationship.

The Misfits asked me what the snake with blue eyes looked like. I said, "He is bald, and he is built." The two characteristics I find irresistible in a man. The Misfits decided they would invite their apartment neighbor—a bald, built guy—to my Super Bowl party. They did, but he didn't show up.

You know who did show up? The snake with blue eyes that I was addicted to. He didn't actually attend my party. He went to someone else's party and stopped by my place on the way home. What a snake.

I had a hard time resisting him due to the blue eyes. It's like how drug dealers give you the first hit for free to get you addicted. I don't know if drug dealers actually do that, but it seemed like a good analogy.

My party was winding down, and the snake with blue eyes showed up with his irresistible bald head and built body. Ugh. Addiction sucks. He awkwardly hung out with me and the few Misfits still at my party.

After calling it a night, the Misfits called on their way home to the island and said, "What's with the Russian?"

I laughed and said, "He's not Russian!"

They explained, "Well, it was awfully suspicious how he showed up all awkward and bald and out of place!"

From this point forward, the snake with blue eyes was known to our group as "the Russian." I am happy to report that is the end of the Russian's story in my life.

My sexual abstinence, combined with the assistance of the Misfits, cured my addiction to the snake with blue eyes. I had zero interest in engaging with him. He still tried, and that was how I knew I had recovered from that addiction.

I met up with the Misfits for another Sunday of day drinking after the Super Bowl party. The Super Bowl party was also our fantasy football trophy ceremony. I asked them to please help me find someone "bald and built" to date. Their apartment neighbor came up again. They said, "Steve's bald and built and seems like a nice guy. We'll invite him to your birthday next month in March."

During this time of recovery in my life, I was recovering from the devastation of Jeff leaving. I was trying to locate my self-worth, so I immersed myself in becoming the best mediator I could be. Again, I don't do anything half-assed. Mediation provided a focus on learning, and the Island of Misfits provided lots of high-conflict people to study!

Steve

Just before completing the practicum to become a "full-fledged volunteer mediator," I met Steve. This was exactly one year after Jeff left. Steve was the bald, built apartment neighbor that didn't show up to my Super Bowl party. Steve appeared to have his shit together. He legitimately had a substantial income and looked good on the outside.

I had just completed an alternative dispute resolution conference at the University of Washington School of Law. This was a conference where we could earn continuing education credits and learn about the versatility of "alternative dispute resolution." This was my second year attending, and it tended to run around my birthday.

The conference ended on a Friday, which was my actual birthday. My mediator friends came to meet me at the island restaurant for my birthday along with the Misfits. Steve had been invited by the Misfits in an attempt to deliver me a "bald, built guy" for my birthday.

Steve lived in the apartments above the island restaurant. In an attempt to avoid an awkward meeting, Steve sent a very nice bottle of champagne to my table. My friends and I were all drinking it, and I got up to go to the bathroom. While I was in the bathroom, Steve appeared in the restaurant.

One of my mediator friends was also named Amy. Steve was standing on the outskirts, thinking she was me. When I came out of the restroom, my bartender friend grabbed me and pointed Steve out to me. My bartender friend was very impressed with the bottle of champagne Steve had sent down, so he wanted to make sure I knew who sent it.

I walked over to Steve and introduced myself and thanked him for the champagne. When I meet people, especially in a dating scenario, I look deep in their eyes. I can see things in the eyes that people don't know they are showing me. At the time, I wasn't certain what I saw in Steve's eyes, but I sensed it was straight-up FEAR with all capital letters.

When Jeff left, in an effort to restore justice to my devastated psychology, I promised myself that I would never be with a man that had not "surrendered." In recovery groups, "surrendering" is a gesture of humility. It is a surrendering of yourself to the will of the universe. It is embracing powerlessness as a functional method of "letting go" of that which is out of your control.

By the time I met Steve, I had all but forgotten this promise to myself. I was so desperate for a man in my life that I was willing to accept whatever Steve was. I saw that *fear*, and I ignored it. That kind of *fear* only existed in someone who had not surrendered.

I met Steve in March of 2018. In April of 2018, Steve was sitting in my kitchen, and I was making him dinner. We were chatting and getting to know each other. I had regained my cooking passion and was thrilled to have someone to cook for.

After Jeff left in March of 2017, I had stopped cooking while I was recovering. I missed Jeff so much, and I missed our cooking together. I had to rediscover this passion on my own terms, which happened gradually over the year of cooking for the Misfits and all our parties.

As I was cooking for Steve, a text message came in on my phone. After we ate, I checked my messages. It's always good for me to check my messages when my kids are at their dad's house in the event that they are messaging that they are on their way over. My jaw hit the floor when I saw that it was Jeff's first message to me in a year!

Jeff's message had no apology in it. I had promised myself that I would never speak to Jeff again unless he apologized to me. An apology from him would indicate to me that he had grown enough to at least be friends again. Since there was no apology, I ignored the message.

I was very busy falling in love with Steve, my next unhealthy relationship. Thank God for this distraction; otherwise, I might have caved and messaged Jeff back. I had no desire to message Jeff back. I was so proud of that accomplishment that I declared myself "recovered" from my addiction to Jeff. Little did I know, it wasn't Jeff I was addicted to. I was addicted to unhealthy relationships.

Cooking for Steve and receiving the first message from Jeff was eerily cathartic. How did Jeff know I was falling in love with someone else? The universe works in mysterious ways. Steve kept encouraging me to go call Jeff. This should have been my first indicator of how controlling Steve is—which, by the way, is the opposite of surrender.

I kept explaining to Steve that I had no interest in speaking to Jeff until he had apologized to me. Steve kept reassuring me that it would be okay to call.

Ya, I get it. Shut the fuck up. I'm not calling him, and I'm certainly not calling him because you want me to. Fuck off. I didn't say any of that, but I probably should have.

After I made Steve dinner, I expected sex in return. That's when Steve informed me that he would not be having sex with me that night "for my own good." I was like, "What the actual fuck? You better get upstairs and fuck me." He refused and left that evening without giving me the sex I wanted.

I had been abstinent for three months, and if he was going to be my boyfriend, he was going to need to put out regularly. Any guys reading this book would be like, "What an idiot!" My "high maintenance" was that I wanted more sex than Steve wanted to put out. Steve had it really tough with a hot and demanding girlfriend. Poor guy.

This earned him the nickname "Moral Cowboy." Before Steve left, I explained to him that having or not having sex is a two-way conversation. He doesn't get to decide for me; he only gets to decide for himself. That night, he was deciding for me because he wanted to appear to be honorable and respectful. I explained to him that it would have been "respectful" to fuck me because that was what I wanted. Instead, he was trying to control my vision of him being honorable and respectful rather than actually being honorable and respectful.

That conversation was my second introduction to how controlling Steve is. My third introduction to how controlling Steve is happened about six weeks into our relationship. I was joking with the Misfits about Steve's "secret." I sensed Steve was hiding something, but what? When I was in Steve's apartment, it smelled like cigarette smoke, so I was joking with the Misfits about him being a closet smoker.

By the way, my grandmother was a closet smoker. I know a closet smoker when I see one. My grandmother would smoke hunkered down by the HVAC vent in the house. She would inhale and then blow the smoke into the vent. Truly a ridiculous scene for a grown woman in her own house.

Remember I saw something in Steve's eyes the night I met him? I was still processing through what I saw at this point. I decided to try this closet smoker persona on him and see his response. Well, he was so offended by the fact that I smelled cigarette smoke in his apartment that he literally moved apartments within two weeks of me saying that. And get this. He never told me.

The next time I went to his apartment, it was a completely different unit on the sixth floor, not the apartment a couple doors down from the Misfits. I was astounded that he was able to entirely move himself and his apartment without my knowledge. He never said "moving day" or "I hate that you smelled cigarette smoke, I'm moving." Not a single indication, ever.

When I found out, I definitely should have ended this relationship. It's one thing if you are not aware of the red flags. It is an entirely different thing to know you see a red flag and not stop. It wasn't a yellow flag: proceed with caution. It was a red flag. Hard stop.

Honestly, had I not ignored all these red flags, I would not have put myself through all that misery. What you allow continues. I allowed Steve to lie by omission by not breaking up with him. Then again, had I not allowed myself to make myself miserable again by ignoring red flags, I wouldn't have learned that misery is actually what I am addicted to.

I am not addicted to unhealthy relationships. I am addicted to misery. I know it seems ludicrous, but it really is a thing. You can get addicted to emotional states.

Over the next two years, Steve and I would go through months of spending significant amounts of time together. I would become so frustrated with Steve and his controlling behavior that I would break up with him several times over the course of our two-year relationship.

About a year into my relationship with Steve, I got the apology I was looking for from Jeff. That was two years after Jeff left. He wrote me a beautiful apology and emailed it to me. I received that email while Steve and I were standing on the beach, throwing the ball for the dogs—an activity that Jeff and I used to do together. Another oddly cathartic experience.

At this point, I was not happily in love with Steve, but I was in love with Steve. I responded to Jeff's beautiful apology with this:

Jeff,

I thank you for this gift. This gift is appreciated with so much love and understanding. This beautiful apology has given me the gift of letting go of the tiniest bit of anger that I could not let go of on my own. This beautiful apology confirms that you are the great man that I saw.

A year sober is the most amazing accomplishment and such a gift you have given yourself. It has clearly stilled the waters so that you can see a similar reflection to what I saw. I am so happy for you.

I wish you the absolute best.

Amy

Six months later, I was in full remodel mode of my house. My house was twenty years old and was in need of updating. I was trying to decide how to proceed because Steve and I had been dating for a year and a half, and I wondered if Steve and I would be moving in together.

The conversation about moving in together with Steve was similar to how the conversation went with Jeff about treatment. He avoided the conversation for months, and then when I forced him to have the conversation, he forced a yes out of his mouth. But his behavior told a different story.

Remember how much I learned about passive-aggressive behavior in my divorce and with Jeff? This relationship with Steve was no different. Steve was scheduled to move in "sometime after the paint was dry" on the remodel. That would have been October or November 2019.

When October rolled around, Steve told me that he had let his down-and-out buddy move into his place in early September. By the time Steve told me this, his buddy had been living at Steve's place for six weeks! Steve had not mentioned this significant change and purposefully hid it from me.

I would ask him how his friend was doing, and he would say things like "I haven't talked to him" or "he hasn't called me back." I would ask Steve if he wanted to invite his buddy over for dinner, and he would say "not tonight." His buddy was living at his place, and he hadn't talked to him? Those were blatant lies to cover up the fact that his buddy was living with him.

It wasn't a problem for Steve that his buddy was staying at his place since Steve was "living" at my place. I put "living" in quotes because Steve never kept a single thing at my place. There were all kinds of empty drawers and cabinets for him to use. The only things he had at my place were two things I bought for him: an electronic toothbrush and deodorant.

The only reason Steve came clean about his buddy was because he got caught in this "lying by omission." I was so sick of taking care of Steve and him not taking care of me that I told him that I only wanted to see him on the weekends. When he was forced to be at his apartment with his buddy, that caused his controlling constitution to break. Now he had a roommate instead of a buddy living at his place while he lived at mine.

Six weeks after he let his buddy move in and two weeks after Steve was demoted to being his buddy's roommate, Steve broke down and told me. I tried my best to be understanding, but when I found out about this kept secret, he may as well have told me he was molesting my daughter. I am not exaggerating.

I felt like my mother must have felt when the school counselor told her about the ten years of sexual abuse that had been going on under her nose. My brain automatically goes to that place with secretive behavior. It is lying by omission, and it is no better than stating a blatant lie, which he also did to cover up his secret. This was like my stepdad saying, "It only happened a few times."

This is how sensitive I am to secretive behavior. Sorry, not sorry, guys. You won't get away with secretive behavior and be in a relationship with me. Grow the fuck up and take responsibility for the choices you make and the things you do. Cue another breakup.

As I was cleaning house after the remodel and nursing the wounds that Steve gave me, I found a small pile of things that belonged to Jeff. I emailed Jeff a picture and asked if he wanted these items. Jeff and I agreed to meet for coffee, where I brought him these items.

It was just like old times. Man, I missed Jeff. He had such an energy about him that I love! We are both very fast processors, and a friend of mine reminded me of this. She said, "It must have been nice to speak with someone that processes as quickly as you do."

She was exactly right. I don't meet a lot of people who process as quickly as I do. This is a trauma-induced response, by the way. What fires together, wires together. My synapses fire rapidly because I am constantly assessing danger and safety. At any rate, Jeff and I were back on speaking terms. I missed having him in my life, and a certain edge to Jeff had been softened.

About six weeks later, as the holidays were rolling around, Steve and I got back together. The problem with these unhealthy relationships is that these guys can put on a good show. It is very convincing when they say that they have changed or that they are going to change. But when it comes time to put their money where their mouth is, these guys fall short. Follow-through is not their strong suit.

Steve and I agreed to "pretend everything was fine" and get through the holidays. We spent November and December together as the family I was hoping to create for the future. I had been very clear with Steve that come January, I needed a firm move-in date.

When January rolled around after a lovely holiday season together, instead of delivering a move-in date, Steve delivered me another set of problems. Being the effective problem solver that I am, I insisted that this set of problems be solved a certain way. After all, he was relying on my expert opinion, and rightly so.

This was regarding a parenting issue. His adult child was sick and needed help. I knew how to help his adult child, and his adult child came to me for help. When I prescribed to Steve what he needed to do to be a good parent, he did the bare minimum. Specifically, Steve did everything I told him to do for his son. What Steve didn't do was take responsibility for his own role in his son's health.

This was a deal breaker. I could not be with someone who I don't respect as a parent. I lost all respect for Steve in those moments. Not only was Steve not taking responsibility, he was also blocking me from taking care of his son the way I knew his son needed to be cared for. I will not allow my parenting to be blocked by someone whose parenting I don't respect. Steve and I parted ways in January 2020.

Fast-forward to COVID-19. Jeff and I had been emailing and texting periodically in an attempt to communicate. We went on a motorcycle ride, and I showed him around the remodeled house where he had once lived. This was all in an effort to get to know each other again. Strap in, people. This is not a love story. It is a story of recovery.

The thing is, as I was writing this book, I had the impulse to ask Jeff some questions. So I wrote him an email. I asked him about growth and recovery. I asked him if sobriety was challenging. It's possible I might have been fishing for the benefits of sobriety. I'm not sober, and I'm trying to discover if there is a reason to be.

Periodically during this pandemic, I would have two-week periods of complete sobriety, and it felt really good. Then I would have a couple drinks on a Friday or Saturday, which eroded my desire to not drink.

My book is kind of about being a high-functioning alcoholic in search of a strong reason to be completely sober. Well, that's obviously not the whole story, but I have not yet reached the tipping point of the benefits of sobriety outweighing the benefits of drinking. I think I was trying to hot-wire the answer from Jeff since he's been sober for a lot longer than I have ever been able to accomplish.

Jeff replied to my email, and his answers confused me. Instead of hot-wiring the answer about the benefits of sobriety after a couple years of sobriety, I was more confused than before I asked the questions. Actually, his response convinced me that absolute sobriety is not the answer for me.

There was something else I realized. I didn't know Jeff anymore. I am sure some of the essence of who we were still remains, but when we are out of contact with someone for years at a time, context changes. When Jeff and I got together and rode motorcycles or chatted over coffee, it was just like old times. I miss having him in my life. He is one of the funniest people I have ever met. We laughed a lot when we were together.

The pain of our relationship, though, has left a permanent scar on the romance. As I grew up and matured over the few years we were apart, the open wound he left had healed. Thinking about Jeff in a romantic way is like biting into something that tastes horrible, and you spit it out.

I say this not because I'm mad at Jeff but because I'm embarrassed about my behavior. Not the behavior that Jeff tried to shame me about but my actual behavior. I look back on my unchecked, immature infatuation with Jeff, and I'm embarrassed. I behaved like a boy-crazy teen.

To be clear, I want to spit out the relationship because I don't want to be that person anymore. I have grown up, and I see clearly how my behavior led to problems. I see clearly that I allowed Jeff to treat me in a way that caused me pain. What I allowed continued.

For me to see it clearly, it took Jeff treating my son the way he treated me.

I love Jeff dearly and want nothing but the best for him. He wasn't willing to take responsibility for his destructive role in the relationship and in the family. That was how he broke my heart.

I know I will never love another like I loved Jeff. I am grateful that he gave the senseless, boy-crazy obsession of mine a place to land. We had a lot of fun. Now I have grown up and moved on. I have matured, and I am grateful for the time we had together. I am grateful that Jeff broke my heart so I could dive deeper into recovery.

My relationship with Steve became my overdose on unhealthy relationships. It is very difficult for my brain to comprehend that a fifty-three-year-old adult male behaves so irresponsibly in a relationship. Lying by omission and being an irresponsible parent are not characteristics I am willing to tolerate. Additionally, he had periodic temper tantrums like a two-year-old. It was insanely childlike.

Had I stopped at the red flags rather than ignore them, I would not have learned what I needed to learn. Had I not stayed in the relationship with Steve, I would not have gotten the full overdose of misery that has facilitated my abstinence from relationships. Had I not overdosed, I might have been in hot pursuit of another unhealthy relationship. Instead, I'm deeper in my recovery, and I'm writing this book.

I'm an Alcoholic

Speaking of taking responsibility, as mentioned, I'm an alcoholic. I also mentioned that I don't want to stop drinking. Here is my reasoning. Alcoholism is the least of my problems. It is not the thing that is destroying me. I am destroying me. I'm doing it slowly enough that, hopefully, the self-care will outrun the destruction.

I have spent too much time and focus on whether or not I'm an alcoholic. I would self-justify that I'm not an alcoholic by explaining all the differences between me and an alcoholic. I would stop drinking to "prove" I'm not an alcoholic. I would say, "I'm not an alcoholic. I'm a problem drinker." What the fuck is the difference? I resisted and rejected the label until I couldn't anymore. I'm too realistic and no-nonsense to keep denying my alcoholism.

Another reason I denied it was because of the stigma associated with alcoholism. There's an image we all assign to alcoholics based on our own experience with them. There is absolutely zero logic and justification that aligns an alcoholic as "different from" the rest of us.

Somehow, we try to justify high-functioning alcoholics as better than "regular alcoholics." That high-functioning alcoholic is still "different" from the rest of us because he is an alcoholic. Albeit a high-functioning alcoholic, there is still something wrong with him that is not wrong with us. We also try to assume that all alcoholics have the same problem: alcohol. We even "allow" people to be alcoholics that "had it tough."

We all try to find the line of demarcation between me and an alcoholic. That line does not exist on a personal level. On a global level, maybe. On a personal level, we are all human, and we all have "defects of character" and "shortcomings." Defects of character and shortcomings are inherent to the human experience. It is how these defects of character and shortcomings are managed that sets us apart from each other.

Part of my efforts here are to move focus from alcoholism to problem solving. Alcohol has caused some problems in my life, but it has also benefited me. In fact, the reason I don't want to stop drinking is because the "benefits" of alcohol still outweigh the "problems."

One of the benefits alcohol provides me is a friend to hold my hand through responsibilities. I have never had a partner who was helpful. I've only had partners that fucked shit up. I have always been the responsible one. Daily drinking allows me to work long hours even when I'm tired. Alcohol has always been my energy pill, my liquid motivation.

For those of you who have husbands that do *any* portion of the responsibilities, you may not need alcohol to hold your hand. You have someone sharing in the responsibility of a life together. I have only had a husband and boyfriends that created more work for me, not less. So I drink.

I get a drink, and I get shit done. I'm not the kind of alcoholic that drinks to relax. I drink to accomplish tasks that I'm too tired or too unmotivated to do. I don't drink to avoid responsibility. I drink to take care of responsibility.

I have always been the "party mom." Even as a teenager, I wouldn't drink, and I would clean up after everyone. I would make sure no one drank and drove. Now I've mastered my drinking so I can drink and all the responsibilities still get taken care of.

I'm talking mastery here. Shit doesn't just get done; it gets done well. I complete a task drunk better than the average person completes it sober. That's fucking mastery.

I often wake up in the morning forgetting all the shit I took care of the night before. Laundry is done. Projects are completed. Kitchen is clean. Food is prepped. Seriously. It's kind of funny.

It would kind of suck if I woke up and shit was all fucked up. The kitchen is a mess. Laundry is screwed up. Shelves are crooked from assembling them drunk. But no. I'm a goddamn master of accomplishing tasks under the influence or not.

Another benefit of alcohol is that I relax enough to have fun. My social inhibition comes down just enough that I drop my professionalism, classiness, and seriousness. I become a lot more fun. I have mastered my drunk persona so well that most people find me more relatable. When I've got my serious, professional, "taking care of business" persona on, I'm quite intimidating. Especially when I've got my athletic body on.

What allows me to fly under the radar as an alcoholic is that I'm not the type of alcoholic that gets fall-down drunk. I'm not the type of alcoholic that lacks awareness and the ability to problem-solve. I'm the type of alcoholic that drinks regularly and with conscientious intention. I keep up the appearance that "I've got my shit together" because I actually *do* have my shit together. It's easy to mistake me for a nondrinker.

Additionally, I'm never the drunkest person in the room. It's probably a survival mechanism developed to keep the attention on someone else's display as opposed to mine. I'm a sophisticated alcoholic, not a sloppy drunk.

All of my exes have alcohol to thank for keeping me in those relationships far longer than I should have stayed. I stayed with the father of my children for nearly twenty years. We divorced when my children were seven, nine, and seventeen. If I didn't have alcohol around buffering the pain of raising my kids, his kid, and him all on my own and on my dime, I might have flown into a codependent rage. I think it is better for all of us that I didn't. Thank you, alcohol.

Here's the deal. Alcoholics are not all bad. And sometimes, alcoholism isn't the problem. Sometimes being an asshole is the problem, and the alcoholism hides that problem from themselves. It certainly doesn't hide it from the rest of us. We all know that guy, the one who becomes a complete asshole when he's had a couple of drinks. This was Jeff, by the way.

Alcoholism is not my problem. Alcoholism has obscured my recovery, but it has not prevented it. Alcoholism does not cause problems in my life. It solves them. No wonder I don't want to quit drinking.

I am not discounting that there are alcoholics where alcoholism *is* their problem. Alcoholism is a very prominent problem that prevents people from entering recovery. And there are all kinds of other addictions as well. Whatever your drug of choice, the bigger problem is that it prevents you from living a conscious life with conscious choices.

My main focus is my journey through recovery. Not recovery from my alcoholism specifically but recovering my "self" that I was before all the things happened in my life that buried that "self." Alcoholism being one of the things burying that "self" (purposefully present tense). My other addictions have also been burying that "self."

We become addicted to that which takes our pain away. Emotional pain is caused by loss. Loss of anything is loss. Even growth is loss of the self before the growth. Recovery is about recovering the lost self from underneath the rubble of losses. Recovering individual authenticity from the rubble of all the pressure to conform.

This is the first time in my adult life that I have been comfortably single. After divorcing the father of my children, I was so uncomfortably single that I forced Jeff into an intense relationship. My intensity was so unchecked. That is what I'm realizing right now as I write this. I don't regret it because I truly love Jeff and loved what we had, except for the parts I hated.

After Jeff, I was also uncomfortably single and on a focused search for a partner to share in the burden of my life. I was at the height of my addiction to unhealthy relationships when I became addicted to the snake with blue eyes in the year I spent hunting for someone. Then I trapped Steve.

Steve was perfect, except he was severely lacking in awareness—both self-awareness and awareness of those around him. This lack of awareness was like a teenager's lack of awareness. I'm raising teens right now, so it became difficult to overlook. I drank heavily during this relationship, and I overate to manage the pain of being with someone who looked like an adult but was really a teenager in a convincing adult costume.

In the beginning of 2020, I found myself severely overweight, depressed, and being awfully hard on myself. I decided to take responsibility for my pain instead of numbing it. I broke up with Steve, the chaos causing my pain and misery. I also decided to take responsibility for my depression and get prescription help. Lastly, I decided to try to cut myself some slack on my weight until I was ready to deal with it.

Then came the coronavirus. My schedule got wiped clean. I have never, in my adult life, not had my day jam-packed with responsibilities. This was the first time I could not excuse myself from writing. Years ago, I had "stopped the glorification of busy" and became intentional about every day. Even still, I had daily priorities that circumvented writing.

Once the coronavirus closed the world down, I had almost zero responsibilities in the day. The kids did not need transportation anywhere. Most of the business I do was shut down when the courts shut down. My home was well stocked, so I did not need to run out and hoard toilet paper and hand soap. I even had a plentiful stock of disinfectant wipes. I had almost no priorities other than making my children a couple meals a day and feeding and exercising my dogs.

I have spent all of 2020 getting comfortable with being fat and single. My weight gain helps me stay single. It has been my way of being avoidant. I don't feel good about my body, so I'm not motivated to engage in sexual relationships. This is a good thing, considering I spent all of 2017 in hot pursuit of a man to have reliable sex with. The Misfits would laugh at me because that was all I wanted: sex, regularly scheduled, into my busy days. You would think this would be easy to find. Nope.

In early 2020, my weight gain was affecting my self-esteem. Once I stopped being hard on myself, I realized that my value was not tied up in my weight. I pulled my mind together and decided to do things that promote healthy self-esteem. I wanted to test the theory about whether or not I could be comfortable with being heavy.

I began managing my drinking better. This helped me get great sleep and restore my mind. I called my doctor and got a prescription for an antidepressant. I took charge of my day by organizing my priorities and writing! Lots of writing.

I've been able to do the mediation work I love virtually. I can thank the coronavirus for forcing my mediation business online. I don't know if I would have pursued an online format if it weren't for the coronavirus. Working with people to help them resolve conflict brings me a tremendous amount of pleasure. I pride myself on facilitating growth and resolution. My weight gain does not bother me in my business relationships.

In fact, I can thank the coronavirus for a lot of things. Most importantly, I can thank the coronavirus for my focus. The isolation the coronavirus extorted put my focus where it needed to be—on my writing and where my addiction really was. I am not addicted to alcohol; my problem addiction is to unhealthy relationships. This addiction was much harder to detect and was obscured by the illusion that alcohol was my problem. Writing about all this has brought me clarity and understanding that I've never had before. Thank you, coronavirus.

Today, I feel completely comfortable being single. I have never felt this way. Ever. In fact, I am so comfortable that I can recognize now that I was pursuing unhealthy relationships like a drug. I was so desperate for a fix that I was making some bad choices. Being in a relationship was more important to me than being at peace. I can only see that now that I have abstained from my drug of choice: unhealthy relationships. I have Steve to thank for my overdose on unhealthy relationships commanding my abstinence.

Once your brain stops craving your drug of choice, you know you have recovered. I have quitting cigarette smoking at nineteen to thank for this realization. Quitting smoking was the most difficult addiction to break. I would occasionally break down and have a cigarette or a pack when I was drinking. Each time I would overdose on cigarettes, I would feel so sick that I wouldn't smoke for months. Then I would relapse again. Until, finally, twenty-five years later, my brain has zero desire for a cigarette, even when I'm drinking.

Relapse was a part of my process. Overdose was a part of my process. Relapse and overdose might be purposeful and necessary parts of the process of recovery. They certainly have been for me. Relapse and overdose have served as purposeful reminders of the things that make me sick.

Steve was my overdose on unhealthy relationships. It wasn't a relapse because I didn't know I was addicted. This is the only explanation I have for how I have become so comfortable with being single. My brain is in that "sick" phase of addiction. I've learned enough to do my best to not relapse.

I consider my weight gain a relapse. I don't feel comfortable being heavy, and I don't want to get comfortable being heavy. Maintaining this heavy weight for the last year and a half has been a purposeful overdose. I've been wondering about the purpose of this overdose, and I've isolated what I think is the answer.

My overweight overdose was not a conscious choice. It is the consequence of the aggregate choices I've made over the last two years. I overate and overdrank to numb the pain of my relationship with Steve. I stopped exercising and drank more to manage my workload. This has all led to a sixty-pound weight gain. It has been a purposeful and necessary part of the process. I have my addictions to thank for rescuing me from the grip of shame.

I am able to label myself as an alcoholic because there is no shame in being an alcoholic. There may be shame in being the type of alcoholic that makes bad choices, makes a fool of himself, and wreaks havoc on his relationships, but I am not that type of alcoholic. I don't believe that alcoholics can be differentiated as "different than." Instead, I believe alcoholism to be a human characteristic just like any other human characteristic. It is no different from a biological determination of male or female, black or white, nice or mean, healthy or unhealthy, or alcoholic or not alcoholic.

Alcoholics

To understand how I have my addictions to thank for rescuing me from the grip of shame, it will help to understand how I was able to draw that conclusion. It begins with understanding addiction, and it concludes with understanding recovery. To begin, we have to stop separating ourselves from others.

Our brains have a natural and biological sorting bias. From caveman days, our brains needed to instantly detect safe from dangerous. In the beginning, categorizing and separating was a survival mechanism.

These days, our brains are still susceptible to this bias. However, humans have developed the capacity to elevate this separation bias to the executive functioning parts of our brain and consider logically, rationally, and morally the implications of separation. We are also able to logically, rationally, and morally override the bias and prevent separating ourselves from others.

The delineation of alcoholics from the rest of us is not an accurate delineating factor. I've learned this because I have spent far too much time trying to determine whether or not I'm an alcoholic and avoiding the obvious answer of "yes." My brain preferred to keep alcoholics in a separate category from myself.

Once I took responsibility for the idea that I can't separate myself from alcoholics, I began to wonder, *So what?* Another terrific thing our brain does for us is self-justify our decisions. So began the self-justification of how my alcoholism was different from the alcoholism of others.

Alcoholics cannot be lumped into "unhealthy" or "bad" or "problematic" sets of people. There are some alcoholics that have a drinking problem, and there are many alcoholics that don't have a drinking problem. I suspect that there are, actually, many alcoholics that are enormously beneficial to our world.

Problem drinking is not the delineating factor of bad people versus good. The real problem is deeper. The real problem requires a deeper understanding. When you truly begin to understand alcoholics, you understand that alcoholics drink away their unwanted feelings. For some, the unwanted feeling is sadness or anger. For me, the unwanted feelings are joy and responsibility.

If you are an alcoholic, you will always be an alcoholic, even if you stop drinking or have never had a drink. Being an alcoholic is a description of a characteristic about a person, just like eye color or gender. If someone says, "I'm an alcoholic," this is not license to judge the person about her drinking. Just like you wouldn't judge someone from their eye color or gender. The next question, for a deeper understanding of the characteristic, would be "What feelings are you trying to drink away?"

Over the last several years, I have contemplated "alcoholism." I have determined that there are three categories of people in this world. These are as follows:

1. Healthy people (drinking or nondrinking)
2. Alcoholics not in recovery (drinking or nondrinking)
3. Alcoholics in recovery (drinking or nondrinking)

I've come to realize that "alcoholism" really isn't about the alcohol. Alcohol is the easy logical answer, but it is not the complete answer. If it was, then removing alcohol from the equation would "solve the problem." The reality is, removing alcohol from the equation simply gives you another equation, another set of problems to solve. In fact, it gives you the problems that you were avoiding solving by drinking.

Instead of having problems related to drinking, like chronic low performance at work or not feeling good, the problems might look more like unhealthy relationships and being unfit. If alcohol was the problem, what explains the chronically late people who don't drink?

If alcohol is the problem, what explains the unhealthy relationships and lack of fitness in nondrinking people?

Conflict comes in all shapes and sizes. Sometimes we are in conflict with others, and sometimes we are in conflict with ourselves. When we are in conflict with ourselves, this is where recovery is needed. Whether it be about drinking or overeating or whatever your issues are, alcoholism creates conflict in an already problematic situation.

Healthy People (Drinking or Nondrinking)

I suspect these people make up less than 1 percent of the world population. This is not a scientific analysis and could be attributed to a sampling problem. The reality is we pay attention to problems—in ourselves or in others. A healthy person is not someone without problems. A healthy person is someone who knows how to resolve problems. Healthy people are effective problem solvers.

Healthy people are people who do recovery well naturally. They are people who grieve their losses and accept that grief is a part of life. They follow through with every part of the grief cycle, which allows them to reach acceptance organically. They may have had terrific parents, or they may have had not-so-terrific parents. Either way, they developed a disposition in life that allows them to appropriately grieve their losses and experience joy in their lives.

Some healthy adults may have been born into a healthy family system that allows them to sustain a healthy family system as adults. These healthy people learned healthy boundaries and healthy relationships, with themselves and with others, through a family system that modeled health. They learned to resolve conflict to prevent escalation.

Healthy adults may develop organically if they are born into a healthy family system that does not avoid conflict. They do not hide problems, and they do not "keep up appearances," knowing full well there are problems. They resolve conflict through compromise and equitability.

No one person gives or takes more at the expense of another. Autonomy and individuality are accepted and honored. These are people who have the serenity to accept the things they cannot change, the courage to change the things they can, and the wisdom to know the difference. They live well-balanced lives, are liked by most, and they don't overdo or underdo things. They learned this organically through their family system.

Do you know anyone like this? Me neither. That's why I say I suspect these people make up less than 1 percent. Maybe I've just never met one. And there are billions of people on the planet, so I can't say there are none.

Children born into unhealthy family systems require recovery to become healthy adults. Whether the family system is mildly unhealthy or severely unhealthy. These family systems can be labeled "mildly dysfunctional" or "severely dysfunctional" or anywhere in between on the spectrum of dysfunction. The unhealthy messages learned as children need to be unlearned.

These family systems may or may not have alcoholics in them. There may be no drinkers in the family system, and that does not mean the system is healthy. The system may be full of alcoholics, and that does not mean the system is unhealthy. The health of the system depends on how many people in the system have recovered or are recovering.

Healthy messages are taught through recovery. This is where "treatment" can be creative. Recovery doesn't look the same for everyone. There is no right way to do it. You cannot step neatly through the steps and become recovered. Recovery is fucking messy. This is why recovery sucks.

Alcoholics Not in Recovery (Drinking or Nondrinking)

In recovery groups, we call nondrinking alcoholics "dry drunks." This is a negative term of endearment that alcoholics in recovery groups use to explain the people in their lives who don't drink but are still assholes. These people might be former alcoholics or may have never had a drink in their lives. This may seem confusing, but the confusion comes from the focus being on the alcohol rather than on the recovery.

How can someone who has never had a drink be an alcoholic? This is a question of semantics. Instead, I think this category of people could be called "never ever recovered." My grandfather was one of these people. He never had a drink, but man, was he an asshole. So it doesn't have to do with drinking or not drinking. People can still be dicks even if they don't drink.

What separates this category of people from healthy people is that they are not in recovery. What that means is that they have not properly grieved the losses in their lives. They may have "accepted" the losses, which is the final stage of grieving, but they "hot-wired" acceptance by going around the other stages.

The problem with hot-wiring acceptance is that the pain of the loss stays stuck in your chemistry and subconsciously undermines relationships, especially the relationship with yourself that is called self-awareness. This is why "dry drunks" should be called "never ever recovered." They may not drink, but their behavior in relationships is not healthy. This is why they seem like assholes. "Never ever recovered" is a compassionate way to look at the assholes in your life.

Another common problem with this group of people is they may use recovery groups as a cover for "being in recovery." Instead of doing the actual work of recovery (which is hard!), they attend groups and say they are in recovery. They may even feel like they are doing the hard work of recovery by not drinking. Sometimes not drinking is so difficult for people, they think that is the hard work.

Recovery is an entirely different set of problem-solving equations. I can assure you that you can be in recovery and drink or not drink. Recovery is a process independent of drinking or not drinking. Recovery is a process of self-discovery, discovering the authentic self that was buried by the rubble of socialization and idealization.

Recovery from alcoholism is not necessarily about the alcohol. For some people, it is essential that they do not drink, but quitting drinking altogether is not necessary for some. Additionally, some people don't drink, but they have all the same relationship problems of an alcoholic. The "problem" with this group of people is not the alcohol. The problem with this group of people is lack of recovery.

Alcoholics in Recovery (Drinking or Nondrinking)

Those of us in recovery might still be drinking, and some may find it necessary to not drink at all. That is a personal choice. Sometimes, alcoholics judge those of us who are still drinking as being "less than." This is why I don't feel like I can go to an AA meeting.

People in AA meetings have a desire to stop drinking. I don't. I have a desire to recover, and I don't believe stopping my drinking altogether is the answer for me. I believe I have progressed further through recovery than a tremendous amount of people (drinking or nondrinking), which is why I'm writing this book.

I have an analytical mind and a strong process. This is how I have successfully minimized the "problems" alcohol causes. The problems alcohol causes are problems such as not feeling well the next morning or weight gain. From my perspective, these are the least of my problems.

My problem with weight gain is associated with alcohol, but alcohol is not the sole cause of my weight gain. Weight gain is a complex issue associated with the logistical elements of alcohol, but it is not the only cause. I gain weight when I'm drinking regularly because of the accumulative effects of alcohol over a sustained period of time, not from a few nights of drinking.

My current weight status is my "heavy" set point. I reach this set point when I am drinking daily. It is not *only* the alcohol causing me to reach this set point. It is the calorie consumption of the alcohol, but it also includes the effects the alcohol has on my body and mind. I have also been able to drink daily and maintain a healthy weight for years at a time. This would lend to the conclusion that alcohol is not my weight-gain problem. However, it would be ludicrous to not consider alcohol as, at least, part of the problem.

For us alcoholics, too much emphasis is put on alcohol being "the problem." As I have continued to test this theory over the last ten years, I have discovered that alcohol is not the problem for me. The real problem is the underlying cause of my alcoholism. Alcoholism is a symptom of a deeper problem.

Lumps are a symptom of a deeper problem, such as infection or cancer. Alcoholism is the mental lump of "lost growth." Similar to how a lump is an outward symptom of infection or cancer, alcoholism is the outward symptom of a lack of mental maturity. Alcoholism is an outward symptom of having an inadequate problem-solving toolbox.

Alcoholism showcases what needs to be recovered. Alcoholism is the lump that developed from shortcutting maturity by becoming an adult without developing the mental problem-solving skills necessary in adulthood. Alcoholics may use alcohol to avoid responsibility rather than resolve problems effectively. Alcoholics may postpone maturity by drinking instead of growing up and taking responsibility.

Recovery is about recovering the child that got lost along the way. It is about accessing the point in time where that child was led askew. Recovery is about a compassionate grown-up who knows *exactly* what that child feels like, returning to that time and helping that child into maturity. That child needs to be recovered and grown up. Not by someone else but by her own grown-up self. That child needs the compassionate grown-up to gently pressure her inner child in a positive direction and apply that pressure relentlessly.

Were You Raised by Wolves?

Her child needs to learn to depend on adult problem-solving skills rather than inadequate childlike skills. We all know how children solve problems. They sweep dirt under the rug. They hit, they take, and they run away. They call names. They fight. They scream. They hide.

This is not "bad behavior." This is purposeful behavior to get what they want. These are the only skills they have in their problem-solving toolbox to solve their problem. If the problem is being scared, a child might solve that problem by hiding. Sometimes a child might solve that problem by hitting. Either way, it is likely a temporary and inadequate solution to the problem.

As children grow into adults, they hopefully have an adult role model teaching them more problem-solving skills than hitting, hiding, and calling names. Hopefully, every child has at least one healthy adult who is helping her grow her "problem-solving toolbox" and fill it with more adequate and useful tools. Hopefully, this role model teaches her that childlike problem-solving skills often solve a lesser problem and create a cascade of other problems too.

When a child hits another child, a cascade of problems occurs. First, the child being hit is hurt. Second, the hitting child either feels good about hitting or bad about hitting. Both are damaging to a healthy self-esteem. Children have to learn to control the impulse to hit to prevent the cascade of problems.

In order to control the impulse to hit, children have to have another tool to reach for that is more effective at getting them what they want than hurting someone else. If this other tool is never developed, hitting is the only problem-solving technique this child will employ because it is the only tool she has. This explains adults that hit to get what they want. They never developed more effective tools while growing up.

Children's brains are much smaller than adult brains. Their brains are not as capable as an adult brain. The purpose of development and growth is to train the brain to move the body purposefully. Therefore, children cannot be expected to control impulses without proper training. If children do not get the proper training, their problem-solving skills remain inadequate and underdeveloped. As adults, their prefrontal cortex did not get the proper training, so their animal brain runs their body instead of their executive functioning. Hence the expression "Were you raised by wolves?"

As mentioned, part of growing up is learning to control impulses. Self-control is a sign of maturity and of prefrontal cortex development. Alcoholic adults need to control the impulse to drink to prevent the cascade of problems that result from overdrinking. For some, this task is impossible while drinking, so these alcoholics choose to not drink. A very smart problem-solving technique for these individuals.

However, some of us alcoholics know our limit. We might flirt with that limit, but we know the line that we cross over that prevents self-control. In order to be a healthy alcoholic, I must know this line well and avoid flirting with it at all costs. Which I absolutely do.

I don't just work hard. I work for mastery. "Anything worth doing is worth overdoing" is my motto. This goes for being a healthy, responsible adult as well. I have been working toward mastering being a healthy and responsible adult, which, coming from an alcoholic, has been a long journey that has no finish line.

This is how I prevent my alcoholism from running my body. I can't prevent the neurochemical impact or the chemical impact of alcohol. I can control how often and how much I drink. I can be a healthy and responsible adult and still be an alcoholic. The pivotal word here is *adult*. Healthy and responsible adults have a full "problem-solving toolbox" even if they are alcoholic, as long as they are in recovery.

Alcoholics not in recovery are simply children in adult costumes. They have not recovered the lost inner child and grown that child up. The objective is to grow children up to be healthy and responsible adults. The problem with alcoholism is the underdeveloped child, not the alcohol. Once this underdeveloped child grows up and gains the problem-solving tools of an adult, the underlying cause of the alcoholism isn't a problem anymore. The underlying problem is the underdeveloped child running the show rather than the healthy responsible adult.

Regardless of how we become healthy and responsible adults, being one is the goal. Alcoholic or not, drinking or not, a healthy and responsible adult has either recovered that lost inner child or never lost the inner child to begin with.

You may not know that you have a lost inner child if you don't have alcoholism identifying that issue for you. However, just because you are not an alcoholic does not mean you don't have a lost inner child. If people around you tell you that you are an asshole, you have lost your inner child. Alcoholism is only one outward symptom of a lost inner child that requires recovery. Being an asshole is another outward symptom of a lost inner child.

It does not matter if an adult is an alcoholic or not if that adult is healthy and responsible. If that adult is satisfied with her relationships, she has done enough recovery. If that adult is unsatisfied with her relationships, more recovery is needed. If her relationships are unsatisfied with her, she has a variety of tools to choose from to solve that problem for herself.

Addiction

Recovery groups often talk about "co-addictions." Basically, if someone is an addict, they don't only have one thing they are addicted to. This is why they call cigarettes a gateway drug. That addiction leads to others.

Addiction is not only a noun to describe a physical or psychological addiction to a substance. Addiction is an expression of how we live our lives. If we are living "in our addiction," our addiction has a major influence on the choices we make from day to day.

Living in addiction means we allow our subconscious to contribute a major influence over our choices. To some degree, it is necessary to abstain from the thing one is addicted to in order to minimize the influence. While one is "in their addiction," they are under the influence of that addiction.

You can be addicted to illegal drugs, legal drugs, alcohol, food, sex, or any other "thing" that, in abundance, harms your body. You can also be addicted to more noble, less harmful activities that, in abundance, harm you or your relationships, such as working, exercising, recovery programs, reading, caffeine, spectator sports, "stuff," and any other seemingly innocuous "more acceptable" activity done to an extreme. My point is, we are all addicts on some level.

I really don't think we should separate the addicts from ourselves. I think we should embrace addiction as a characteristic of being human. No one person is better than another because they are addicted to a more noble activity or thing. We have to stop dividing ourselves into categories of good and bad, better than or less than.

Even perfectionism is an addiction. Perfectionism is about addictively striving for an unattainable goal. Perfectionism is covert addiction. It is highly restrictive as to how one must "act" and "look" and "perform." This addiction is so elusive that it often escapes the attention of the addict himself. Perfectionism is the addiction that prevents authenticity.

We are all human, and we all have a unique experience. I can sense, when I tell someone "my boyfriend left to pursue his alcoholism," they immediately think I am separating myself as "better than." I am not. I am an alcoholic too. When I tell people I am an alcoholic, I also sense that they separate themselves from me as "better than." They wonder why I am admitting such a shameful thing and look quizzically at me. These are their issues, not mine.

Being an alcoholic is not shameful. I am not ashamed of it. That is why I say it out loud. I'm also an addict. If you remember though, I have never used any drugs other than alcohol and weed here and there. The reason I am not ashamed is because I work hard to improve my relationships with myself and others. I refuse to let my addictions define me.

I have never been a fan of weed. I've tried it a few times, but I actually don't like how it makes me feel. I become very paranoid, which is not a good feeling. Also, I really don't like feeling lazy. My brain sends me shots of dopamine (the feel-good reward chemical) when I am productive, not when I am lazy.

Here's the other thing I learned while writing this book. Did you know you can be addicted to emotions? *All* that research and this never occurred to me until recently. I read something on Pinterest, researched it more, and wham! It's a real thing.

Similar to how the chemistry of your brain works to seek pleasure from substances, the brain also seeks "the comfort of home." If "home" is a narcissistic mother, a sexually abusive stepfather, and an absent biological father, guess what my brain has been seeking? The comfort of home.

This has flown entirely under my radar! I have been so hyper-focused on my alcoholism, addiction to Mexican food, and self-compassion that it never occurred to me there was a biological drive undermining my efforts! It occurred to me that my addictions were symptoms of a deeper problem, but what that problem was eluded me.

I have an emotional addiction! Is that even a thing? It is. When I read about it, I contemplated it over and over. I tried to understand what was being said. I read many different articles. It's the only thing that makes perfect sense.

Being addicted to the feeling of "home" means that I am addicted to the misery and confusion of my childhood. My brain gives me a shot of dopamine when I find "home." My brain rewards me. This is how addiction works.

Luckily, I am also addicted to feelings of being productive and useful. My brain rewards me when I feel productive and useful. Therefore, my brain seeks those feelings as well.

Remember the teeter-totter? Here's the biological answer. Chemically, my brain is teetering from the feelings of being productive to tottering for the feelings of the misery of home. My brain is addicted to both states, which means it rewards me in both states. This book is my attempt to overcome these addictions.

Daily Poisoning

Alcohol is, literally, poison to our bodies. However, our amazing bodies have an adaptive measure. The chemical formula for alcohol is -OH. Many of you know this from elementary school science. You also probably know that the chemical formula for water is H_2O. What your amazing body does is take the -OH and add a hydrogen to that molecule to turn it into H_2O! Isn't that amazing? With two hydrogens and one oxygen, now the poison is converted to water!

I tell you, the more I study science, the more I believe in a higher order. How do our bodies know to do this? Natural selection is the answer. Theoretically, people who died from alcohol did not live to pass on their "defective at converting alcohol to water" genes. Those that did pass down their genes passed this survival method on to the next generation. Thank God, given the way kids drink in college today. And don't get me started on weed. I could write an entire book regarding how I feel about weed.

As far as daily poisoning goes, the data seems to show that I sleep better overall when I'm not drinking. Whether my drinking is a "problem" or not, alcohol definitely creates problems. Especially over time. Drinking is definitely a way that I perpetuate my own suffering.

I keep myself miserable or on a path to misery when I drink regularly. I don't "have" to give it up. I just want to feel good about myself, and I want to feel physically good. That is literally impossible when daily dosing with poison. It's straight up logic. It might not be what I want to hear, but it is truth.

My theory is that I need to have a majority of the days of the week need to be nondrinking days. It's not that drinking causes me to behave poorly, it's that it causes me to be fat, lazy, and depressed.

It's hard to find motivation when you feel like shit, especially when it is self-inflicted.

This is not to say that I always want to be perfectly present and sober, but I do want my athletic body back. I do want to feel good. I do want the presence of mind and spirit that accumulate over several days of not drinking. Daily dosing with poison prevents feeling good.

Daily dosing with poison is my way of "not taking care of myself." It is my way of throwing an "I don't wanna" temper tantrum about being responsible for myself and treating myself well. I don't want to take care of myself. I want someone else to do it for me. This is immaturity at its best.

I need to get to acceptance that there is no one but me to take care of me. Always and forever. I can do it however I want, but it is up to me. I guess the denial is slowly being removed. The longer my life goes on with no one saving me, the more I realize it is my fucking responsibility. Responsibility blows.

On the other hand, there is some part of me that does not want to perpetuate my own suffering. This time alone, not in a relationship with an unhealthy man, gave me the gift of realization that my suffering is my own fault. I create it with the choices I make. Now that there isn't a man around creating my suffering, I create my own suffering by drinking and being overweight.

It's almost like deliberately depriving myself of health and wellness. Actually, not almost. It *is* deliberately depriving myself of health and wellness. So I guess I'll ask myself every day if the choices I'm making are the price I want to pay for today. Today, do I want to deprive myself of health and wellness?

The problem with daily poisoning is that it keeps me at a low-level depression, a low-level sickness that is undetectable relative to serious pain. It keeps me tired because good sleep is interrupted. It keeps me feeling just a little shitty but not so shitty that I don't want to stop daily poisoning altogether.

The thing about daily poisoning is that it deprives our bodies of sleep. If sleep deprivation is a torture method used to get information out of people, why would we do this to ourselves? I mean, we wouldn't waterboard ourselves or voluntarily shock ourselves. We wouldn't hang ourselves from our arms until we get the performance out of ourselves that we are looking for. Yet we voluntarily sleep-deprive ourselves. For what?

What is it that Brené Brown says? You can't shame or belittle people into changing their behaviors. So why do we torture ourselves? If shaming and belittling don't work, why would torture work? Torture is extreme shaming and belittling.

If shaming and belittling don't work, then why do it? Torture is against the law, but we continue to torture ourselves and justify it as acceptable. Whatever justification is used, it cannot be denied that sleep deprivation, at the very least, is low-level torture.

Sleep deprivation is highly corrosive to our brains and bodies. In addition to being a form of torture, long-term sleep deprivation is linked to all kinds of ill health. Hypertension, obesity, and depression, to name the most prevalent few. The first line of defense against ill health is to get plenty of good sleep.

When I poison my body daily, I throw my healthy equilibrium off. A few drinks one or two nights in a row isn't enough to throw my body out of whack, but the sustained daily drinking is. This is my personal analysis, not a public service announcement.

If I drink too much in any one particular day, that can also throw my healthy equilibrium off. That's when I wake up the next day and say, "I'm not drinking for a few days." Gratefully, I don't overdo it very often. However, if that's my cue to stop daily dosing with poison, then I need a new cue. Otherwise, I'll only stop daily dosing with poison every few years.

Generally, if I have one night of overdoing it, a couple days later, I'm right back at it with friends or coworkers or whatever justifiable purpose. I forget. I forget how bad it feels to overdrink. I also forget how bad it feels to overeat. The pain is only great enough to remember until the next time I overdo it.

Sleep deprivation is a low-grade-pain way to kill ourselves slowly. I spent a long while being intensely angry at my abuser for many reasons. This one, for me, was unforgivable. Interrupting my sleep for your sexual needs is just not okay. I carried this one with me into my marriages. It would absolutely infuriate me if my husband woke me up to have sex.

I cannot think of anything more disrespectful and narcissistic. It's one thing if you and your partner are on the same page, and you don't mind being woken up to have sex. It is entirely disrespectful to *know* it infuriates me and do it anyway.

So now that I don't have an abuser waking me unnecessarily for his sexual needs, I torture myself with daily poisoning. I keep myself sleep-deprived and waking every morning tired and minimized. This leads to overeating to dull the pain of being tired and having no energy. This is a natural response to being tired. My body wants calories to give me energy.

Additionally, being sleep-deprived lowers my inhibition. Where I might have the willpower to forgo the plate of nachos in favor of a healthy serving of vegetables and lean meat on a well-rested day, on a sleep-deprived day, the nachos win. Not just a well-portioned side of nachos. I'm talking supreme nachos with a pound of cheese, freshly deep-fried chips, an overdose of jalapeños and hot sauce, and as much guacamole as I can eat.

First things first. When beginning a healthy start to a "clean-living" lifestyle, get enough sleep. Go to bed at the same time and wake at the same time every day. This creates a healthy equilibrium that sets everything else in clean-living motion, such as eating well, working smarter (not harder), and exercising regularly. Sleep is highly restorative for both bodily functioning as well as brain functioning.

Single and Not Looking

This is the first time in my adult life I don't have a man fucking shit up. From the age of nineteen until the age of forty-nine, I have had a man in my life. If he wasn't "in my life," I was in hot pursuit of him. This is the first time in my life that I have been at peace with *not* having a man in my life.

There were a variety of reasons I was driven to have a man in my life. One of them being, life is tough, and it is so much more pleasant with someone. In theory. It is only more pleasant if you have the same standard of living, lifestyle, and goals. If not, you are swimming upstream to your goals.

This is the first time in my life I feel like I am letting the current take me where I am going. The men I have been choosing up until now created a tidal wave of force against what I want for my life, lifestyle, and goals. Now I am effortlessly flowing toward my goals. This is not what I am used to.

Since my divorce six years ago, I have been talking about writing. At the point of my divorce, I identified myself as an athlete and as a writer. Self-identity is everything when it comes to getting what you want out of life. You have to know who you are and what you want.

I have always enjoyed writing. For the last twenty years, especially, I have done a lot of writing for myself to work through issues. I have also done a shit ton of writing to my "partners." They loved my writing, but they hated what I had to say. Truth telling, fact-splaining, and reality testing are surefire ways to piss people off for the simple reason that they are being held accountable when they don't want to be responsible.

What I realize now is that was all part of a process that led me here. It led me to wanting to reach a broader audience. My writing wasn't convincing my partners to change. My writing was helping them understand their behavior and how it was negatively impacting me, but they weren't willing or able to change.

Now here I am with a clear vision of what I want to write about. I'm writing regularly for me and for you. I have a strong desire to be "known." I don't feel like anyone truly knows me. Part of my mission statement in writing this book is "I want to be known by me."

Daily poisoning maintains a low-grade pain that undermines success. It slowly erodes my goals and achievements. I'm tired and less alert. I can't maintain the amount of attention necessary to keep writing coherently. It impacts memory, and my body feels fat and lazy.

I'm not getting the benefits from exercise and healthy eating because those goals are eroded as well. I really have no reason to daily poison other than to maintain a habit that is causing a slow and methodical destruction.

I self-justify my drinking as being "not that bad," and it's not from a judgmental point of view. But it is "that bad" from a self-destructive point of view. The destruction is so slow and such a low-grade pain that it is virtually undetectable as self-destruction. But there is no way of getting around the results. It is slow, numb self-destruction, intentional or not.

The results are that I'm less focused and less alert when I'm drinking daily. It is an indelible outcome. Daily poisoning is dying a slow painless death rather than living a life. Daily poisoning keeps the pain level flying below the radar so I don't notice that I've spent years weighing myself down.

Years have gone by self-justifying why I haven't done this or haven't done that. All I do is obsess about drinking or not drinking. I just want the obsession to stop. I have to have a more significant reason than "feeling good" or "feeling better." For me, the system needs to be repaired, and alcohol is not what is throwing the system off.

Fucking Narcissism

I have been attracted to narcissistic people due to narcissism being a foundational element in all of my parents. Narcissism wasn't only tolerable, it was subconsciously preferable. This is the worst crime that is committed against children. As children grow into adults seeking narcissistic adults, the child unwittingly perpetuates her own suffering.

Abuse is very narcissistic. It is getting the narc's needs met at the expense of the victim's well-being. As children, the brain is developing. This brain development lasts approximately twenty-five years. Twenty-five years!

If a child's brain develops with narcissism being "normal" and "safe," brain functioning is programmed to tolerate this toxicity. A relative relational simile is the sea anemone and the clown fish. The sea anemone is the toxic narcissist. The clown fish seeks shelter in the sea anemone, oblivious to the sea anemone's toxicity. The clown fish even helps the sea anemone by cleaning house! This symbiosis works great for the sea anemone and the clown fish, but humans are negatively impacted by the toxicity of a narcissist. That negative impact is compounded if the toxicity goes undetected.

Additionally, the developing brain, in a way, becomes addicted to narcissism. It seeks out narcissism for a dopamine reward. Narcissism is "home," and our brains seek "home" when we are adults, regardless of whether the home was toxic or not. When our brain registers that something feels like "home," it rewards us with feel-good chemicals. This is all entirely out of our control. It is entirely autonomic, just like breathing and a heart beating.

Thankfully, our developed brain has the capacity to restructure its functioning. This is called "plasticity" in the neuroscience biz.

Our biology is built to adapt to change, but change is hard. "Not changing" is the path of least resistance, which is often preferrable. However, if change is desired, we are all entirely capable of change.

However, changing something that is happening autonomically requires a deep understanding of the process. It requires an awareness of the process, and it requires an awareness of what can change, what needs to be changed, and what will change.

God, grant me the serenity to accept the things I cannot change, the courage to change the things I can, and the wisdom to know the difference.

All the men in my life have been problematic as a result of their narcissism. None of the men in my life were "bad" men, nor were they complete assholes. Simply stated, they were incapable of seeing beyond their own noses. Whenever I would insist that I be considered, they fundamentally didn't know how to consider anyone other than themselves.

Narcs are very charming. That is how they hook you. When they are charming, it camouflages their narcissism. However, the way you can tell is if they keep making the same "mistake" that hurts you. It is not a "mistake." It is their behavior.

If their behavior causes you discomfort or pain and they do not change their behavior, that person is more concerned about himself than about you. Your pain doesn't matter because he is not in pain. Narcs, fundamentally, are incapable of seeing beyond their own best interest.

Norm was a kind and gentle narcissist. We laughed a lot, and we played a lot. We have great kids, and he parents well enough in a separate household. His inability to contribute to the well-being of the entire family was proof of his fundamental inability to see beyond what he believed was his own best interest.

Jeff was an alcoholic narcissist. The alcoholism made him an asshole while the narcissism prevented him from seeing my perspective. Jeff choosing to leave to pursue his alcoholism was proof of his fundamental inability to see beyond what he believed was his own best interest.

Steve was a kind, responsible, and generous type of narcissist. He appeared to be a kind, responsible, and generous person when he was around. However, Steve was just like a kindergartener who was on his best behavior at school, and he would lose his shit when he got home from school.

My home was "school," and his apartment was "home." Steve would constantly leave so he would not have to maintain his kind, responsible, generous performance all the time. This way, whenever he was overwhelmed with appropriate adult behavior, he could escape home and misbehave however he wanted.

It took me two years with Steve to figure this one out. I had to decide if his behavior was something I could live with. He showed me over and over that his behavior was not changing, even though my requests were specific to his stopping the hurtful behavior.

For two years, I tried to tolerate the pain. I have a high pain tolerance. He would throw his temper tantrum and leave. The temper tantrums were also rather painful as they were directed at me being the problem. According to him, I was being unreasonable or irrational because I had one simple need: "Please stop hurting me." I was unreasonable and irrational.

This is how narcs turn the responsibility on you rather than taking responsibility for their own behavior. Believe me, if there was anyone that was "high maintenance" in that relationship, it was not me. I was the one that took care of everything and did everything around all his special needs. Believe me, he was well taken care of. He just didn't want to take care of me.

I guess I just want an adult for a partner, and what I'm finding is that there are a lot of children in adult costumes all around us. I can't tell if it is a sampling problem or a universal problem. I mean, we all act childish at times, but being an adult requires that you be able to identify your behavior as childish and gather up some maturity to be accountable for it.

Plus, we are more susceptible to childish behavior when we are sleep-deprived. We live in a culture that honors sleep deprivation as a measure of success, as long as you can justify the sleep deprivation as a byproduct of how hard you are working.

For me, the pain has to get loud enough. Maybe I just need to be in pain long enough. When I'm dulling the pain with alcohol, I stay in pain much longer, but the pain is less intense. All the men in my life have alcohol to thank for keeping me in those relationships much longer than I would have if I stayed sober.

Heavy

My life is heavy. There is no doubt about it. It's not just my body that is heavy. It's my entire life. It's no wonder my body matches the environment it lives in.

As a result of my settlement, my life became overwhelmed with "stuff." I kept expanding my space to make more room for more stuff. With each kid came more stuff.

I did the best I could to keep the stuff organized. I have exceptional organizational skills. Anyone with children knows that organizing is a task that takes hours to execute and minutes to destroy.

I bought my house in 1999. I built my husband a shop and two sheds for his tools and our family stuff. Our family expanded to two kids in 2004 and was going to expand further at the end of 2006. In 2006, I added a quadrant to our home.

I say "I" even though it was technically a "we" at the time. However, I'm giving my inner child a voice, and she is very selfish. She wants credit for everything. Since I'm writing this book, I'm giving her credit for everything because that is certainly what it felt like at the time.

Even though studies show that we are all prone to overestimating our own proportional contribution to household chores, it is indisputable that I contributed more. I might say I contributed 90 percent and he 10 percent. He might estimate that I contributed 60 percent and he 40 percent. Either way, we would both agree that I contributed more than him. And if he doesn't agree that I contributed more, he can write his own book.

Without question, I feel like I did 90 percent of all household and child-rearing responsibilities. He would do what I would ask, but I had to ask. He would perform the "ask" inadequately enough that, over the years, I developed an "it's easier to do it myself" atti-tude and "if I want it done to an adequate standard, I have to do it myself." I am partly to blame for the 90 percent. I enabled my husband to spend the majority of our last few years together playing online strategy games and smoking a lot of weed, neither of which helped his motivation to get off the couch and help me out or get a paying job.

I built a very heavy life full of lots of stuff and lots of people. Yes, these are my rich-white-girl problems, but they are my problems all the same. Abundance is not problem-free. Abundance creates its own set of problems.

Many people are not cut out for responsibility. Life is messy. Cleaning up diarrhea and vomit is unpleasant, but someone has to do it. Men that gag and women that say "I'll do it" are codependent. That's me. I'm codependent. I've got dogs and kids. Life is messy.

My drinking has a lot to do with how heavy my responsibili-ties are. I don't have a partner to "share" the responsibility with, so I shoulder the entire burden. This also leads to feeling sorry for myself that I have to shoulder all this burden on my own.

Having a beautiful large home is definitely wonderful. However, taking care of a huge yard, cleaning a huge house, and paying for everything by myself is a huge burden. But I built this life, so it is my responsibility.

Problems are always going to be a part of life. When you set down one set of problems, you pick up another. I would just as soon keep my problems of abundance rather than set them down for prob-lems of scarcity.

There is nothing more powerful to help me feel like "I'm killin' it" than when my body is looking and feeling great. That doesn't mean I don't hyperfocus on perceived and insignificant flaws. I do. I just talk myself out of it by saying, "You've squeezed your ass into twenty-six-inch jeans. Get over it."

I know you think I'm being ridiculous. I know you are think-ing that all your problems go away when you can squeeze your ass into twenty-six-inch jeans. But I assure you, all the problems are still there. It's just that now you can deal with your problems in twenty-six-inch jeans and cross "weight problem" off your list of problems.

Sometimes we keep certain problems around to prevent us from dealing with other problems. For instance, I kept problematic men around so I could focus on their problems instead of focusing on my problem. My problem was that I didn't know who I was without a man in my life.

To be honest, I have systematically gotten rid of all my problems except my own personal problems. I have either successfully resolved the conflicts with the people in my life, or they are not in my life. No one is causing any of my problems. I am the only one responsible for my problems.

Outside of being a couple or being a fit single, today, I don't know who I am. I'm not coupled, and I am overweight. I am having an identity crisis. I have not fully identified with my whole self just yet.

My Garage

When I first got my settlement twenty-two years ago, the accumulation began. I was dating the man that would become my husband and the father of my children. We were going to build a life together, and it began with consolidating our homes into one. He was living with me while he transitioned out of his first marriage and into a life with me.

We went house hunting together, but I was the buyer. We were not buying a house together. I was buying a house for us to live in. The first house we looked at ended up being the house I bought. We looked at many homes in a wide area range. I wanted to make sure I was buying the house that I wanted to live in for the rest of my life, and ensure that I did.

I didn't think it would be a good idea to buy the first house we looked at. I would have wondered what we missed out on if we didn't see all the buying options. This first house had been on the market for nearly a year. That concerned me because this was a spec home built by a builder, and it was the first new home on the street. The other homes surrounding it were built in 1965. Was this why no one was buying this house?

This house was "builder grade" everything. There were very few special touches, and there were several things I wanted to change. Nevertheless, I decided it was the best home for the money, and I put in an offer. At the very same time, someone else had made an offer. The builder decided to go with my offer since it was a cash offer and full asking price. I've always felt a little bad about grabbing this house out from under this other couple. However, this house turned out to be the greatest investment I could have ever imagined.

The home I bought was a large home in downtown Bellevue. At the time (1999), Bellevue was extraordinarily undeveloped. It was so undeveloped that I could not get a pizza delivered to my house. That is how "rural" we were. My home is about one mile from a major shopping center that was built in 1946 and was the main attraction in Bellevue. Today, Bellevue is a bustling mecca, but back then, I couldn't get a pizza delivered.

Norm and I lived here, and we raised his daughter and our kids together in this home for eighteen years until our divorce. When we divorced, not a single person noticed in our neighborhood.

Why? Because I was the face of the family. I was the one at school events and the community figure. I was the one taking care of everything. I was the one keeping up appearances. That's how good I was at keeping up appearances. My husband went to rehab and had been gone from our home for seven months. Then we were divorced, and not a single person knew about it.

I had to tell a very social friend of mine on purpose so she would spread the news. I gave her explicit instructions to tell everyone and anyone. It felt weird walking around like nothing had changed when I had gone through a traumatic severing of a family into two households.

In the very beginning of our marriage, I made it very clear to my husband that my bottom line was that "I need to be able to park my vehicle in the garage." I bought a home with a three-car garage to ensure that I would be able to park in it. It is absurd to me that people with garages don't park vehicles in them. Don't get me wrong. I get it. I just wanted to establish my standard, which was that "at least my vehicle will be in the garage."

Living in the Pacific Northwest, we get a lot of rain (not that I should need to justify my position). This is one reason parking in the garage is a necessity. Combine that with me being somewhat of an efficiency expert, and not being parked in the garage equals getting soaked along with being the only one to carry in all the groceries, the kids, and all their stuff.

In order to maintain this order to hold this space open for my vehicle, I kept building more and more storage on my property to house my husband's stuff. When I bought the house, part of the deal was that the builders would build a shop off the back of the house. They did. Once that was filled, I had a shed built to capture the overflow.

Once that shed was overflowing, the side of the house filled up with stuff. In an effort to get that stuff put away, I had another shed built. We were running a business out of our garage and shop, so more structures needed to be built to keep at least one garage bay open for me.

I can only tell you now, looking back, what a hamster on a wheel I was regarding solutions to the perceived problem. The perceived problem was that there was not enough room for all this stuff. It seemed like a logical solution to build more structures to hold the stuff. It's not like we were hurting for space. Looking back, I can now see how I preserved my denial instead of facing the real problem, which was my husband's accumulation problem.

I knew he had a problem with accumulation before I married him. I believe it was an effort to support him that I married him anyway. If you give a kid a credit card and tell him his only limit is that one bay of the garage is off-limits for storage, welp. You get overflowing buildings breeding more overflowing buildings.

I did a final addition to the house when I was pregnant with my daughter. We were under construction for my entire pregnancy. By the end of my pregnancy, I looked at my husband and said, "Get them out." I couldn't take it anymore. I needed to nest. I needed to create the space for an addition to the family. I needed him to do something for me. I had managed the entire construction process.

I added on a significant wing to my home. Each addition I have done has made a portion of the home more useable. Portions that we were not using at all or using as "catch basins" became entirely useable.

When we were first beginning our separation, Norm would drive up to the house, open the garage door, and pull into the garage. The one convenience I insisted on, and he's taking advantage of it now that it isn't a demand anymore. It is a gift.

A glorious space available for a car. When he would come over to visit with the kids or grab some stuff to take to his apartment, he would pull into the garage. I'm sure it was to maintain his own denial, to pretend like nothing was different and that nothing was changing. Because that shit is real, and it does not feel good.

However, for me, I needed evidence that things were changing. That things are not the same. That he acknowledged and understood boundaries beyond "one bay of the garage." He didn't.

Looking back, I can tell you that now. Boundaries were like gooey tar to him—no clear understanding of where you end and I begin.

I'd been down that road before of trying to explain to him about boundaries. He looked at me confused and with sad eyes, so I would feel sorry for him. Of course, none of this was conscious. It was just how he learned to get some attention. Honestly, it had worked until now; so of course, he would keep doing it.

I didn't want to get into a mom-splain, so I set up bike racks in the garage so that he couldn't pull in. I rode bikes to school every day with the kids. This was how they got to school and home together. Bikes. Instead of having to haul bikes all around all the clutter, I cleaned the space up and put the bike racks in the middle of one of the bays.

At the time of our divorce, I owned two houses. I could not order him to get his stuff out fast enough. It was the only accomplishment I wanted in the divorce: for him to get his massive amount of accumulation and get the fuck out. I had to give him deadlines, and I even gave him open rein. Take *anything* you want. I had money. I would replace anything he took that I wanted.

So when he wanted his half of the knives, it really ticked me off. I am the cook. I am the one who uses the knives. To solve my own problem, I set the entire block of knives out with his stuff. I went and bought myself a new block of knives that I loved even more.

It would take me six years to completely remove all the remnants of all the men in my life. What remained was their influence, and I made it mine. Norm influenced me to grow my space. Jeff influenced me into high-performance vehicles and especially motor-cycles. Steve influenced me into taking ownership of it all.

Now there are no men influencing my space. My garage is clean and full of well-maintained vehicles. I have a Ducati SuperSport S in one garage. I have my son's car in one garage. I have my Range Rover Sport 550 horsepower Autobiography in the last garage. Right behind it is a beautiful fold-up dual ride-up motorcycle trailer. There is literally nothing else in my garage. I could not be prouder.

The Beginning of the Transformation

In the year prior to this showcase display of a garage, I spent significant time and energy on updating my house. I ordered a garbage dumpster and had it in my driveway for two weeks. I cleaned out every corner of my house including the attic. I cleaned out every shed, the side of the house, and every corner of my garage, workroom, and shop. I got rid of everything that I didn't use on a regular basis. If it was not beautiful, necessary, or meaningful, I got rid of it.

This was an extraordinarily cathartic experience. I updated every square inch of my house and made every space useable and beautiful. I have no more catch basins. I love my space, and I especially love my new office. All just in time for the coronavirus to sequester us in this beautiful home.

I couldn't help but be in love with my home. When stay-at-home orders were put in place, I didn't mind. "Home" is now a safe place. It is mine. It is where me, my children, and my dogs live happily and peacefully. We get stuff done, and we enjoy being together. It has been a dream come true for us.

I don't stress out about the kids' school and how this situation is going to impact their education. This is life. Learning to deal with what life throws at you is as much of an education as any. My kids going to school is a small portion of their education. I am setting them up for success by allowing them to be emotionally intelligent people and develop their own interests and passions. My kids are amazing people who, I believe, make the world a better place.

When the coronavirus struck, it initially impacted me heavily, as it did so many people. Interestingly though, the longer it went on,

161

the better I felt (which seems opposite of how it impacted others). It seemed like the longer the coronavirus sustained, the more agitated and frustrated the populace became. It seemed like everyone was thinking, *Fine, fine, fine. We'll wear masks. Just open everything back up!*

I couldn't care less if everything opens back up. I love having my kids home. I love cooking. I love how much more time I have in a day because I don't have to drive anywhere. I love working from home. I love my home. I love the new normal that is being established.

Part of why I am not agitated is because money is not an issue for me. The coronavirus has not financially destabilized me as it has so many people. This I am grateful for.

Another reason I am not agitated is because stay-at-home orders suit me. I am an excellent cook. Home is where we all love to be. We love each other, and we don't fight because I am a conflict resolution specialist. We solve problems. The trauma I have experienced has prepared me for every moment of this.

Lastly, the reason I am not agitated is because the coronavirus forced me into a security blanket. The coronavirus became one of those heavy blankets that emergency medical technicians put on you to calm you down and keep you warm. It created a massive security blanket for my heavy life.

Nearly all my "work" had come to a halt. At least half my job was playing taxi driver for my kids to school and all their activities. With everything being shut down and everyone being required to stay at home, I had nowhere to go. As a conflict resolution specialist, the courts being closed also eliminated the majority of my schedule. At home, with no "work" to do and no man around fucking shit up, I got down to writing this book. The heavy blanket of the coronavirus stilled everything so I could focus.

This is the first time in my life that I feel entirely congruent with my higher purpose. When I work with clients, I feel congruent with my higher purpose. Working with my kids on issues that come up, I feel congruent with my higher purpose. Talking with friends and family and socializing, I feel congruent with who I am.

When I write, I feel congruent with my higher purpose. Writing this book is a bigger reach. Instead of writing to the men in my life and explaining to them how they are fucking shit up, I'm writing to you and revealing for myself how I have become the woman and mother I am today. I'm giving myself the gift of reaching out to share my experience in a meaningful way.

Essentially, this book is about dissonance. We all experience dissonance when we hold two seemingly conflicting thoughts in our heads. Dissonance is an uncomfortable feeling that our brains avoid by playing all kinds of tricks on us to reduce it. This is why self-awareness is the key to unlocking incongruent behavior.

It is a fact that our subconscious runs a lot of our behavior without our knowledge. That's just it. The trick our brains play on us is the very comforting delusion that we are aware of our behavior. While we can be aware of our behavior, what is not as easily understood is the motivation behind the behavior.

This is where a lot of assumptions close the gap. In my life, people see my abundance. They see my beautiful home, my stunning personality, my super cool vehicles, and they see someone "who has it all together." What they don't see is the motivation behind my overperformance.

To close the gap, people make up stories in their heads about how it is possible for me to be living so high on the hog and be a single mother *and* still have it all together. I'm not frazzled, and I'm not struggling. I have my shit together, and that creates dissonance for people who don't have their shit together.

Here are the stories I've heard:

1. We assumed you took your ex-husband for everything he had.
2. We assumed you got money from your dad being an author.
3. We assumed you had family money.
4. We assumed you hit it big in the dot-com era like so many.

More often than not, the story people tell themselves is that I am not responsible for my wealth, but someone else is.

The reality is that I am responsible for my wealth. I am also responsible for maintaining my wealth despite everyone trying to take it away from me. I mean this both literally and metaphorically. I have lived a very abundant and wealthy life. I have maintained and preserved my wealth instead of squandering it away. One purpose of this book is to reduce the dissonance and reveal where my wealth comes from.

Resentment

Who here has woken up at some ungodly hour of the morning to some kind of disaster? A baby is screaming, and there's diarrhea and vomit everywhere. Maybe it's the baby. Maybe it's the elderly parent. Maybe it's the dog or cat. There's diarrhea or vomit everywhere, and you say to yourself, "I didn't sign up for this."

No doubt. You didn't know that was the contract you signed when you hatched a human out of your vagina. You didn't know that was the contract you signed when you were born into a family where the kids take care of the adults. You didn't know that was the contract you signed when you took that dog in off the street or paid $5,000 for that fancy show dog.

Ignorance is no excuse. You may not have known that was the contract you signed, but it is the contract you signed. Fuck parents who bring children into this world to take care of the adults. That's your fucking job. It is literally how the biology works.

When you bring a child into this world or you adopt a pet, *you* are the responsible party, whether you read the contract you are signing or not. Whether there is a contract or not. Whether you understand the contract or not. There is an implicit moral code that humans abide by or anarchy results. Parents clean up the diarrhea!

One morning, I woke up at 2:30 a.m. to a funky smell. My three-year-old chocolate Labrador retriever was not on the bed where she normally resides throughout the night. I'm not a fan of dogs sleeping in the bed, but that was before when the bed was crowded with a pseudo partner. Now my king-size bed is big enough for me and the dog, and I'm good with that.

I felt around on the bed, and I couldn't find Lexi, so I flipped the light on and stepped out of bed. Straight into a muddy puddle of diarrhea. I hopped to the bathroom, trying to not hit the trail of diarrhea to no avail. In addition to the trail of diarrhea Lexi left, now there were footprints of diarrhea to the bathroom.

I clean my feet up and the tile floor and decide to temporarily subdue the diarrhea mess on the carpet. I go downstairs. I gather towels and pet-stain neutralizer. I'm working on the temporary fix when my son walks in. Yes, he is still up at 2:00 a.m. playing video games with his friends online. Remember, it is the coronavirus schedule.

He says, "Oh gawd."

I say, "Ya."

He says, "Lexi just peed in the playroom."

Ugh. I go downstairs, gather more towels, and spray the spot in the playroom. Thank you, Lexi, for staying in one spot. I stand on the towel for a few minutes and get that spot cleaned up.

I go back to bed. Lexi snuggles up. We sleep until 6:30 a.m. She is curled up by the door. I get up. I let her and her sister, Luci, out. I usually don't let them out before seven since Lexi barks and disturbs the neighbors. They go out, and the 6:30 a.m. event is pretty uneventful.

I climb back in bed to try to grab a bit more sleep. Lexi wakes me at eight. I brush my teeth and head downstairs. As I'm walking down the stairs, I'm saying, "Oh my gawd, Lexi." I can smell more diarrhea. Thank gawd it is the same trail as upstairs on the carpet, but it's on the hardwood floor. Win.

I grab bags and cleaning supplies and scoop up the diarrhea, getting it on the outside of the bag and on my hand. I eventually get the entire mess cleaned up and head into the kitchen to make coffee. I start my coffee and breakfast and prep breakfast for the dogs. I grab some pumpkin out of the cabinet since this is excellent for managing diarrhea in dogs.

I use the can opener and open the can of pumpkin, which sprays on my white sweatshirt when the pressure of the can is broken with the can opener. I open the can and toss the lid in the sink, where more pumpkin splatters on my white sweatshirt. For some reason, my coffee didn't come out right, and I'm thinking, *Ugh, could this day begin any worse?* Of course it could.

Fast-forward seven days. I had been cleaning up diarrhea four out of seven days. Luci ended up getting sick after Lexi. Luci is almost thirteen years old, so her explosive diarrhea is in one spot, and then she leaves a trail of six to nine feet from the explosion. When this happened at 1:00 a.m. on a day when I needed to wake at 5:00 a.m. for work, I did a quick cleanup job and put wet towels over the affected area. It was extraordinarily difficult getting back to sleep with that smell stinging my nostrils. Somehow, I was able to get back to sleep. When I awoke at 5:00 a.m., I found three more trails in a different room.

After I completed my work assignment, I checked my messages. My daughter had sent me this message: "How do I get diarrhea out of the carpetttt." I called her to find out that she YouTubed the solution and used soda water per Oprah's suggestion. I called a carpet cleaner on my way home from my work assignment. This was Thursday, and they couldn't get out until Monday. I decided I would clean the mess up when I got home.

By the time I got home, my house cleaners had placed paper towels over another soiled area in the same room. When I got home, instead of cleaning, a few friends came by for an impromptu gathering for drinks and chatting. Wet towels were on all the soiled areas and were covering the smell up quite well. We all took a quick tour, and my friends got a good laugh at the work ahead of me. It could wait until tomorrow. That night, I closed the door to that soiled room, only to find that overnight, Luci had soiled three more rooms in the same fashion.

Every time I step out of my room or into the house from outside, I can tell if there is a fresh soiling. I have a highly acute sense of smell when it comes to yuck. This is why I can smell any food and tell you with confidence if it is okay to eat or drink.

The next day, I completed several hours of work prior to attempting to attack the mess. I had a small spot cleaner that was highly underpowered for this project. However, I couldn't leave the mess for the carpet cleaners on Monday. I had to at least get up what I could. I spent the next hour and a half on my hands and knees in shit. Could my day get any worse from that first day? Yes. Yes, it could.

Fast-forward two days later on a beautiful Sunday morning in the PNW. It's 8:00 a.m. and 70 degrees out. Today is supposed to reach a high of 95. It's unusual for the PNW, so we enjoy these days when we can. I'm drinking my perfectly made coffee and telling my coffee, "I love you."

I see Lexi silently go racing across the yard after a bunny. My Lexi is an elite athlete. She is high performance, and my first thought was *That's odd that she's not barking.* Then she doesn't come back to my line of sight, and I think to myself, *Oh my god. I better check and see if she got it.*

She did. There the bunny lay with Lexi standing over it, wondering why it wouldn't play anymore.

I look at her. She looks at me and reaches down to bring me her kill. She's not sure if she should be proud or if she did something wrong.

My next thought is *If it is not dead, someone needs to do a mercy killing.*

I'm not cut out for that kind of work. I can do just about anything, but I can't kill something intentionally, even to put it out of its misery or suffering. I can't kill bugs or spiders. I carry them outside to suffer their fate instead of at my hand. I absolutely hate fishing. I have too much empathy for living things suffering at my hand.

I begin scanning through my phone to find someone who can take care of this. My first thoughts turn to who I know that would be willing to kill something. My next thoughts turn to who can get here quickest to put this bunny out of its misery. My first message is to the kids' dad. Then I realize, most of the people I know are partiers (including their dad). None of them will be awake this early on a Sunday morning.

Yes, it is 8:30 a.m. Partiers are a lot like teenagers. They either sleep until noon or sleepwalk around their house until noon. My next four messages go to my neighbors who have husbands. While I am praying, quite literally, for an eagle or coyote to come take this bunny, my neighbor messages me back and loans her husband to me. I have never been so grateful to be a part of a community that I love!

By the time Scott got here at 9:00 a.m., rigor mortis had set in. I'm sure that was the longest half hour of that bunny's life. Let it be known. Lexi can catch you bunnies. Stay away, Peter Rabbit!

I don't know about you, but days that start like this can go fuck themselves. As I was in the middle of all this I was thinking, *I need to write about this*. There are some days where these irritations don't bother me, and there are some days when it seems like my irritability is off the charts.

When I had a partner, I could blame my irritability on him. I could feel like I was the only one who did anything around here. I could feel like I was the superior person because I always took care of everything. I could be resentful of my partner that he wasn't helping out.

On the mercy killing side of things, I was still resentful. Not toward anyone in particular but just generally that there was no man around to do the mercy killings. Norm could have done the mercy killing. Jeff could have also, but these two were way too much maintenance to keep around for the occasional mercy killing. Steve could not have done the mercy killing, so his high maintenance was definitely not worth keeping around. Generally, I was resentful at no one in particular, and I was resentful that I had to message all my neighbors for help.

What I have learned in recovery is that anytime I am feeling resentment, I need to root around for what I am not taking responsibility for. Yes, it would be nice if I and my partner shared equally in the diarrhea cleaning of our babies, but that's not what happened. Instead of resolving the conflict and staying in bed and forcing him to clean up the diarrhea, I sealed my own fate as diarrhea-cleaner-upper. Then I resented it.

As far as mercy killings, I suppose I resent the universe for creating a situation where mercy killing is necessary. I resent that my biology is not designed to kill something. I resent that some people are capable of killing things unnecessarily. Yet that is the same characteristic that allows them to kill things when it is necessary.

The thing about resentment is that it is tied closely to codependence. Resentment is the byproduct of codependence. Resentment is all about not taking responsibility for the choices you have made as an adult. I resent my husband because he's not helping out, but I'm the one doing all the work, so when can he step up? I resent my boyfriend for leaving me, and now I have to take care of the dogs by myself. They are my dogs. My responsibility.

Who's to Blame?

We desperately want someone else to blame. This is a part of being human. Quite often, there is someone or something to blame. However, if there is a problem that is impacting your life, you can rest assured that you are, at the very least, a part of the problem. While it might be easy or appropriate to blame someone else, it is also your responsibility to figure out what part of the problem is your responsibility.

If the problem is a shared problem between you and someone else, chances are good that you both contribute some portion of asshole to the equation that results in "the problem." Therapy can tease the problem apart and allow each of you to determine your role in the problem. You'd be surprised how changing your role changes the problem. It may not make the problem go away—in which case you may need to make the other person go away.

The reality is, by definition, if there is a problem in your life, it is your problem. It is your responsibility to resolve the problem. We want someone to blame because we don't want to be the person blamed. In fact, when we blame someone else, they often become defensive. Which means they turn around and blame you, someone, or something else.

Defensiveness is an extremely toxic behavior in relationships. I didn't know this at the time, but after historical analysis of my most important relationships, defensiveness was categorically a problem in all of them. There is covert defensiveness too, which is harder to detect.

Ultimately, defensiveness has to do with not taking responsibility for your own behavior. Defensiveness is a way of avoiding responsibility. Defensiveness is a way to shift the blame from you to someone or something else.

If you are an asshole, your responsibility in a relationship that is important to you is to stop being an asshole. Being an asshole means that you treat someone in a way that harms them. If the relationship is important to you and that person can be clear with you about what is harming him or her, it is your responsibility to change your behavior.

Enabling behavior is when someone allows another person to avoid personal responsibility. An enabler's responsibility is to take responsibility for himself or herself. An enabler's responsibility in the problem is to establish boundaries and not allow himself or herself to be mistreated.

If there is a conflict, assuredly, one of you is an asshole, and one of you is an enabler. Usually, in conflicts, you switch back and forth between asshole and enabling to keep it extremely confusing as to who is the asshole and who is the enabler. Chances are good that you are the asshole some of the time and the enabler some of the time.

Before I started therapy, I didn't recognize a problem as a problem. It was a situation clothed in "normal" clothing. It was my first husband saying, "No way. You aren't qualified for anything else. You won't make as much money anywhere else. You have to take the management job." And my internal dialogue was telling me I was capable of so much more. My self-concept bumped up against his fear of scarcity.

Therapy Was a Means to Align My Self-Concept with Reality

There is quite a bit to unravel when your brain develops in an extremely confusing environment, when you don't know that what you've been taught is "what not to do." The only way you will ever figure this out is if you develop the ability to look at your relationships objectively.

You must look at your relationships and ask yourself if you are satisfied with your most significant relationships. If you are not satisfied, then you have to determine what you are going to do about it. You have to develop an understanding of what is in your control and what is not.

You cannot make people more functional than they are. You can ask them to contribute more, but if they don't, you've got to figure out what you are going to do about it. You can try to force the issue, but this often backfires.

One of the most important concepts I learned in therapy is that children are children. They are not little adults. They are little humans that are learning how to have a healthy relationship with themselves as well as with others. The other thing I learned is how bad most of us parents are at allowing children to be children.

Childish behavior is so annoying. I believe we develop an intolerance for our children to have childish behavior when the adults around us are childish. The problem is that it is appropriate for children to behave childishly. They are children, and by definition, they are immature. Some of their maturity is under parental influence, but much of it is time and growth.

Healthy Relationships

Children are inherently narcissistic. Not the bad kind of narcissism—the natural kind. The kind that developmentally teaches us we are important in this world and we matter. Children, hopefully, outgrow this narcissism and realize that there are other people in this world that matter too. That other people have feelings too, and you may hold the power to injure the feelings of others. This is the tricky and complex navigation of relationships.

In my developmentally consistent stage of narcissism, I was taught that I did not matter. I was taught that I only mattered for what I contributed to my parents. They did not teach these lessons with their words; they taught them with their actions. They taught me that narcissism was how love feels.

When my children reached the developmentally narcissistic stages, I did not power-struggle with them about who was more important. Instead, a medium of communication was created so I could help them understand that they are important. They matter *and* so do others. My ego was not in competition with theirs.

Ultimately, I think that navigation from this developmentally typical stage of narcissism into a healthy level of narcissism in our adult lives is a major factor in all kinds of relationships. This path has become so murky and tangled with self-love, self-acceptance, and self-care that we cannot tell the difference between typical healthy narcissism and atypical unhealthy narcissism.

There is a huge difference. I only know this because I've been in search of a soulmate for my entire adult life. Instead, I have ended up with what feels like a psychology degree in narcissistic personality disorder. Not only have I read a dozen books and articles, I have had more than my share of practical experience with narcissists.

Not only was I raised by narcissists, I have chosen narcissists for partners. I am a magnet for narcissists, so I had to learn how to turn that magnetism off. I don't want narcissists in my personal life, but I can work with them in my professional life without issue.

This is partly how I turned the magnetism off. I've learned to identify narcissism fairly rapidly. I get a lot of practice in my line of work as a mediator. The reason for this is that narcissists don't have a full problem-solving toolbox. They have very few behaviors to choose from when things don't go their way. Therefore, I come across a variety of levels of narcissism in the art of dispute resolution.

The main thing everyone needs to know is that we are all susceptible to narcissistic behavior. What makes narcissistic behavior toxic is when a person is unwilling or unable to see his own narcissistic behavior. Additionally, narcissistic personality disorder is a particular extreme of narcissism deeply rooted in psychology that is particularly untreatable. Whereas narcissistic behavior is less deeply rooted and somewhat more changeable.

Psychologists and psychiatrists say there is no "cure" for narcissism. While there may be no "cure" for narcissism, the antidote for narcissistic behavior is reality-based self-awareness. Awareness of your own tendency to behave narcissistically allows a person the opportunity to change that behavior in an important relationship.

Narcissistic behavior is more like a changeable characteristic, while narcissism is much less changeable and evades the owner's awareness. By definition, if you are self-aware, you aren't a narcissist; however, you may still have narcissistic behavior. A key defining factor of a diagnoseable narcissist is the lack of self-awareness.

Another key defining factor of narcissism is lack of empathy. Narcissists lack the ability to put themselves in your shoes. Think of my stepfather. While he was molesting me, he looks up and sees tears pouring down my face and asks, "What's wrong?" As ludicrous as this sounds, it was a genuine inability to consider that what he was doing was harmful to me and causing me pain. This is narcissism in its purest form.

What complicates things even further is that just because a person thinks he is self-aware, this does not mean he is. Just because a person says he has empathy, it does not mean he does. Self-awareness and empathy are demonstrations of such behaviors, not statements of fact.

I believe it is impossible to have a healthy relationship with a narcissist. By definition, narcissists are only in a relationship with themselves. However, as demonstrated by children and healthy adults, some narcissistic behavior is both necessary, expected, and manageable. What makes a relationship unmanageable is the inability to change for the greater good.

From my perspective, I don't think relationships can succeed or fail. Relationships don't have binary outcomes. Relationships are an ongoing experience that continues even after death for the living. I am still in relationship with my stepfather even though I have not spoken to him in the last thirty years. There is an indelible connection that was corroded by his narcissism, and the connection still exists.

This is also true for all relationships I have had. I do not have a life partner, and that has everything to do with the level of narcissism in each of the partners I have chosen to date. I do not look at a single relationship I have had as a failure even though there is very little conversation between me and my previous partners. I learned what I needed to learn from each relationship, and I moved on. Today, I've learned enough to explain to you what I know went wrong and how I ended up where I am today.

I am grateful to have experienced all my significant relationships. They have all been toxic, and therefore, I had to establish healthy boundaries between me and them. However, I am grateful for every one of them, including my relationship with my stepdad. My singular reason for being able to say this is the result of a shit ton of therapy.

Every relationship was a desperate search for unconditional love. A desperate search for "the goods," the cherished treasure, the holy grail. The feeling that makes life worth living. The feeling that life is good, enjoyable, worth living, and worth living well.

Unconditional Love—
The Holy Grail

I grant my children with the honor of being the ones who taught me what unconditional love feels like. Madison, Parker, and Josephine—without them, I don't believe my life would have the meaning and purpose that it has today. My children saved my life from dwelling on the surface and allowed me to become a seeker of depths.

If parents were supposed to be the ones to give children unconditional love and the feelings I experienced as a child was what unconditional love felt like, no thank you! Unconditional love sucks. However, if what I experienced as a child in my family growing up was *not* unconditional love, maybe I've got it all wrong. Maybe if what I experienced as a child was what happened when parents were unable to give unconditional love, then maybe unconditional love exists. Maybe I've just never experienced it. Well, that makes a lot more sense.

I remember standing over my newborn son with him on the changing table. He was probably a month or two old. I remember wondering about the feeling I was feeling. At this point in my life, I had been "wondering" about my feelings. My relationship with myself was changing, and one part of that change was understanding my feelings. By the time my son was born, I had developed a very good understanding of basic feelings.

By this time, I had been using www.helpyourselftherapy.com to change my relationship with my feelings. I had also been doing therapy two to three times weekly with Madison, individual therapy, and couples therapy. Between Tony (at helpyourselftherapy.com) and all the therapy I had been doing, my relationship with my feelings was changing. I was identifying and understanding my feelings with much more awareness and comprehension.

I'm standing over my newborn son, and I'm thinking to myself, *What is this feeling I'm feeling?* It was a wonderful feeling that felt good and connected and intense. I thought to myself, *I think this is what love is supposed to feel like.* I had never felt anything like this. It was at that moment I realized that love was all that was needed to make this relationship work.

But that's because I was the adult, and this little guy was entirely dependent on me for his every need. I do wonder if I would have felt this intensely about my son if I hadn't already been raising my step-daughter, Madison. She was five by the time he was born. She was in kindergarten, and I had been established as her primary caregiver by this time.

Madison spent very little time out of my care except for when she would be at her mom's. We had a variety of joint parenting arrangements throughout Madison's life. I carried most of the burden of raising Madison without the benefit of biological bonding.

This unique disposition created somewhat of an emotional contradiction. I was burdened with all the responsibility without the organic emotional connection. Madison and I have a very strong emotional connection, but it is more manufactured as a result of my caregiving and my taking responsibility for coaching her into being the best adult she can be.

Raising Madison for five years allowed me to feel how burdensome children are when the organic emotional connection is not present. Don't get me wrong, I never felt as though the burden was unwanted. Sure, I wish her mom and dad would contribute more, but I had no issue paying for everything and doing everything.

I do not regret one single minute of raising Madison. I love Madison, and I will always love Madison. I believe she is a stronger, more successful woman today than she would have been had I not raised her for eighteen years. She is twenty-two now, and we have been estranged for a few years. I suspect, if Madison ever recovers (a.k.a. grows up), our connection will be restored.

Raising Madison was different from raising my biological kids. I don't know if I would have noticed this subtle distinction had I not raised Madison for five years before having my biological children. When my biological kids came along, a platform of emotional understanding opened up to me that I didn't know existed. I was able to feel emotion much more powerfully than before they came along.

I believe they helped me be an even better mother to Madison. The unconditional organic love I felt for them rippled into my relationship with Madison. I have never related to my stepdaughter as anything other than my biological child. Having my own biological children caused an emotional congruence between biological children and non-biological children for me. This is why I always tell people who are contemplating having children that they are making an "uneducated decision."

The emotional platform that opens for a biological parent is something no human being has ever experienced until parenthood of any stage. That's not to say that just because the platform opens, every parent gets on the platform. It is to say that a particular platform of emotional connection opens up that the parent can use or not use.

For me, this emotional platform was one of deep and meaningful connection that I have never felt before. I had done all the emotional work through therapy and awareness, which allowed me to step on that platform and use it to its fullest potential. Intensity of feelings amplified exponentially.

This also means feeling deeply in the opposite direction also. Basic physics tells us, for every action, there is an equal and opposite reaction. This is Newton's third law of motion. I believe this law applies to emotion as well. For every glorious and magnificent good feeling, there is an equal and opposite feeling of yuck. What is the opposite of unconditional love? Shame.

My feelings for Madison differed by only a fraction from my biological children. I believe the reason for that is biological. I did not have the experience of carrying her for ten months in my body and the autonomic nurturing and connection to the fetus that occurs.

179

When my son was born, I was able to identify this fraction. This fraction intensified my mothering instinct. This fraction sharpened my skills and honed my native genius.

Native genius is something a person does exceptionally well and comes extremely naturally to that person. I listened to a woman describing how to determine your native genius. She said that it is the thing that you do, which you do well without effort or thought, and you suddenly realize six hours have gone by. I loved this concept, and it occurred to me that mothering is my native genius.

Is it possible that my gift that I contribute to this world is being a good mother? Is it possible that this is my purpose and what gives my life meaning? Is it possible that I am good at something my mother was terrible at? Is it even possible for me to be a good mother given that I have never had a good mother as a role model?

Sure as shit, I am a good mother. In fact, I am an exceptional mother. I don't say this to compete with other mothers. I say it to own it as one of the greatest gifts I have ever been given. It is, without question, my native genius. There is no other explanation.

I figured this out fifteen years ago. I have tethered to it through all these years. This is why mediation is my passion. Mediating two clients in conflict is not much different from teaching two two-year-olds to get along. I'm not exaggerating. Most people who are in a conflict that they are unable to resolve on their own, to some degree or another, are acting like children.

I spent a significant part of my youth in search of the holy grail and wondering, *What is so great about life?* As an adolescent, I contemplated suicide as a means of asking, "Would anyone even notice or care if I was dead?" I've never been the suicidal type. I'm also not the depressive type, but this contemplation came up periodically.

This would be another gift that would prevent my self-destruction. Instead, I searched for the holy grail, and I found it. The love I have for my children, all three of them, has been the greatest experience of my life.

I Must Be a Mermaid

There are at least two levels of living. There is surface living, where you just go along with everything and don't ask questions. Then there is deep living, where one is in search of answers to mysteries that compel their research. The tattoo I have wanted to get is a picture of a mermaid with part of her face obscured by a beautiful mane of long flowing hair. The caption reads, "I must be a mermaid. I have no fear of depths and great fear of shallow living."

I don't know why I haven't gotten this tattoo. I guess it's because I sense I might have some regrets at some point. Either I won't like the artist's work and it's indelibly printed on my body, or maybe it's the thought of paying someone a lot of money to cause me pain and discomfort for many hours for an imprint on my body. It would be much easier and pain-free for me to write about it here instead.

The truth is, I believe this statement will always be relevant for me. I do feel like a mermaid. I do feel like there are many fish in the sea, but I'm a mermaid. I am different. I swim with the fish, but I don't partner with them. I lead them. I need a creature that has a more sophisticated development. Additionally, I clearly fear shallow living and have no fear of living in the deep and meaningful.

In this time of becoming comfortable with being single, I am able to reflect on my relationships in an objective way that I never have been able to do before. I am not trying to find a man, and I am not in a relationship with a man (or a woman). I am comfortably single for the first time in my adult life.

I am a single mother raising two teenagers that I am extremely proud of. They are growing into excellent human beings. The one thing I want to pass on to them is how to be in relationships with other people in a healthy way. In a way that preserves the "self" and honors the other. I don't want them to go in search of a soulmate and end up with what seems like a degree in personality disorders. I want them to understand themselves, the universe around them, and others in a way that is productive and useful.

There was a time when I was contemplating my relationship with Jeff. We had not broken up yet, and I was trying to decide whether or not to proceed with our relationship as it was. The song "Piece by Piece" by Kelly Clarkson stretched my thinking in a way that it has not been stretched before:

> but piece by piece, he collected me up
> off the ground, where you abandoned things
> piece by piece he filled the holes that you
> burned in me
> six years old and you know
> he never walks away
> he never asks for money
> he takes care of me
> he loves me
> piece by piece, he restores my faith
> that a man can be kind and the father could
> stay

I did not feel this way about Jeff. I did not feel that he picked me up. I didn't feel like he took care of me. I didn't feel like he loved me. He didn't "ask" for money, and he didn't "walk away" regularly, but those were the only relevant pieces of the chorus that applied to Jeff. The very first lyric of the song is "And all I remember is your back walking toward the airport, leaving us all in your past." I realized, some months later, that that line was the most relevant lyric of the song.

Once Jeff left and I thought more about the chorus of the song, I realized, *I don't have anyone in my life that does this for me. I never have.* I've had everyone in my life leave: my dad, my mom (emotionally abandoned me), and my stepdad. Jeff and Norm only left because I wasn't going to allow them to take advantage of me anymore. They would only stay if they could take advantage of all the life I provided for them, and they did not have to take any responsibility. "All I remember is your back…"

Then I realized, *You know who does never walk away, ask for money, takes care of me, and loves me? Do you know who restores my faith that a man can be kind and the father could stay? God. That's who.*

I don't believe in Jesus Christ our Lord and Savior. I don't believe God to be some "being" in the sky or a "being" of any kind really. I believe humans developed "God" to embody a concept that is very difficult for human beings to grasp. Especially human beings that aren't deep thinkers.

God is not somebody or something. God is a concept. I'm not opening an argument here. I'm simply stating my views and how I got here.

I don't believe in Jesus Christ, our Lord and Savior, dying on the cross and being the Son of God and all that. I find it absolutely unconvincing that a book written three thousand years ago could be translated to anything understandable in our modern day. Over these three thousand years, there had to be a huge margin for error and inaccuracy.

Again, I don't want to argue about it. You will not convince me that modern-day Jesus Christ worshipers devoutly follow the word of the Bible for its scientific accuracy. People follow Jesus Christ because they believe it is the right thing to do. They follow Jesus Christ because they need something to hold on to rather than feeling like a marble rolling around in a black hole. They follow Jesus Christ because they are followers. They follow Jesus Christ because Jesus provides a positive and constructive influence in their lives.

I do not criticize this. You do you. Do what you have to do to get yourself through this life.

I spent a year attending a beautiful Presbyterian church. I loved the ritual, and I loved much of the teaching. However, just like in twelve-step groups, I would "take what I like and leave the rest." I took notes at every sermon. I tried learning the songs. I still love going to church but often feel like it is too "Jesus Christ-y" for me.

I don't think we should do things based on WWJD. For those of you not in the know, that stands for "What would Jesus do?" The concept of Jesus and how it all gets tied together with right and wrong doesn't work for me. The concept of "sin" is inconsistent with human nature.

As far as the song "Piece by Piece" goes, God allows me to embody the concept of what fills the holes left behind by an absent parent. The concept of a "man" that doesn't walk away. A "man" that doesn't ask for money. A "man" that takes care of me and loves me. A "man" that restores my faith "that a man can be kind, and the father could stay."

I don't believe in Jesus Christ our Lord and Savior, but I do believe in the concept of God as a way to express an experience of what is happening around us. It is a deep and meaningful way of interpreting what is happening and why. I believe in "God" or "the universe" or "quantum physics" or "whateva the fuck"! I believe that something is happening all around us, and if we don't understand it, it confuses us and distorts our thinking.

From a very young age, I remember praying to God. When I was very young, I would pray for good Christmas gifts. Later in life, I would pray for a certain boy to ask me out or for a certain thing to happen. I would pray that I would win the tennis tournament I was signed up for. Even later in life, I would pray for my stepfather to die.

This motherfucker never died. He is still alive today. In fact, he's married to someone my age. If "God" was on my side, wouldn't this guy be dead?

I even relied on science to kill him. He is "type A." He eats spoonfuls of mayonnaise. He drinks heavily. He probably does hard drugs, and he's overweight. I was certain he was going to die for his sins.

Nope. Still alive. What does this tell us? That this is not how "God" or "the universe" or "whateva' the fuck" works.

We want it to be neat and tidy. We want square holes and square pegs. We want bad people to die and good people to live. Here's the problem. We are all some blend of bad and good. People are not black or white. People are not binary. People are complex compilations of their parents. There is no measure for the binary choice of "good" or "bad."

The reality is that there are all shapes of holes and all shapes of pegs. We can't think of people in these condensed versions. People are very complex and, I believe, very good. I think their parents fuck them up, and that's how they become psychologically misaligned with their higher purpose.

This is not a question if God exists or not. This is a question of "what is your relationship" with God, the universe, the higher power, or whateva the fuck. I call it faith. I have faith in how the universe works. I have faith that destructive things are necessary for constructive things to exist. I have faith that how the universe works is not mysterious at all; it's just that we don't understand it.

We've spent three thousand years trying to translate the language of the universe into something that is universally understood. This translation has resulted in myths, theories, and religions. The translation has generated many beliefs and many religions, all of them lobbying for first position of being "right."

I'm not here to argue about who is right and who is wrong. I am here to give my perspective. My perspective is this: I feel better feeling like I have a purpose. I feel better knowing I am not 100 percent responsible for my outcome. I feel better knowing there is some portion of my pain that I am not entirely responsible for. I feel better admitting that I don't understand how the universe works, and I'm searching for the lesson in the pain.

Life is not pain-free. Life can be very painful at times. I know I feel better believing that there is a higher purpose, and I am aligned with it. My pain serves a purpose, and my pain is useful.

There has not been a man in my life who has collected me up off the ground. The money I collected from my settlement picked me up "off the ground where you abandon things." I have never had a person; I had money. That money gave me the resources to pick myself up off the ground. If there was anyone who collected me piece by piece, it was me and however the fuck the universe works.

If there is any man in this world that has made restitution for wronging me, it is my stepdad. Maybe the financial chunk I took from him didn't hurt him, but that's not what I am about. I'm not an eye-for-an-eye kind of person. He made his amends with forwarding financial resources so I could live the life I was destined to live.

Now here we are. I am revealing what no one wants revealed. But why not?

Problem-Solving Team

I am a mother. My job is director of our problem-solving team (a.k.a. our family). My measure of being a good mother has nothing to do with you or how you do things. It has nothing to do with some list of criteria. It has to do with how my kids feel.

I want my kids to feel good about themselves. I want them to be generally happy about being alive. I want them to look at problems as opportunities for a solution. I want them to understand how to engage in healthy ways in relationships. If I can accomplish any of this to any degree, I feel like a successful mother.

I don't care if my kids go to an Ivy League school. In fact, I don't want to pay for that, and I don't think they should either. That is some kind of status symbol that I don't believe in. I want them to find paths where they feel useful and purposeful, like I have found in motherhood. My purpose found in motherhood has led me to a greater purpose of being an iconic mother.

All the men in my relationships came to me to be mothered to their next stage. I repaired some measure that their mothers failed to accomplish. I served the purpose in their lives that my therapists served in mine. Replace the bad parent with a good parent. Therapy taught me how to be a good parent to myself through the modeling of my therapists. I was a good parent to my men and moved them on their way.

Norm never would have accomplished what he has today had I not put an end to that relationship. Jeff literally chose to not do recovery with me. Steve would never have learned to ride a motorcycle and recognize his shortcomings in relationships had we not spent our time together. My stepdad, he chose the right person to wrong.

My stepdad chose a compassionate and connected person. Whether I was compassionate and connected or whether the abuse made me compassionate and connected, we will never know. What I can tell you today is that I am compassionate and connected, and not everyone loves that about me.

My compassion and connection are far too intense for many to tolerate. My deep and meaningful dwelling in this life causes too much discomfort for so many. People can't stand the thought that I thank my stepfather for who I have become. That I forgive him for the torturous ten years of my fifty-year life. That I forgive my mother for choosing a partner such as him. That I forgive my mother for benching my dad in the game of parenthood. That I forgive my dad for not taking good care of me and allowing me to be molested by a family of wealth and privilege.

It is all neither here nor there. I am happy. My kids are well-adjusted. I'm figuring shit out. My heavy weight causes me tremendous anxiety, not because of how I look but because I am worried I will die.

Then I think about how much I wanted my stepfather to die. He had so many more traits that, scientifically, would cause an early death, and he is still alive. At seventy-four! He even spent two years in prison and didn't die! He was not in prison for child abuse or sexual misconduct but for illegal conduct that got him disbarred. If there is anything to admire about this man, it is his willingness to "take one for the team."

Maybe I shouldn't stress so much about my weight. It will come off when I start taking better care of my body. I will start taking better care of my body once I get these words out, once my internal environment seeks continuity with my external environment. I know I am getting close. I'm just not quite finished with this book.

Therapy

One of the benefits of therapy is that it creates structured relationships. The relationships are influenced by individual personality and individual relationship skills, but the environment is structured and less ambiguous. Theoretically, therapy is a way for people with relational problems to have a safe, secure, and healthy relationship. Essentially, you are paying someone to be in a healthy relationship with you.

Therapy is a way for people with avoidant or antisocial behavior to theoretically have a safe person to discuss intimate issues with. People who are avoidant prevent meaningful connection, and then they feel lonely. Therapy is a way for people with avoidant behavior to feel connected and thereby improve on how they relate to others. By improving how they relate to others, they improve the connections in their lives.

Therapy is also a way for people (such as myself) who are "emotional sluts" to theoretically have a structured, educational, and safe relationship to learn from. I speak emotion like a slut hands out sex. I know that *slut* is a negative word, but it is also a descriptive word that I am taking ownership of. I'm not using the description to disparage anyone, including myself. I'm using the word to describe my experience as being an emotional slut in a relatable way.

Therapy is a way for people who have problems relating to others to, theoretically, create a safe and healthy relationship. The reason I keep stating "theoretically" is because some therapists are good at what they do, and some therapists are not. Some therapists serve best a higher percentage of the population, and some therapists serve best a smaller percentage of the population. Some therapists are just terrible at therapy, either because the therapist doesn't "get life" or doesn't "get therapy."

The best therapists are therapists that "get life" and "get therapy" and are able to blend the two in a way that helps patients (or clients). It just occurred to me that *patient* is both a noun and an adjective. I wonder if this is why there is such disparity in the doctor/patient relationship.

In some ways, mediation is similar to therapy in that mediation serves to help two people solve a problem and bring resolution to a conflict of opinions. Mediation provides a safe environment for both opinions to exist and reach toward a resolution that is—at least partly—satisfying to both parties.

The disparity between a "mediator" and an "attorney" can be likened to the relationship between a therapist and a client as opposed to a doctor and a patient. I often describe myself as the "opposite of an attorney." Attorneys are "professional intellectual law fighters" versus mediators being "professional common sense and emotional IQ understanders." I don't fight. I dissolve fights. Attorneys' fight.

Like mediation, therapy is a craft. There are people who pursue mastery of their craft. There are also people who believe they are masters of their craft. The question is this: is mastery of a craft an attainable goal, or is mastery a theoretical impossibility?

We are a society that measures success based on outcome. Depending on the outcome being measured, a different conclusion could be made. A therapist's mastery cannot be measured by how accurate her diagnoses are. Additionally, how do you measure how much a therapist has helped someone? What does mastery of the craft of therapy look like? Which party masters the craft, the therapist or the client?

Mastery can't be measured. This is why there are good therapists and bad therapists. Someone who thinks her master's degree confirms she has mastered the craft is not a good therapist. A good therapist knows that there is no finish line, that there is no one determination of mastery. A good therapist knows that while his or her style works well for some, it may not work well for others.

The same goes for mediation. Some mediators are not even attempting to be masters of their craft. Mediation may not even be their craft. For many volunteer mediators, mediation is the volunteer job while something else is "the craft." A good mediator knows that determination of mastery cannot be determined by one measurement. A good mediator knows that her style works for some, and it doesn't work for others

What am I trying to master? As a mediator, I am trying to master the dance between two people in conflict toward a resolution that is satisfying enough for both parties. When children are involved, I also try to minimize the distress and mitigate the future stress by resolving conflict rather than allowing conflict to influence future relationships. Divorce, done senselessly, divides a family physically and emotionally. I try to mitigate the damage and preserve the intact family.

My process works well for people who show up in good faith and are willing to compromise. My process does not work well for people who are incapable of showing up in that capacity. I do my best to work with people to get them into a good-faith mindset. However, I am not a miracle worker. I cannot (although I wish I could) download what's in my brain to my clients and have all the data import perfectly.

An exceptional therapist executes this import with precision, accuracy, and effectiveness. A good therapist executes the import with some precision, accuracy, and effectiveness. A terrible therapist executes this import with very little precision, accuracy, or effectiveness.

Therapy and Re-parenting

In the middle of 2019, I decided to cancel individual therapy. I would still attend my group therapy, continue to work as a mediator, and continue to do my own self-administered program. While I was still attending group, I did not feel the need for individual therapy. Once I began to feel as though I was equipped to handle healthy relationships on my own, I decided to gradually reduce the amount of therapy I was doing. I decided I didn't need to pay someone to provide a healthy relationship for me anymore.

I have avoided determining the aggregate cost of therapy that I have spent over the years. I've paid for therapy for Madison, me, Norm, couples therapy, trauma group therapy, classes, and psychiatry for all of us. I know the number is a huge number, so I don't analyze it. It was necessary and useful; therefore, what was spent on it is irrelevant. However, this is a legitimate reason to wean myself off therapy too.

Over the years, I have used therapy as a means to solve problems before I got to my appointment. I would consider, during the week, what I would discuss with my therapist and input what I thought she was going to say. Inadvertently, I would solve those problems and discuss the resolution with my therapist.

What occurred over the years is that the voice in my head was replaced with the kind, compassionate voice of my therapist. The hostile, overly critical negative voice that was taught to me by my "nurturing" was replaced with a positive, hopeful, and compassionate voice. Instead of perpetuating the cycle of negativity, I gave myself a new constitution of positivity.

Much of this was because I needed to learn to be the parent I never had. By the time I was a parent, it became necessary for me to be different if I wanted to teach my kids how to take good care of themselves. In order to do this, I had to learn to re-parent myself. By doing so, I learned how to parent my children.

I began treating myself the same way I treat my children. I have compassion and understanding and patience for them; therefore, I gave myself the same compassion, understanding, and patience.

If I wouldn't say it to my children, I wouldn't say it to myself. Without therapy and a healthy structured relationship, I don't know if I would have developed these skills. We treat our kids how we were treated unless we make a conscious effort to do it differently.

Therapy also created a drop-dead date. The appointment was on the calendar, which caused me to process all the things I wanted to discuss. The processing is the purpose of therapy. I did it all before I got to therapy.

In writing this book, something I've realized about therapy is that my drinking and weight issues were symptoms of the things I was discussing in therapy. I was always in there discussing current problems like people who were driving me crazy and discussing how I managed some crisis or other. I learned that I was excellent at crisis management and managing people who drove me nuts. So why did I keep going to therapy?

Well, it lets off the steam. It's a way to burp the baby. It's a place for me to be open, honest, and authentic without the fear of criticism, contempt, stonewalling, or defensiveness—at least not from my therapist. These four horsemen still showed up in group participants, and the structured environment allowed us to deal with the horsemen safely without irreparable damage.

Therapy is where I have kept a historical record of periods of heavy drinking and periods of sobriety. My therapist and group members help maintain accountability and support in a way that I could not find naturally occurring in my world. Therapy is how I have concluded that sobriety is not the answer for me.

Does therapy work? Yes. If you know what you are doing. Why did I need therapy for so long if it "works"? Well, long story short, I grew up in a completely fucked-up family. There was significant sexual abuse over the course of my adolescence. There was a gross level of narcissism among my caretakers. And in the end, I was abandoned to fend for myself. I was raised to be a sheep by wolves in sheep's clothing.

The relationship with the therapist is about replacing the bad parent with a good parent. But you also pay for it. It is structured. It has boundaries. It is *not* unconditional. The conditions are you *pay*, you schedule the relationship, and you get what you get. You may get good care, or you may not.

Doing Therapy Right

For anyone who does not believe in therapy, chances are you're doing it wrong. There is also a better than likely chance that your therapist is doing it wrong. If it's not working, it is either you or the therapist messing shit up.

One way we mess shit up is that we expect to walk into a therapist's office and for that therapist to "diagnose" us with the "cause" of our problem, *and* we expect the therapist to tell us how to fix it. The problem with this entire line of thinking is that this is just not how therapy works. I promise you that if you walked into a therapist's office and that therapist accurately diagnosed you with narcissistic personality disorder (NPD) and told you how to fix the multitude of problems that go along with NPD, you would walk out of that office saying "that therapist is batshit crazy" even if the therapist is 100 percent correct in her diagnosis.

The way that therapists mess shit up is by being prone to human error as we all are. Therapists are humans too, and just because they did some schooling to "teach" them about mental health problems, that doesn't mean they get it. They might think they get it, but there are many that don't. I have personal experience with many therapists I would not recommend.

It's not to say that a therapist is "good" or "bad" at the work they do. It's more like finding the right fit. As humans, we all have different levels of understanding of life, love, and relationships. You have to find a therapist that speaks your language.

Those of us that are English-speaking assume we are speaking the same language to other English-speaking people. The reality is that while it is the same language, our history with the language impacts our understanding. The meaning of many English words depends on the context of the speaker. The understanding of what the speaker is attempting to communicate is also dependent on the context of the listener.

Think about the difference between an American English-speaking person from California versus an American English-speaking person from Louisiana or New York. The words are mostly the same, but the speaker's pronunciation is more easily understood by fellow Californians or New Yorkers. British and Australian English speakers also use many of the same words we use in America. This allows for mostly effective communication between the different regions.

When it comes to therapy, you can't assume that every English-speaking therapist speaks your language. If the "therapy" isn't working, it's *your* job to say, "This isn't working. I don't feel any better." Also, it is important to understand that *you* have to do the work, not the therapist.

What You Allow Is
What Will Continue

When you hire a therapist, you are literally hiring someone to tell you what you don't want to hear. You don't want to hear that you have problems, and you certainly don't want to hear that you are part of the problem. But you are. It's one problem to think that it is not okay to have problems, and it's a whole different problem to expect someone else to fix it for you. You are the problem if you have a problem.

This is the trickiest part of therapy and perhaps the main purpose of therapy—to determine what part of the problem is yours and what part of the problem belongs to someone else. If you grew up being mistreated by your parents, siblings, or friends, chances are pretty good that you will allow this treatment as "normal" and "acceptable," and you will go on to tolerate mistreatment in your adult relationships.

This is where therapy can help you out. Therapy is a tool for you to figure out that you are being mistreated, and you can change the way you allow people to treat you. First, you sort out that the reason you don't feel good is because someone is mistreating you.

Then you sort out that the person who is mistreating you is an asshole and that being an asshole is that person's problem, not yours. Then you sort out that your part of the problem is that you allow the asshole to mistreat you. Then you use what are called "boundaries" to let the asshole know that he can continue to be an asshole, but you won't allow the asshole behavior in your life. Finally, if the asshole behavior continues, more extreme boundaries need to be established, such as physical barriers between you two.

Unfortunately, life is not this easy to decode. There are different tiers of asshole behaviors from mildly rude and inconsiderate to physically abusive. Furthermore, emotional abuse is extremely tricky to identify, and even more so if it is all you've ever known. The bottom line is this: If you are depressed, determine who among you is the asshole and get treatment. Therapy is treatment for asshole behavior *and* enabling behavior.

Admitting That I Don't Have My Shit Together Even Though It Looks Like I Do

I have written millions of words in the last fifteen years. No one has seen them except me and the partner I was writing them to. I have written volumes of books in my mind. There have been a few men in my life that have had both the burden and the fear that comes with reading what I've written to them.

I've never put structure to my writing except to take corrective measures and stand up for myself. I've successfully pushed the boundary between overthinking and deep thinking. I have thousands of pages of journaling, which is unstructured writing.

It was not always corrective measures that needed to be taken. It was often five-page love letters or long-winded explanations provided for understanding. After my divorce at the end of 2014, I began writing the more structured pieces to Jeff, a few other friends, and eventually to Steve. The writing before my divorce was primarily processing through the shit ton of therapy I had been doing and trying to process through everyday life.

There is both a practical side and a deeply meaningful side to just about everything. The practical and pragmatic part of me was saying "get your shit together." The deeply meaningful side of me was wondering why I couldn't get my shit together.

On the outside, most of you would think I've got my shit together. I have people tell me all the time, "You seem like someone who has their shit together." In many ways, I really do have my shit together. And in many ways, I've struggled to maintain that image.

It's not obvious to the onlooker from a distance, but if you were in this mind of mine, you might understand. I sometimes feel like the little woman filing things in my brain has taken too many breaks and keeps coming back to her work and having to reorient.

I have gained and lost fifty or sixty pounds too many times in my forty-nine years. Some people notice. Some people don't. When I'm thin, people think I've always been that way, and working out and eating right is no problem for me. When they see me overweight, people say, "Really? You don't look that heavy." Or they offer other charitable comments like "You are a beautiful person. Who cares about your weight?"

The answer is, I do. I care about my weight. Not because of how it looks but because of how it feels. Being overweight sucks compared to being thin. *This* I promise you. It's harder to breathe. It's harder to exercise. It's harder to be kind and gentle to yourself when you know you are being undisciplined and not treating your body well. My fat rolls on my stomach are in my way when I'm trying to put my shoes on. My fat rolls fall over the top of my too-tight pants.

This time around, I am not buying fat clothes. I am going to suffer through these uncomfortable clothes until I get my body back. Even though I have spent more time overweight than at a healthy weight, my healthy weight is definitely the rationally preferred state. So why can't I maintain it?

If I can be disciplined enough for a year or more to take the weight off and keep it off for some range of time, I can't say I don't have the discipline. I clearly do. I've spent most of the six years since my divorce in a healthy body.

I maintained a fitness of running half-marathons for many of those years, and I was able to knock out six miles on any given day during those six years. I have run a total of thirteen half-marathons, completing the last one in June of 2019. I loved the feeling of being capable of running six miles on any given day. I felt powerful.

Six miles is the perfect distance. I'm not a fast runner, but this is just over an hour for me. Believe me, an hour and fifteen minutes of running at any pace, four to five days per week, is plenty to keep a body physically fit. I only know this because, right now, I couldn't run one mile if you promised me vodka at the finish line. Okay, I'm exaggerating. If there was vodka, I'd run the mile. I can't promise I wouldn't get injured, but I'd run it.

This is another benefit of a thin body over an overweight body: ease of movement. As a result of being accustomed to my thinner body, being in this overweight body feels like I'm wearing a fat suit. No joke. It feels out of place and labor-intensive.

When I was younger, I didn't feel the fat as much as I feel it now. I don't know if that has to do with getting older, denial as a younger person, or the stark contrast to a year ago. I've put sixty pounds on, and I'm not exaggerating. I stopped running a year and a half ago after I ran the Seattle Rock 'n' Roll half-marathon.

It was a grueling run on a hot day that finished through Queen Anne, the part of Seattle known for its steep hills. In Seattle, we don't get much training in hot weather. Believe me, the heat makes a huge difference. I showed up at the wrong start line, believe it or not. *Every* year, it started at CenturyLink Field. The advertising said "Finish where you start." What it didn't highlight was that the start was a different start than previous years.

I had to decide how I was going to get to the actual start line that was actually at the Space Needle rather than Seahawks Stadium. I could walk it. It would get me there just as I was supposed to start. I could run it. Add two miles to the thirteen I was going to run? No thanks. I could go home and call it a day. I called another Uber and got to the start line in plenty of time. These things take forever to start when you have twenty thousand people running.

I think the turning point, for me, came when there was a two-mile hill ahead of me at mile 10. People were trying to run up this hill. My only thought was *This is my thirteenth half-marathon. I have nothing to prove to anyone. I am walking this hill.* I knew I wasn't going to beat my best time, and I was fine with that. I also knew that I was going to eat and drink as much as I wanted when I was done, so whatever.

That was a pivotal day. Nothing could have prepared me for the year and a half after that day. That is what is great about life; there are no do-overs. This last year and a half has been a year and a half of transformation for me. Hard work that I would just as soon avoid. It has been a year of building a cocoon around my soul to protect me during my transformation.

There has been nothing easy about this transformation. After the race, I continued with life as usual. Overeating and overdrinking were consistent habits for me. The running kept my weight in check. Unfortunately, stopping running started piling on the weight. Not fast, but today, I am sixty pounds heavier than I was two years ago.

Another barrier was exiting the relationship with Steve, which I knew was a problem. I knew this relationship was some form of self-torture, but I couldn't quite bring myself to quit. This is where quitting has been a problem. For me. I don't give up. Everything I have ever let go of has claw marks on it.

Once the universe all but beat me over the head with evidence, I finally quit. This is another area where I can thank the coronavirus pandemic for creating a barrier between me and Steve. This, combined with the lack of connection in our relationship, made for a clean exit. My relationship with Steve felt like a forty-year marriage without any benefits. Exiting was painless.

Prior to the coronavirus, my days were filled with driving kids to and from school, building my business, administration of everything around my home, and pretending like I had a partner. When the coronavirus caused statewide alarm, school was cancelled, courts were closed, and there was absolutely nowhere to go and nothing to do.

I had already begun what felt like a depression. I was unmotivated and uninterested in life. This feeling was compounded by the isolation caused by the pandemic. I'm not a depressive kind of person.

Generally, I am enthusiastic and passionate and very energetic. I'm accused of being "loud" or "talkative" when I haven't said a word. I wanted to blame Steve, but I couldn't.

I knew that I exited that relationship for my own good. I knew that I was miserable in the relationship. My misery was justifiable, given that he was unable to commit and unable to take responsibility for his childish behavior. I only had myself to blame for staying in a relationship that made me miserable.

Of course, he was going to stay. He wasn't miserable. He loved having sex and being a boyfriend on his schedule without any consideration for mine.

In June of 2019, I stopped running, which is my stress-relieving exercise. I stayed in an unhealthy relationship that made me miserable for six more months. In January of 2020, I exited the relationship. It is never easy to do, even if it is the right thing. Then in March of 2020, my entire schedule for life was wiped clean with stay-at-home orders. I have absolutely no structure on an already fragile foundation.

Getting My Shit Together

I finally pulled myself together enough to make an appointment with my doctor. I decided that I needed the help of an antidepressant if I was ever going to get my shit together. Due to the coronavirus, we did a virtual appointment. When I told her how much weight I had gained, her jaw dropped.

This was the same doctor who, seven years ago, explained that my weight was impacting my health negatively. Back then, that was all I needed to hear to get to work. I took the weight off over the course of a year and maintained a healthy weight since then. Until now.

I was not offended by her jaw drop. It had taken me three months to gather the courage to call her. I was avoiding her telling me what I already knew. I knew I wasn't healthy, and I didn't want to admit it to my doctor. That made it real.

I would tell anyone else this news about weight gain. That made me believe I was being "open and honest" about it. But I wasn't being open and honest until I admitted to someone when it mattered. This is the difference between maintaining denial and overcoming denial.

Her response was entirely appropriate and expected, given that the last time she saw me was the month before I ran the Seattle Rock 'n' Roll half-marathon. All my history with this doctor has been at a healthy weight after initially losing the weight. The image this doctor had of me was that I was a doer, a go-getter, an unwavering running enthusiast.

Contrast that image with the sixty-pounds-overweight, no-makeup, sweatpants-wearing woman sitting virtually in front of her and bam! Jaw drop. Little did she know that my dormant inner child was going to come to life and rebel against her authority. She had no reason to suspect back then that I was going to lose my shit. How could she? I didn't even know that my dormant inner child was going to come to life and rebel against my authority.

In fact, I didn't know that had happened until I wrote those last few paragraphs. Like I said, I've written millions of words in the past. They've been filed away by the little confused woman taking too many breaks. Or maybe it's that I have never put the structure to my writing that benefits my soul.

I've wanted to write a book for the last six years, but I haven't. I started and stopped many times. Why? Because I didn't know what I wanted to say. Now I do. I'm giving that inner child a voice. She's the one that has been isolated from growing up. I haven't given her a voice, so she keeps speaking up through body fat.

This is the one weight-loss method I haven't tried. I haven't tried truly honoring my inner child for all that she has accomplished and how far she has come. I haven't told her story. I haven't shared her insightful and brave and courageous story.

What Is Recovery?

In the community of alcoholics and addicts, recovery refers to a process of eliminating addiction from your life and focusing your energy on a higher power that guides your life. Not as in a higher power that contrives all the events of your life but a higher order that powers your attitude and behavior. The other day, a friend of mine asked, "Why does there have to be a higher power?" I had to think about this for a while.

I guess the answer is there doesn't. There's doesn't *have* to be a higher power. It's a choice: a choice to believe in a higher order or a choice to believe there is no higher order.

This is not a hypothesis that I am trying to prove. It is not a theory that I am going to support with evidence. It is my philosophical perspective. I am not trying to start an argument about the existence of God. I am explaining how the existence of a higher order supports having a good attitude and growing up.

A higher order is a "system" to tether to so we can avoid the feeling of purposelessness. If life has no purpose, some of us feel like, "Fuck it. What's the use?" Why work hard at sobriety if there is no purpose? Why work hard at maintaining a healthy weight if we have no purpose for being here on this earth? Why endure pain and the harsh realities of life if it is all meaningless?

If everything is random, and there is no higher order to the events that occur in our lives, how can we deal with our grief? How do we emotionally manage the senseless acts of violence? How could we be productive or useful if there was no meaningful existence?

Choosing to believe in a higher power is choosing humility. It is choosing a modest estimate of one's own importance. It is choosing to be easily managed, teachable, and readily taught. It is choosing to be humble and right-sized.

Now I believe it is really important to separate "a higher power" from religion. In recovery groups, we say, "Take what you need and leave the rest." This is my approach. I will often mention "God" or "the Universe" or "whateva the fuck." I have been known to go to Catholic churches, Christian churches, and alternative churches—all in an effort to research the difference between "believing in a higher power" and "a religious following."

I have also been known to say "That sermon was a little too Jesus Christ-y for me." I sometimes feel that Jesus Christ is put on a pedestal, thereby removing his "one of us" status. Also, I believe it is entirely impossible to translate anything that was written three thousand years ago and have it relate to current days. This concept is absolutely ridiculous to me.

I'm not trying to offend those of you who follow Jesus Christ. You do you. Jesus is just not my thing. But that doesn't mean I don't believe in a higher order of things. I do believe life has meaning. I do believe in a lot of the Jesus-Christ-y ideology. I do believe in kindness, and I even believe WWJD is a great tool for our universe. For those of you that don't know this acronym, it stands for "What would Jesus do."

I have created my own acronym, which is WWMHSD. It stands for "What would my higher self do?" The only problem with these acronyms is that one actually needs to stop and consider one's own behavior in order to use it. One would have to ask this question prior to behaving. This is self-awareness that all too many people don't have. Also, the bigger problem is that the people who need to use that tool don't use it.

Whatever. Really. Believe in a higher order. Don't believe in a higher order. Believe in Jesus. Don't believe in Jesus. Make your own choice and leave the rest of us out of it.

I do not care for the hypocritical nature of religion. But that doesn't mean I can't get something out of going to church. I take what I like and leave the rest. There are some pastors I really enjoy listening to and some I really don't. I enjoy going to church. There is something sacred, charming, and satisfying about the ritual. The difference, for me, is that I approach religion with a curious mind, not a critical one.

While my analysis concludes that "many followers of certain religions are outrageously hypocritical," I also don't categorically renounce all religions. What makes me a successful mediator is my ability to see all sides of a conflict. I use very little black-and-white thinking, very little binary thinking. I am the poster child of showing up in good faith. I have outstanding critical thinking skills.

Recovery from My Perspective

Unfortunately, I have spent a lifetime feeling like I don't belong to any particular group. I can't show up to Alcoholics Anonymous meetings in good faith because I don't want to stop drinking. Do I want to stop allowing the effects of alcohol to assist me in making bad decisions? Sure. But do I really have to renounce alcohol altogether in order to do that?

For whatever reason, I have never felt like a part of a group. I have always felt like front-runner. I'm not in the clump of "normal," "average," or "mediocre." I don't have what it takes to be average. I always go the extra mile because it's not crowded. However, it gets lonely out front.

Maybe this is why I like going to church or recovery groups. When I'm in these places, I'm anonymous, and that is not only okay, it is preferable. I think I've always gone the extra mile because I was terrified of getting lost in the masses. Being insignificant. Being unnoticed and left behind.

I have always overperformed to stand out, to make myself unique and better than average. In my adult life, I adopted the motto "anything worth doing is worth overdoing." Blending in is a fate worse than death.

I would say that I have been "in recovery" for much longer than I have been consciously aware. I don't believe I need to recover from alcoholism. I believe I need to recover from a lifetime of ungrieved losses.

Conscious recovery began for me when Jeff left me to pursue his alcoholism. When he sequestered himself away from me rather than work with me on a solution, I lost my shit. For many months, I could not control my sobbing. I was in the grocery store, and the checkout woman asked me how my day was. I sobbed. "I just lost someone close to me, so it's not going very well." I don't have the ability to *not* be open and honest.

There were many days where I would fall to my knees, literally, and sob. I would ask God to take the pain away. I would beg and plead. The pain was so acute that I went to as many Al-Anon meetings as I could. I had never been to a twelve-step meeting before Jeff left me in 2017. Desperate times called for desperate measures. I went to my first meeting and then another. And then another. And then another. The pain went away.

I was part of a group—a group of people who love and worry about the people in our lives with drinking problems. These people had come before me. I wasn't out in front of them. I was in the middle, comforted by their experience and their teaching. I was choosing to be docile, easily managed, teachable, and readily taught. I was choosing a modest estimation of my own importance. I was not being swallowed in mediocrity. I was being healed in conformity.

Do you remember, in Disney's *Tangled*, how Rapunzel's hair would glow golden, and when she wrapped it around Flynn Rider's hand, it healed his wound? Being in the grace of this recovery group felt like being wrapped in Rapunzel's glowing golden hair. My wounds were healing, even those that I didn't know I had.

This was when I began learning the language of recovery. The language of recovery is one we have heard quite a few times. It sounds rather evangelistic to those that don't speak it. The fundamentals of the language of recovery are the Twelve Steps, the Twelve Traditions, and the Serenity Prayer.

These are the Twelve Steps:

1. We admitted we were powerless over alcohol—that our lives had become unmanageable.
2. We came to believe that a power greater than ourselves could restore us to sanity.
3. We made a decision to turn our will and our lives over to the care of God as we understood him.

4. We made a searching and fearless moral inventory of ourselves.
5. We admitted to God, to ourselves, and to another human being the exact nature of our wrongs.
6. We were entirely ready to have God remove all these defects of character.
7. We humbly asked him to remove our shortcomings.
8. We made a list of all persons we had harmed, and became willing to make amends to them all.
9. We made direct amends to such people wherever possible, except when to do so would injure them or others.
10. We continued to take personal inventory, and when we were wrong, promptly admitted it.
11. We sought, through prayer and meditation, to improve our conscious contact with God as we understood him, praying only for knowledge of his will for us and the power to carry that out.
12. Having had a spiritual awakening as the result of these steps, we tried to carry this message to others, and to practice these principles in all our affairs.

God, grant me the serenity to accept the things I cannot change, the courage to change the things I can, and the wisdom to know the difference.

My Recovery

As I began writing "my book" (a.k.a. this book), I began analyzing when my recovery began. Undoubtedly, I began learning and speaking the language of recovery when I began attending twelve-step programs in 2017. However, my recovery began much earlier in life. In fact, I believe that I have been "recovery-minded" my entire life, and that is what sets me apart from the majority.

I don't remember a time when I was not researching, growing, and learning about how to take care of myself as an adolescent, as a teen, and as an adult. I remember many specific events of research, growth, and learning, all of them with a focus on self-care and health. This book is a compilation of these specific events. I was searching for the answers.

In the fall of 2010, my youngest child, Josephine, began preschool at the elementary school where her two siblings before her attended. Her older brother, Parker, was in third grade at the same school, and her older sister, Madison, was finishing middle school. I had already been through the ranks once at this elementary school, began round 2 at the elementary school with my son, and in 2010, I was beginning round 3.

When Madison started in this elementary school, I gave a lot. A lot of time. I was young, enthusiastic, and excited to participate. Each year, I contributed more. Parker was born when Madison was in kindergarten, so he came along with me to my volunteer jobs. First grade was where I met a woman who roped me into PTA.

Between Madison's first- and fifth-grade years, I gave so much time and effort to my volunteer job that I became very well known in the community. So much so that Mrs. Chun, the teacher who had been teaching at the elementary school the longest, asked the other teachers every year, "Who got Amy Hart this year?" I loved helping the teachers out. Eventually, PTA distracted me from helping the teachers out to helping the greater school community.

Believe it or not, there is a lot of business that needed to be conducted with our PTA. For someone like me who takes everything very seriously, combined with the flaw of perfectionism, PTA was the perfect placebo. I worked tirelessly and endlessly on whatever task the PTA needed resolved. By the time Parker was enrolling in this elementary school, I had come to my senses and realized that all the work I had done would become further and further removed with each new administration of PTA moms.

I would not classify myself as a PTA mom. The reason is because I took the business seriously. PTA was not a popularity contest or a fashion show. It was a serious book of half-a-million-dollar business being run by PTA moms. No offense to the amazing people who have given their blood, sweat, and tears. They did the best they could. However, this was where I began to realize a serious business can't be run effectively with volunteers.

I'm sure there are some successful boards of directors that are volunteers and serve their mission statement. However, most PTAs are not run by this type of volunteer board. Most PTAs are run by reluctant, ambivalent, uninformed, overwhelmed moms who are doing it because no one else will.

When Josephine entered preschool at this elementary school, I met a group of moms that would become my closest group of friends. Peggy, Margo, Vui, Sabra—these are the friends I am still in contact with regularly ten years later. The friends I developed during Madison's education are all still friends as well, but they are more like acquaintances these days.

One day, I was walking home after drop-off, and Margo was walking back to her car. We were in a conversation, and I suddenly felt embarrassed about something I said. I don't remember what it was, but I remember going home and researching embarrassment. At the time, I relied heavily on www.helpyourselftherapy.com.

To me, it is not weird at all that I felt a feeling. I didn't understand it, so I researched it. However, I guess it never occurred to me that not everyone does this. Not everyone is so curious about their feelings that they run home and research them rather than give themselves a hard time about the feeling.

Here's what I learned. Feelings are just that: feelings. They come and go on their own terms. After years and years of research and a background in science, I've come to understand that "feelings" are neurochemical reactions in our brains that send instructions all over our bodies to tell our bodies how to react.

It's fucking crazy. Seriously. Your body reacts in a fraction of a second before you have time to think about it. These are primary outcomes from the initial neurochemical incident. A secondary outcome is when you've had some time to think about what you are doing. A tertiary outcome is when enough time has elapsed that you have had time to consider alternative outcomes and make a decision about the most desirable outcome when that neurochemical incident happens again.

When I felt the embarrassment, instead of judging myself for feeling embarrassed, I wondered about that feeling. I wondered why I was feeling it. I wondered what it meant. I wondered if I could override that feeling and not feel embarrassed, or did I need to return to the scene of the crime and make repairs? Was I justifiably embarrassed, or was I embarrassed for no reason?

I realized that I was embarrassed for no reason. It was spontaneous embarrassment with no other root than the possibility that I may have made a mistake. Kind of like how one might feel if she tripped on her way to the stage after an introduction in a public forum. Most of us would feel embarrassed. But why? It's one thing to trip and fall to the floor. It's another to simply trip and catch your footing immediately without consequence. Either way, I would feel excruciating embarrassment.

Excruciating embarrassment? Really? For an inconsequential trip or a slight fumble in words? What warrants the excruciating part? What justifies the intensity of that feeling? Come to find out, excruciating embarrassment is shame.

The research on embarrassment led me to researching shame and guilt. Shame and guilt are embarrassment's nasty, horrible parents. Turns out, shame and guilt are manufactured feelings. They are not genuine, authentic feelings that occur organically. They only occur by force.

Shame and guilt only occur when a parent, parents, or other caregivers have forced a developing child to feel these feelings as a guide for behavior. "You should be ashamed of yourself." "You are being naughty!" These are very common statements that parents use to force their children to feel shame and guilt respectively. Unfortunately, most parents who raised children in the sixties, seventies, and eighties didn't know any other way to parent. Why? Because they were parented this same way.

Guilt is a feeling about behavior. It is about doing something wrong. Shame is a feeling about being wrong—not wrong about something but fundamentally wrong as a human being. We learn to associate these feelings with the things that our parents psychologically beat into us.

I feel a flood of shame when I look in the mirror and "look fat." I can't help it. The neurochemical reaction happens, and the outcome is a primary outcome of shame. My mother, grandmother, and grandfather psychologically beat into me that being "fat" is the worst fate on earth. My dad backed them up, and my stepfather reinforced this ideology.

Currently, I'm in the secondary outcome of taking time to consider this reaction. I literally look in the mirror, and shame floods over me. Instead of allowing that feeling of shame to occupy my emotional real estate, I add other feelings into the mix. I look myself in the eyes in the mirror, and I tell myself, "My value is not determined by the scale. I provide value to the lives around me regardless of what the scale says." This is a process. Everything is.

My hope is to gain a tertiary reaction of determining an alternative outcome to looking in the mirror and seeing a shameful heavy body. Instead of shame flooding, I would like to feel beauty flooding regardless of what it "looks" like. I would also like to look in the mirror and see that slim athletic build that fits everything in my closet. However, right now, this is my work. My work is to develop a tertiary outcome to looking in the mirror and not liking what I see.

The Biology and Reality of Recovery

The reality is that life is a strange paradox. Recovery is about aligning who you were (before this hostile world imposed its influence on you) with who you are destined to be. It is about aligning your external world with your internal world. Emotionally intelligent mothers raise emotionally intelligent children that allow for better alignment results.

Today, my mother and I have a relationship. I don't depend on her for anything. The only thing I count on is her "advice." She's quite a bit of lip service and no action. I can also count on her when I want to feel "unimportant." There is no one on this planet better at making me feel unimportant.

The good news is that since I can count on her for my fix of being unimportant, I can stop doing it to myself. I can stop looking for men that make me feel insignificant, undervalued, underappreciated, and unimportant. I can stop finding jobs with bosses that don't value me. I can stop making myself miserable when I don't have someone around to make me feel miserable.

It took me writing this book to see that correlation. If I never sat down to write, I don't know if I would have discovered that. I certainly didn't understand it until I just wrote it.

I entered therapy to understand why I would gain sixty pounds and lose sixty pounds. I entered therapy to understand the fluctuation. Why not just stay overweight or stay fit?

In writing this book, I discovered the answer. My last six years of recovery have really paid off. Hitting recovery groups allowed me to genuinely embrace the Serenity Prayer. The Serenity Prayer is a prayer my first therapist told me. For the last ten years, and especially for the last three, the Serenity Prayer has been my mantra.

God, grant me the serenity to accept the things I cannot change, the courage to change the things I can, and the wisdom to know the difference. As of this moment, God has granted me the wisdom to know the difference.

This is why I could not surrender to alcohol. Alcohol does not have power over me. I am stronger than alcohol. Mexican food does not have power over me. I am stronger than Mexican food. Unhealthy relationships don't have power over me. I am healthier than an unhealthy relationship.

This is what I proved every single time I lost the weight. Every single time I lost the weight, I would need to sustain healthy habits over time. It was easy to make those changes and get that train rolling. Then the train would pick up speed and get me to my destination. There was a lot of track to cover, but I would cover it. I would prove that I had control over alcohol, Mexican food, and the assholes in my life. I would be fit and healthy, and I loved that feeling.

Why wouldn't I stay there? Why would I fall back into my unhealthy habits? That was the question that needed to be answered. The easy answer is this: I wasn't in control of my addictions. And here's the tougher question. Why not? Why can I control them for years at a time and then not control them for years at a time? Why was it years, not months? Why was it years, not days?

I don't think I would know the answer today if I hadn't done everything I've done up until this very moment, including getting my body back up to 180 pounds. My fit body hid this nasty feeling of shame from me. Today, I've learned enough to understand it and label it properly.

When I reported this to my therapist, she said the strangest thing to me. She said, "What do *you* have to be ashamed of?" She helped me see that this shame was not mine. It did not belong to me.

How can I carry someone else's feelings? Do you know the answer?

I'll give you a hint. It's called being an empath. Empaths feel other people's feelings. So did the abuse "make" me an empath, or was my being born an empath what allowed me to tolerate the abuse?

The question is always nature and nurture. I don't think the two can be separated. Ever. I believe the universe works in mysterious ways, and it is best to accept it. Otherwise, you will find yourself down a rabbit hole and deterred from your higher purpose.

Those of you that are empaths know what I am talking about. I feel other people's feelings. If I am connected to you, I can feel them. Not all of them, but I can understand a lot more than what you are saying. I am a very connected person.

A woo-woo friend of mine once said, "You are very 'of this world,' and I am not." She was referring to the fact that I am pragmatic and practical, even about all the spiritual stuff. She is very wise about the spiritual stuff but can never find her keys.

Being an empath is a blessing and a curse. I am limited only by my own depth of feeling. However, my depth of feeling is pretty fucking deep. Understanding and employing this gift has been a lot like Elsa's learning to control her ice-making power in Disney's *Frozen*. Now I understand why "conceal, don't feel" made me want to sit Elsa's parents down and explain to them how parenting works. And also maybe give them some tips on water safety.

My therapist is exactly right. I don't have anything to be ashamed of. I'm telling you everything. I'm not ashamed to call myself an alcoholic. I'm not ashamed that my body is overweight. I'm not ashamed of my behavior. Except for that time that I drank too much and behaved completely inappropriately at a bar. I apologized to the manager the next day and assured him it would never happen again. Why is this nasty feeling of shame in my body?

I'm sure all the therapists out there are saying, "Of course! You were sexually abused. All victims of sexual abuse hold the shame of their abusers." But let me tell you this. It took me thirty-two years to get here and most of the way through this book before I was actually able to understand what that means and apply it to my life. It literally took everything up to this point and me telling my therapist that I identified that horrible feeling as shame for her to help me with that connection.

That fucking shame has been lurking in the deep dark corners of my soul, fucking shit up without my knowledge or consent. This is where the Serenity Prayer comes back in. The wisdom to know the difference. I can control my weight gain or loss. I can control my consumption of alcohol. I can control if I stay in a shitty relationship or not.

What is not in my control? How my fucking brain seeks home. How my fucking brain got wired to seek misery. How my goddamn biology is driving the bus to Miseryville.

You can intellectualize this all day long. Lots of people might say "I told you that!" or "I could have told you that!" Talking about feelings and feeling feelings are entirely different. Until you actually feel this shit in your soul, you won't know what I am talking about.

My biology is out of my control. The complex functioning of my brain and body are out of my control. I have huge amounts of gratitude for my biology taking awesome care of me despite the ways I abuse my body. I am hugely grateful that my body functions amazingly at 180 pounds and even more amazingly at 135 pounds. I am hugely grateful that my body detoxifies the alcohol I drink so I can participate in one of my favorite activities. Thank you, biological body. You are my best friend. I will take better care of you. I promise.

So here's the deal. Here's the golden rule. Life is not about controlling your addictions. It is about embracing them—understanding them as a reflection of a part of who you are without your addictions defining you.

It is about not being ashamed of your addictions. It is about accepting and embracing them. I can "control" them. Until I can't. Instead, snuggling up to my addictions and allowing them to be a part but not all of who I am will be the key to my success.

The Grief Process

When talking about recovery, we have to talk about the grief process. You may be familiar with this well-known five stages of grief model, or the Kübler-Ross Model. Apparently, there has been some criticism of this model because there is no evidence to support this idea beyond a reasonable doubt. Honestly, people. Get some fucking faith. It's a fucking infrastructural understanding of grief, the noble grandparent of sadness.

Here's what people don't understand. We experience grief regularly. Grief is a constant in life. We live in a hostile environment. Some people live in a hostile physical environment, and most of us live in a hostile emotional environment. If understanding the grief process doesn't work for you, leave it alone. It is intended as a conceptual understanding of the neurochemical reactions that are occurring in your body without your consent. It is *not* a theory that needs to be tested. Believe it or don't believe it. Make your own choice and leave the rest of us out of it.

Sadness is the feeling that occurs in you when something is lost. Think of the temper tantrum of a two-year-old who loses a helium balloon. I remember Josephine and Madison both screaming and crying when a helium balloon left their grip and became irretrievable. Sadness. That is what it looks like.

Grief is what occurs when sadness is not processed fully. The five stages of grief give the most appropriate and comprehensive understanding of what your body is going through without you needing a medical degree to understand it. Loss must be processed completely to acceptance for the sadness to be processed fully.

No matter what the loss is. No matter how catastrophic or how trivial the loss is. No matter if what we lost was something we loved or something we hated. Loss is loss. Our bodies biologically process the loss unless we don't allow our bodies to do so.

Denial

In the beginning of processing a loss, denial is often experienced to one degree or another. Generally, this is an unconscious nonacceptance of the loss. It might look like shock, or it might look like inappropriate laughter. It is a natural and organic stage of losing something or someone.

Denial serves an important part of the process. Denial buffers us from the pain of loss until we have brought enough resources online to deal with the pain. It allows us to prepare ourselves for the pain of the loss. The greater the pain of the loss, the more severe the denial can be.

Many of us know people who are in denial about one thing or another. Knowing that one stage of processing loss is processing denial helps us acknowledge our denial. Denial, left unattended, can become debilitating and lead to very bad decisions. Denial, in and of itself, is not a bad thing unless it prevents one from processing the pain the denial was serving to initially protect.

In order to process the pain, one has to accept that denial is part of the process. Learning to identify denial and admit to the loss is instrumental. Admitting that the loss hurts begins processing of the pain.

Anger

Anger is the nasty little bitch that reminds you that you don't get to control everything. Whenever I find myself angry, I ask myself, "What am I trying to control that is out of my control?" Everyone has experienced the anger and frustration of technology not working the way it is supposed to. Even something as simple as a remote control not working—on a bad day, a button push can send me into a flying rage.

Anger is also a natural and organic part of processing loss. Obviously, the loss is out of your control. If you would have had a say in it, you wouldn't have experienced the loss. If it was under your control, you would still have the thing you lost.

Knowing that anger is a part of the process helps us to identify it. Labeling anger takes the sting out of it. Allowing yourself to be angry allows you to process the anger. Knowing that it is a natural part of processing loss explains why the anger is there in the first place.

Anger, left unattended, can create problems. Maybe you have heard that anger is the tip of the emotional iceberg. In this case, it is. Anger is the surface emotion for the deep underlying sadness of an unprocessed loss.

Depression

This is the part of the process where you don't feel motivated. You may feel sad. You may have a hard time getting out of bed in the morning. You may be wondering "what's the use?" or "what's my purpose?" You are experiencing a life without the thing you lost.

Depression is another organic and natural part of processing loss. As you learn a new normal and experience the pain of the loss, it makes sense that depression is a part of the process. Experiencing pain sucks. It draws a lot of energy out of our bodies, leaving our bodies feeling depleted and depressed.

Depression leads us to the "well of despair." There is plenty of despair at this well, and depression leads us to the "well of despair" every time. Knowing that depression is a part of the grieving process and knowing that it leads to the "well of despair" allows us to process through the depression rather than set up camp and residence at the "well of despair."

Do not drink from the "well of despair" if you don't want to set up camp. Treat the "well of despair" as a temporary tourist attraction. You can look, but don't touch. Keep moving on the path, and you will find other wells that are full of much better substances than despair. Look for the wells of joy, contentment, and grace. Drink from those instead.

Bargaining

This is the part where you beg for things to be different than they are. You beg for the thing you lost to be returned to you. You beg for anything—clarity, restoration, relief from the pain.

Bargaining is also an organic and natural part of the processing of grief. When Jeff left, I was begging God to take the pain away. Did God? You decide for yourself. The pain went away, eventually.

Bargaining is the part of the process where you begin to consider accepting the loss. Instead of resisting the loss, you are at least acknowledging that you've lost something, and you are letting the universe know that you will do anything to get that thing back. From my perspective, this acknowledgment is the most critical part of bargaining. Admitting that something is gone is most of the battle to acceptance.

Acceptance

This is the part where you exit the process. The process is not linear, and it is, actually, quite messy. I like to think of it as more of a spherical process. The stages of denial, anger, depression, and bargaining are all wrapped in a protective coating of acceptance when the loss has been fully processed.

All the stages inside the protective coating are experienced until the protective coating of acceptance is developed. There is no particular order, and there is no particular pattern between the stages. Sometimes they are all experienced at once, and sometimes they are neatly processed from one stage to the next. The development of the protective coating of acceptance is your unique creative expression.

223

Where problems occur is where the protective coating of acceptance hides feelings that have not been fully processed. If anger, sadness, or denial get trapped in the protective coating before they are completely processed, those unprocessed feelings scream for attention. They will need to be mined for in order to process them fully and circumvent their destructive influence.

This is what happens when someone tries to hot-wire acceptance rather than allow acceptance to naturally occur. Each of the stages of grief occur naturally and organically. If we allow our bodies to process the grief naturally and organically, acceptance will naturally be reached. If you force yourself into acceptance before your body has processed the feelings that come with grief, the protective coating of acceptance will obscure the cause of your pain.

You have organically and naturally reached acceptance when you have learned to live without the thing you lost. You have reached acceptance naturally when your life has improved, even though the loss is still a reality. Organic acceptance is when you feel "recovered" from the loss, and you have established a new normal where the loss has less influence than who and what are still with you in this biological life.

Search and Rescue

There is no way to hot-wire acceptance. You can try to force yourself into acceptance, but there is no way to bypass the feelings without consequence. You can't just feel the feelings once and say you're done. You have to let your body do what it was built to do. It was built to process the loss without your interference.

There is no way to bypass denial, anger, depression, and bargaining. These feelings show up on their own terms without your consent. Your only job is to allow these unwanted visitors a place to stay until you are ready for them to leave. When you are ready for them to leave, invite them to leave. Use gentle pressure in a positive direction, and apply it relentlessly when you are ready for these unwanted guests to leave.

Trauma is a series of significant losses. Everyone experiences trauma differently. Something that is traumatic for one person may not be traumatic for another. Human beings are exceptionally resilient. This is due—in part, if not entirely—to the grief process that our bodies and minds go through when processing a loss.

Any loss may need this complete process. No matter how ridiculous it may seem to you, you may need the full processing to reach acceptance organically. There are significant losses that obviously require full processing, such as the loss of a loved one. There are many less obvious losses, such as the loss of an abusive relationship or the loss of an addiction, that need to go through a complete grief processing. And finally, there are things we didn't even know we lost that we need to grieve.

This is what recovery is all about. To one degree or another, we have all lost some self-worth, childhood innocence, and self-esteem along the way. Those of us that experienced trauma, especially, have lost things we didn't know we had. I never knew I lost my self-worth. I don't remember having self-worth. I don't remember losing childhood innocence. I don't remember having childhood innocence.

The other important factor here is that many people deny their trauma and losses because those are scary words. Many people think, *I didn't have it as bad as…therefore, I don't deserve to feel sad or angry.* Many people also think, *It wasn't that bad…therefore, I don't have anything to process.* Sorry, folks. This is called intellectualizing. It is what people do to avoid feeling strong feelings. If you've ever said anything like this to yourself, I promise, you have some recovery to do.

What is recovery? Recovery is recovering the authentic self from the rubble of losses. These could be acknowledged losses or losses of things you didn't even know you lost. The losses piled up and buried your authentic self under all the rubble. Recovery is a search and rescue mission for your authentic self. It is a recovery of the self that was not too scared or too hurt to process grief organically without your interference and avoidance.

Step 1: I Admitted I Had a Problem

What I've come to realize is that I don't have "a problem." I have a system of problems that are rooted in shame. Rooted in a seed that I didn't know had been planted. A system of problems that became a briar patch of misery and suffering.

The main indicator of my system of problems has been my weight fluctuation. My weight fluctuation wasn't between a size 2 and a size 4. My weight fluctuation has been between a size 2 and a size 18. It has been between 135 pounds and 200 pounds. I have never actually seen the scale tip two bills, but that's because I stopped stepping on the scale in the 190s.

Generally, around 180 pounds is where my tipping point is. The last time I was 180 pounds was about seven years ago. Since then, I have hovered in the 135- to 160-pound range for the last seven years. Until my last relationship. The relationship with Steve sent me back to the 180s, which is where I find myself today.

I don't blame Steve for this weight gain. It is true that Steve treated me in a way that left me feeling miserable. In turn, I overate and drank more heavily to emotionally manage. This response was my addictions making my decisions for me. I stayed in a relationship that made me miserable so that I would have a justifiable reason to overeat and drink heavily.

Any person using rational reasoning would come to the conclusion that ending a relationship that made me miserable would be the rational decision. That's the problem, though. We all think we are far more rational than we actually are. Believe me, through the entire relationship, I felt as though I was being completely rational. What I didn't know was that my addictions were making the decisions, not my rational brain.

This is why I don't blame Steve. I blame myself. I have put this weight on throughout the course of our relationship and added even more weight after ending it. I knew I was gaining weight, and I knew why. I couldn't bring myself to make the changes that I needed to make. That's on me.

The relationship with Steve caused me a lot of pain. Instead of eliminating the cause of the pain, I consciously chose to endure the pain and stay in the relationship. I consciously chose to eat and drink my pain away while enduring the pain Steve caused. He didn't cause physical pain. He caused emotional pain, which, as you know, is much harder to detect. Plus, some part of my constitution believed that emotional pain and relationships were inseparable.

I gave Steve many chances to stop causing me pain. I explained in excruciating detail how he could participate in a way that would not cause me pain. He tried. He really did. But my pain outweighed his effort. I finally mustered the balls to break it off for good.

Ideally, the other four times I broke it off with Steve should have been an indicator of the health of the relationship. Each time, however, I would do all the dirty work. Then I would justify his shitty choices for him. I would forgive him, and then we would carry on again for several more months before there would be another painful incident.

What I learned in this relationship is that if a man cares about me and wants to be in a healthy relationship, his efforts will match mine. I learned that the words coming out of his mouth did not match his subconscious drive to sabotage the relationship. I would do his dirty work for him and break up with him so that he would not be suffocated by my love and attention.

I learned that I did not feel important in the first three months of the relationship, and that did not change over two years. I was deprioritized anytime someone wanted to spend time with Steve. His ex-wife, his ex-mother-in-law, his dad, his brother, his sister, his friend, and his business associates all took precedence over me.

No matter how well I treated Steve and gave him my adoration and attention, he never reciprocated it.

I'm grateful to Steve for giving me an overdose of an unhealthy relationship. Similar to how a scary overdose of alcohol would create a period of abstinence from alcohol, I had such a strong overdose of tolerating Steve's immature and childish behavior that I just don't want to be around irresponsible men anymore. I'm completely sick of irresponsible men that have no clue how to be in a healthy relationship and who have no interest in learning.

I can't tell you how many times I start my journaling with "I've got to pull myself together." I also start frequently with "I've got to get my life together." This is fairly ironic because my life is really pulled together. Honestly, I've never fallen apart. It just feels that way.

At 180-plus pounds, I feel like my life has fallen apart. Realistically though, that is an irrational thought. My life is no less put together than it was a year ago. In fact, my life is way more put together!

At the point of writing this, I am almost finished with this book—a task I have wanted to do for at least five years! I have remodeled my home, and I love it! My kids and dogs are well-adjusted. I have no conflict and no drama. All my relationships are as healthy as the least healthy person, and I am the healthier of the two. My life is entirely manageable and on the exact trajectory that I want.

The first step of recovery has to do with admitting there is a problem and that your life has become unmanageable. I have taken this step with all my singular problems, whether it be drinking, overeating, or unhealthy relationships. At any point that my life felt unmanageable, I took this step and problem-solved from there.

This irrational feeling that "my life has fallen apart" simply because I am 183.4 pounds is part of the system of problems. The irrational belief leads to rigorous change. The rigorous change would lead to feeling good about myself, thereby obscuring the shame lurking in the shadows, ubiquitously and covertly influencing the system of problems.

The shame has me reaching for food, alcohol, and unhealthy relationships. The primary driver is the feeling that "I'm not good enough," and the alcohol, food, and crazy-making drama of unhealthy relationships bury that feeling of inadequacy. Addiction buries shame under the rubble of the addiction, thereby preventing the shame from being excavated and incinerated.

This time around, I have identified a different problem. The problem is not that I am heavy. My life is not unmanageable because I am heavy. I have proven time and time again that I can manage weight loss and maintenance of a healthy weight. This time, I have identified the problem as the lurking shame.

I have needed to spend this time in my 183.4-pound fat suit to expose that shame. When I look in the mirror, that shame floods over me. In doing so, I am able to rationalize it and extinguish its power.

It's not my shame. It does not belong to me. Yet it has been undermining my decisions without my knowledge or consent. It has been contributing to my feeling that life is unmanageable even when my life is perfectly manageable!

Shame makes me feel inadequate because I don't have a partner. It makes me feel inadequate because I am 183.4 pounds. It makes me feel inadequate because I am a heavy drinker. Rationally, these are not things to be ashamed of.

I felt my life was unmanageable every time I was heavy, so I lost the weight. Every time I spent a significant amount of time sober, I felt my life was unmanageable due to my drinking. Between my first husband, Norm, Jeff, and Steve, I felt my life was unmanageable because I didn't have a man. Shame convinced me to make my life manageable by accepting an inadequate partner.

How fucked up is that? Shame is lurking in my deep dark depths, making me feel inadequate. So what do I do? I spend thirty years with inadequate partners, not realizing that I am completely adequate. It is my inadequate partner bringing the unmanageability to my life, not *me*!

Right now, everything in my life is perfectly manageable. I have spent all of 2020 without a partner fucking shit up and making my life feel unmanageable. I have developed a career. I have written this book. My kids are growing into responsible contributors. This time around, I'm not going to force regimented, rapid weight loss.

I'm going to try something new. If I want the result to change, I have to change the pattern. I do love my routine when I manage my drinking. I get up early. I run. I carry on a productive day. I feel good. I rest. I repeat.

I'm not a high performer when it comes to exercise. I'm mediocre. It is probably the only thing where I have allowed myself to have a mediocre performance. However, I'm consistent and constant. I don't run fast, but I do run consistently.

Please don't try to clarify and say, "Oh, then you're a jogger." This drives me crazy. I run eleven- to thirteen-minute miles. Distinguishing me as a jogger instead of a runner is run-shaming me.

I identify as a runner. If your definition of *runner* is different from mine, please don't impose your definition on me. I run. I'm a runner. Just because I'm not an elite athlete or meet some arbitrary criteria of what constitutes a jogger from a runner does not make the classification relevant. I run more than anyone who doesn't run and more than most.

I know I like my routine when I'm in good shape. I feel good, and I look good. It is a great way to start every day. So why can't I stay in this place indefinitely? Because it is also hard work. It requires time and energy, which are limited resources. Time and energy tend to be frivolously spent, especially when in the throes of addiction. I have prioritized writing this book over a regimented exercise routine.

I feel confident that I am going to get back to my healthy 135 in the near future. However, before I go there, I need to learn everything there is to learn about being overweight. I need my overdose of being overweight. I assure you, I am almost there. The way I physically feel in this fat suit is exceedingly less desirable than how I physically feel in my trim athletic body.

My pregnancies account for two of the weight-gain incidents. These were seemingly more legitimate reasons to gain weight, but not that much weight. After my first pregnancy, I figured it would be wise to have another baby before losing the weight. The universe apparently had a different plan. I miscarried at thirteen weeks. The waterfall of emotion that flooded me convinced me that I better lose the weight and take some time before getting pregnant again. I did and began my second pregnancy at a healthy weight and with a mindset of only gaining an appropriate amount of weight.

This is not what happened. I ended up gaining the same amount of weight as I did with my first pregnancy. However, in my first pregnancy, I gained the weight in the beginning and developed toxemia. My first birth was an emergency C-section. During my second pregnancy, I gained the weight in the last half of the pregnancy. When it came time to schedule my C-section, my doctor asked if I wanted "my tubes tied" while she "was in there."

I couldn't believe that at thirty-five years old, I was making this life-altering decision. I had to decide, before giving birth on a scheduled day, if I wanted to end my reproductive career. I had to make a permanent decision for myself and my family.

It took me about two days to decide that I couldn't go through pregnancy again. I loved the end result of pregnancy, but I absolutely hated being pregnant. I hated losing a baby in between pregnancies. I hated how my mind felt when I was pregnant.

My anxiety was through the roof. Carrying a life inside me that I was 100 percent responsible for was overwhelming. If you think about the shame that was lurking undetected in my mind, it makes sense that I didn't have confidence that I was capable of building a baby all on my own. It makes sense that my large body activated this shame.

Do you recognize the pattern here? My mind and body were in distress, and I overate to compensate. Pregnancy is a justifiable reason to "eat for two," but I was eating for me, my baby, and my shame-driven addiction. I justified my addiction by allowing myself to overeat because I was pregnant.

Knowing now how my life unfolded after deciding to have my tubes tied, I do not regret that decision at all. It was time for me to know my limits. Two successful pregnancies and one failed effort was my limit.

I don't mean to be insensitive to those that have difficulty getting pregnant. My heart goes out to you. We all have different paths and different lessons to learn. My lesson was about determining what was in my best interest, and tubal ligation was it.

I can't wait to get back to running. I do my best thinking while running. I can't sit and meditate. Running is the closest I come to the benefits of meditation. I'm a kill-two-birds-with-one-stone kind of person. Meditation, while hugely beneficial to the body and mind, feels like a waste of time to me. I would rather "meditate" while I run, which I call "active meditation."

Each time I have gained the weight, I have learned the logistical lessons. Carrying an extra thirty, forty, or fifty pounds is a lot of work. It is hard to get that body moving. It is hard to put on shoes. Gravity becomes an enemy.

I know that I hate being overweight, and yet that's not enough to convince me to continue with my healthy weight management. Being fit and feeling good is also not a good enough reason to maintain my weight. I guess I am in search of what will be a good enough reason. I'm sincerely hoping that this is the last time I go through this.

I believe it will be, and I'll tell you why. Not only am I doing things differently, I've grown up significantly. I believe I am finally an adult. Not just a regular adult—a responsible and healthy adult. My body just doesn't reflect that right now. I have a sign in my office that says "The first fifty years of childhood are always the hardest!" I will be fifty in March 2021, so I'm counting on it all getting better.

This time around, at 180, I learned something more than the logistics. I believe I needed to gain the weight to experience what I have been experiencing for the last six months. I've excavated the shame that was lurking in the deep dark corners of my athletic body. My athletic body hid that shame from me. I couldn't actually feel the shame.

It has been a very long time since I felt this feeling of shame. Actually, when I used to feel this feeling, I couldn't identify it. Seriously, I am a very cerebral person, and I've taken a cerebral approach to understanding all my feelings.

The identification of this one eluded me. I would feel it. It felt awful. I would wonder about it. I would wonder what created the feeling and how to label it.

Up until about six months ago, I called this feeling "profound loneliness." That label seemed to fit the situations well when I would feel it. I almost always was looking in a mirror when I would feel this feeling.

Back when I was studying embarrassment in 2007, it led me to all my research on shame. Brené Brown was instrumental in helping me understand intellectually about shame. Also, my research on sexual abuse concluded that it was highly likely that I had shame surrounding the abuse. Honestly, I thought I got the shame stuff resolved a while back.

In the last few years, when I felt this particular feeling and chalked it up to "profound loneliness," it motivated me to get out of whatever relationship I was in. If I felt "profoundly lonely" in a relationship, there was something fundamentally wrong with the relationship. This was the surface-level feeling that motivated me to make a change.

This was much easier said than done. When I was married, I tried for many years to align our relationship with something that resembled a healthy relationship. Eventually, I got to a point where I realized, *This guy doesn't even know a healthy routine for himself.* I had learned that a relationship can only be as healthy as the least healthy person. He was bringing our average way down. It took a full two years to go from "let's work this out" to our divorce being final. This was January 2013 to December of 2014.

Then with Jeff, whom I was head over heels in love with, I knew we needed to break up when he wouldn't even have a conversation about treatment for his alcoholism. Breaking up was the most devastating outcome to me. It was a typical and expected outcome to him. His indifference was the devastating part.

Then with Steve, the exact same pattern that had been in my previous two relationships emerged. I overate and overdrank to numb the pain. The pain of being in a relationship with someone and still feeling profoundly lonely. The pain of being in a relationship with someone and not feeling important. The pain of being in a relationship with someone who is indifferent about being with you.

Here's how my athletic and fit body hid shame from me. When I was thin, I didn't feel adequate. I felt extraordinarily inadequate when I was heavy and confusingly inadequate when I was thin. This dissonance was created because I could not hold two concepts simultaneously that seemingly conflicted for me.

I could not hold the concept that I was thin and inadequate at the same time. Here's the math my brain was doing:

- thin = adequate
- fat = inadequate
- thin ≠ inadequate
- fat ≠ adequate

Compound this math with how people treated me when I was thin, and it makes for a convincing costume of an attractive woman that feels completely adequate. So convincing that I even convinced myself that I must be adequate even though I didn't actually feel adequate.

I'm an attractive woman. I have a curvy figure and intense eyes. People generally like me, except when they don't. I've tied too much of my analysis regarding who likes me and why to how I look. Being heavy or fit does not change how people feel about me. It changes how they perceive me, which, in turn, affects how they feel about me.

Folks, we have zero control over how others perceive us. We can do everything in our own control to impact another's perception, but ultimately, their perception is 100 percent under their own control. This is why we should never tie our perception of ourselves to someone else's perception of us. It is difficult to maintain this separation and still maintain self-awareness. The trick is to take nothing personally.

People treat you the way they do due to their own issues, not yours. It has been tricky for me to determine that people treat me one way when they are intimidated by me and another way when they desire connection with me. When someone wants to benefit from what I have to offer, he or she treats me differently than when that person feels overpowered by me. This is about them, not about me.

Keep in mind that I have an addiction to unhealthy relationships. Getting lots of attention from men while in my "fit and adequate" costume created the illusion that there was no reason that I couldn't have any guy I wanted. This superficial judgment is the key to unlocking another unhealthy relationship. Out of desperation for a healthy relationship, I engaged in a relationship with Steve.

Finally, someone who is financially stable. Someone who is bald and built and has his shit together. Finally, someone who takes his health seriously. A mature adult taking responsibility seriously—or so it seemed.

Clearly, the lens I look through gives men these qualities even when it is evident that they do not possess these qualities. Steve was someone who looked the part. When it came down to putting his money where his mouth was, the relationship came to an abrupt halt.

My vision is enhanced by reading behavior. It's like watching a standard feed versus a high-definition feed. My addiction narrows my vision to standard definition instead of high definition.

My addiction was the lens I was looking through when evaluating each of my partners. My need to feel adequate was the driver for a relationship. Shame was the driver for my need to feel adequate. Shame made me feel inadequate even when I was actually perfectly adequate.

My need for "a fix" was a need "to feel adequate." This need created the desperation that filtered out what I did not want to see. This is how shame undermined my competence and drove me into any relationship, especially an unhealthy one.

With an unhealthy relationship, my focus would be on the problems of the relationship instead of the real problem: shame. Shame was making me feel inadequate even when I was perfectly adequate. It was the man in my life who was making me feel miserable. It was shame that was keeping me in a relationship with a man who was making me miserable.

The real problem was that shame was driving me into bad relationships so I could get a superficial fix of feeling adequate. All the while, the unhealthy relationship was creating all kinds of emotional pain for me, causing me to indulge my addictions. This is how addiction is self-sustaining if the addiction is not raised to conscious awareness and dealt with appropriately.

While I was still identifying shame as profound loneliness, I did feel profoundly lonely in my relationship with Steve. I felt lonely because Steve was not around. I was lonely because he preferred to be apart rather than together. It was like he was doing me a favor by being my boyfriend and allocating time to me. This would make anyone lonely, so it made sense that I felt lonely.

However, toward the end of my relationship with Steve and in the months that followed, I would feel that awful feeling of shame when I would look in the mirror. What was weird, though, was that I could not label it as "profound loneliness" anymore. I was not any more alone than I had ever been. I was not actually feeling lonely at all. I was enjoying my own company and enjoying the work I was doing. I was not lonely, so what was this feeling?

It finally dawned on me. That feeling was shame. It fit perfectly. Shame is profound embarrassment. It is a feeling that you don't belong. That you have no people. That you are alone, and you are not connected. That there is abundance out there, but none of it is for you. Shame is not a feeling you can intellectualize your way through. Shame is a feeling you need to feel your way through.

I needed my big body to bring this feeling to the surface. It was buried deep under my athletic body, under my overachieving and healthy self-esteem. It's been lurking in the dark, subconsciously driving my addictions. Now that the feeling has been excavated and is being examined, I don't believe it will be subconsciously driving anything anymore.

This examination has helped me identify how much shame I associate with being overweight. Turns out, that is a very small part of the puzzle. The huge part of the puzzle is how much shame I associated with *not* having a partner. That was the shame driving the addiction to an unhealthy relationship. I didn't realize that my belief was that "*any* relationship was better than *no* relationship."

Today, I have found peace in believing that "*no* relationship is better than a shitty relationship." No relationship is better than a relationship where I am not appreciated, understood, and valued.

No relationship is better than a relationship where someone else is doing all the sabotaging and blaming me for the destruction. Yes. No relationship is waaaaaayyyyy better.

It took sitting down and getting serious about writing this book to discover a lot of what I have discovered. My shame has kept me small. My addiction lens manages my denial and my self-worth.

Whenever I would consciously tell myself it's time to write my book, that lurking shame would say, "No one cares what you have to say." Whenever I would consciously tell myself I'm a good strong person, that lurking shame would tell me that I don't matter. Whenever I would try to convince myself that I am destined for greatness, that lurking shame would tell me I'm being unrealistic and living in a fantasy world.

This still happens many times throughout the week. I write anyway. Sometimes I sit down to write and think, *This is garbage.* But I keep writing anyway. Sometimes I sit down to review what I've written, and I say, "Amy, it's really good. It's really fucking good."

I struggle too, people. Don't think I don't just because I look put together.

My perfectionism tells me that I don't look put together when I'm fifty pounds overweight. The reality is, I am put together. I'm just fifty pounds overweight. It doesn't make me any less valuable. I'm still me, and I'm still passionate about the service I provide.

The weight will come off. This time, however, shame will stay right where I can see it. It will not be able to lurk in the dark and subconsciously sabotage my efforts. Shame will not be driving my addictions; my conscience will be in the driver's seat.

This time, my weight loss will not be driven by an unconscious search for adequacy. I will not hustle for my worthiness through a regimented weight-loss program. I will lose the weight when I am ready to reach for a healthy future—when I am ready to maintain a healthy home by myself and for myself.

Steps 2 and 3: I Surrendered

When Jeff left, I promised myself I would never be with someone who had not surrendered. I literally typed a sign to remind myself of this every day. In the two years I spent with Steve, I was trying to determine if he had surrendered or if he would be willing and able to surrender. When I remembered the promise I made to myself, I broke up with Steve because it became clear that not only had he not surrendered, he was never going to in a relationship with me.

My overthinking has brought me to a place of surrender. That is the beauty of it. My overthinking developed my deep thinking, which brought me to surrender. Ultimately, this is what my book is about. Recovery sucks because it involves surrendering. Surrender is the difference between addicts in recovery and addicts not in recovery.

Sometimes I find myself being judgmental about other people's recovery. The problem is, surrendering is hard to do. It is a daily practice, and we all forget. "Accepting the things I cannot change and having the courage to change the things I can" requires a lot of energy and a very conscious effort. When I'm being judgmental, it is me forgetting that I have surrendered.

The concept of not being in control is too much for most people to contemplate and handle without an embodiment such as God or religion. Aside from opposable thumbs, contemplation of our existence is another distinguishing factor between human beings and the rest of the animal kingdom. That I can even share my ideas and contemplation with you is a whole other level.

I have a fundamental belief that people either impact each other positively or negatively, constructively or destructively. I believe that my support throughout my twenty-two-year relationship with Norm and Madison helped them be better people today than they would have been without my influence. These relationships are still ongoing; they just look completely different than they did twenty years ago.

I feel like my relationship with Jeff helped him be a better person—a better father, a better presence in life. Subconsciously, he was destructive and negative, but my conscious positivity and hopefulness mitigated that negative impact. Ultimately, I believe the loss of our relationship was Jeff's overdose that catalyzed his three years of sobriety and a shift toward positivity.

I believe I've spent my time in these relationships to learn that I am a positive and constructive influence in people's lives. Recognizing this helps me feel adequate, to actually feel it. Rather than ignoring that nagging feeling of shame that makes me feel inadequate, I'm acknowledging that shame and inadequacy got unjustifiably wired to my sense of self.

I actually feel adequate. I have a lot to be proud of and nothing to be ashamed of. I am useful, honorable, compassionate, and I'm trying to have it make some difference that I have lived and lived well.

I have barfed all my shame out in this book. I have told you everything. There is something about putting it on paper and putting it out in the world in a real way that offers healing. It allows me to feel atoned. It is my philosophy and way of existing in this world that allows me to feel good about my existence, who I am, and who I have always been.

As I've mentioned, I don't believe in Jesus Christ our Lord and Savior. I also don't believe in Jesus, the Son of God. I don't believe God to be some being in the sky or a being of any kind really.

I believe we developed "God" to embody a concept that is very difficult for human beings to grasp, especially human beings who aren't deep thinkers. God is not somebody or something. God is a concept.

I don't think we should do what Jesus would do. I like the idea for people who have a hard time managing their anger and who can't behave well, but for a deep thinker like me, I need more than WWJD to help me make decisions.

The concept of Jesus and how it all gets tied together with right and wrong doesn't work for me. The concept of "sin" is inconsistent with human nature. Human beings are error prone. Additionally, we have, inarguably, the most sophisticated brain of all known life-forms.

We don't operate exclusively from our animal brain. We have this entire prefrontal cortex that wraps around that animal brain like a hand covering a fist. Like a baseball glove around a baseball. Human beings are capable of training our own brains.

We can teach our prefrontal cortex to override animal brain reactions. This happens naturally when raised in a healthy, loving environment. It is, basically, called maturity.

Do you know why babies are so small? It's because an adult-size head with an adult-size brain cannot fit through the birth canal. As mothers, the greatest gift we give is life. Our bodies take care of and grow a baby from one cell to billions of cells. In utero, a baby's every need is taken care of effortlessly and powerfully by the mother's reproductive system. The only thing the mother has to do is consume nutrients.

Of course, this is a very simplistic model of human reproduction. However, the point is that our bodies are built to survive. Even if you have no idea what you are doing as a mother, you can grow a baby without incident. The vast majority of pregnancies, wanted or unwanted, are successful in producing an infant that will survive into adulthood.

An embryo's every need is taken care of in utero. The embryo floats around in the embryotic fluid, growing, eating, and sleeping without any power source except for the mother. It takes ten months to grow a baby, and then wham! It's a traumatic squeeze through the birth canal, alarming severing from the mother, and a chilling first gasp of air that most likely leads to a loud cry for help. Who wouldn't cry for help after that production?

So begins the human journey on Earth, where everything, including the sun, is trying to kill it. Earth is a hostile environment. However, the human brain has developed over the course of hundreds of thousands of years. Humans have taken a naturally hostile environment and created an unnaturally hostile environment, all through the evolution of the human brain.

The prefrontal cortex continued to develop from generation to generation, giving the human being more and more control over its environment. We discovered how to use the power of the Earth to make fire. We discovered how to turn fire into light. We learned how to transmit signals over long distances so we could communicate with one another. We created the wheel and then the vehicle, and then we created transportation that flies. We created vehicles that float and weapons to kill prey. We developed procedures such as cooking to prevent illness and later developed industries around all of this.

Human beings developed from a prehistoric existence to a documented history. Even if you don't believe in evolution, and even if you believe there is inaccuracy in the recorded details of human evolution, there is no denying that human beings have developed significantly over the period of your lifetime.

The development of technology is evidence enough of human ingenuity. Today, technology is obsolete as soon as it is released. Cell phones, twenty years ago, were "bricks," and twenty-five years ago, they were built into a small suitcase. Today, cell phones are disposable, even the ones you spend $1,000 on.

Here's the thing. With this level of complexity and organization, there must be some higher order to all this. Not some higher order that we need to worship and praise, but a higher order that we must surrender to. Maybe there isn't a higher order, and all this organization is happenstance. Even if it is all happenstance, understanding how it works is powerful.

This is not a question of right and wrong. It is not a question of justice or injustice. Believe what you want to believe. I'm telling you what I believe and why I believe it. Proving me wrong doesn't do anyone any good. However, considering what I have to say and why I say it does not do anyone any harm.

If you look at the organization of the human body alone, there is a crazy level of organization that happens organically, from the initial sperm meeting the egg to the growth into a fully functioning human being. Human beings have been trying to recreate this in an artificial environment and still are unable to do it successfully. We can't create anything even close to the sophistication of a human being. We can't create anything even remotely similar to the functioning of the human brain. This is why I don't believe in God as a being. I also don't believe in God as a mystical being because that is just nonsense. I'm way too pragmatic for that.

I believe that all these stories about the gods and mythology are exactly that: myths designed to teach generations of humans right from wrong and good from bad. This is why there is not one universal book of right and wrong, good and bad. We cannot all agree. Some believe the one book is the Bible. Different religions believe in different books of right and wrong. There is no universal language of right and wrong. Right and wrong are determined by a consensus of trillions of people.

Interestingly, our bodies are made up of trillions of cells. These trillions of cells coordinate and work together to keep you alive. No matter how self-destructive you are, no matter how knowingly or unknowingly you cause yourself harm, trillions of cells conspire against self-destruction.

This is the organization one must surrender to. What does it mean to surrender? Well, it means that you acknowledge that you are not in control of everything and that there is some higher order that determines if you live or die. It is not some superior being that strikes a lightning bolt down on specific people for specific reasons, saying "fuck you" in particular.

Live Your Life on Purpose

Part of living is dying. You don't get control over the dying part, only the living part. What you do with your life is up to you.

Are you going to work your whole life reaching for a finish line that you never really reach? Are you going to keep moving the bar every time you get close? The finish line is death. Are you racing for it or living your life on purpose?

This is what recovery is all about: surrendering. It is about getting your human body back to the spiritual place that you were in your mother's womb. Back to the spiritual place you were before the hostile world gradually convinced you that you are not worthy. Back to the spiritual place you were before you formed habits around performing to validate your worthiness. Back to the spiritual place you were before you knew fear, grief, sadness, anger, and pain.

If you are alive today, you are worthy. This does not excuse bad behavior. People are not their worst behavior. In the simplest form, a murderer could still be a good father. We are human beings. *We* are error prone. We make mistakes. We live in a complex world with a complex hierarchy of right and wrong. We cannot be reduced to simple forms.

Just because you "accept" Jesus Christ as your Lord and Savior does not mean all your sins will be forgiven. It may, but I don't think so. I don't think you will show up to the pearly gates. I don't think anyone will. I think that is all made-up folklore to convince people to behave a certain way. There isn't even a universal understanding of what you need to do to be let into heaven.

My dad said to me once that he hoped I would accept Jesus as my Lord and Savior so he could spend the afterlife with me. WTF? How about this life? Why don't you want to spend this life with me?

If you didn't want to spend this life with me, what makes you think you want to spend the afterlife with me? Does not compute. Sorry, Dad. This life is a sure thing; the afterlife is make-believe.

Surrendering is about admitting that there are certain things out of your control. You can't control other people. You can't control what other people say or do. You can't control when you die. You can't control the universe around you. Surrendering is acceptance that the only control you have is over what you do and what you say. The rest is up to the universe.

God, grant me the serenity to accept the things I cannot change, the courage to change the things I can, and the wisdom to know the difference.

I learned the Serenity Prayer long before I entered twelve-step work. I've continued to say this prayer whenever I feel "in my addiction." Throughout my twenty years of recovery and especially in the last ten, I've been acutely aware of waking up at 3:00 a.m. I've decided this 3:00 a.m. waking is the universe summoning my attention. I say this prayer to get me back to sleep.

In any ordered structure that promotes healthy living, the first order of business is to get enough sleep. Sleeping is a passive way to restore your body's equilibrium. A number of biological processes for repair and restoration occur during sleep. If maintaining a healthy weight is important to you, get enough sleep.

If you can maintain a healthy weight without enough sleep, you are working against your body rather than with your body. Your body requires sleep to restore the damage that the hostile universe has done, including exercise. It's not that the universe is "against" you. It's that there is always give and take. There is always push and pull. There is not progress without adversity.

This is why you have to learn to work with the universe. It's not you against the universe. It's not the universe against you. This is why it doesn't make sense to me when people say, "God took my [insert anything] away. That is why I don't believe in God." Umm... you believe "God" took your [insert anything] away, so doesn't that mean you believe in God? Maybe you don't believe in a "loving"

God. Maybe you believe in a hostile and revengeful God, but that is still a belief in God.

A revengeful God doesn't make sense though. As much as a loving God doesn't make sense to people who have lost loved ones, a vengeful God doesn't make sense either. Explain to me all the people on death row. Explain to me all the people in prison. Explain to me all the people who have not been caught for their misbehavior. Wouldn't a vengeful God strike down on these people with a "fuck you" in particular?

When I prayed for God to strike down my abuser, why wasn't my abuser struck down? How did my abuser defy all the odds of a type A personality with a high-stress environment, eating spoonfuls of mayonnaise, drinking heavily, probably doing illegal drugs, and sexually abusing a child in his household? How in the fuck is this fuckin' guy still alive and married to someone my age? This alone is argument for the nonexistence of a vengeful God. In fact, it might even be proof of the existence of a loving God. Perhaps the universe knew better than me that killing this motherfucker was not the answer.

Surrendering is about taking a guess at what your purpose is and living a life to fulfill that purpose. "Live your life on purpose" is my motto. Big or small, serve your purpose, and your purpose will serve you.

Here's the thing. Surviving is fucking hard. When you are dealt a bunch of hard shit in the beginning of life, it is goddamn hard. You can count on the fact that you will be dealt some hard shit in your life. Count on it. It has nothing to do with God. It has to do with the fact that life is not all rainbows and unicorns. It is challenging and messy and complicated.

You are given what you need. You just have to accept what you are given. Learn your lessons. Grow up. Live your life on purpose.

Steps 4 through 12

Maybe he wronged the right person. Instead of wronging someone who would take revenge, he wronged someone with compassion and connection. Maybe he wronged me because I was the right kind of person to wrong.

Maybe his victimization of me was actually an expression of love and fondness that I didn't receive from my biological parents. I know it is fucked up. I know it is ugly and messy. And such is life. Life is not the pristine ideal that we make up in our heads. Life is a dissonant deviation from that pristine ideal.

I turned my abuse into something that works *for* me rather than against me. I live a great life, not a down-and-out, clinging-to-the-bottom-rung kind of life. I cannot explain it other than how I have.

I can tell you it was much harder straightening out my relationships with my mother and biological father than it was straightening out my relationship with my stepdad. The relationship with my stepdad was blatantly abusive. My relationships with my biological parents were covertly and inconspicuously abusive. This complicated the search to detect the source of my addictions.

I have been more the victim of reverse judgment than negative judgment. Reverse judgment does not feel good either. "Reversing" the judgment is still judgment. It is still a separation of you from them.

Whether it be a separation because they feel I am better than them or whether it be a separation because they feel I am less than them, either way, it is a separation that the other person controls, not me. I'm not the one doing the separating. If it were up to me, I would find ways that we were similar, not different.

People don't know that I was sexually abused throughout my adolescent development. People don't know that I was raised by a narcissistic mother. People don't know that my biological father was a wonderful man to his other family and entirely absent from my life. People don't know that I'm an alcoholic. People don't know that I am a multimillionaire.

Welp, now you all do. Now you know. I feel better getting this off my chest. I feel better knowing that you know the truth. I feel better knowing that you have more data to determine if you like me or not. I feel better knowing that you know what I know.

Some people who value monetary wealth and don't know that I am a multimillionaire treat me as "less than." People who suffer from their history of sexual abuse separate me as "better than" because I am no longer suffering. People who were also left by their fathers separate me as having a better father than they had. People who have had narcissistic parents believe their own parents must have been much worse than mine, which is why I was able to recover and they have not.

I don't know the answers here. All I know is that separation does not feel good. This is why judgment doesn't feel good. Judgment is a separation of what is different between me and you. Judgment makes us fundamentally different from one another and not congruent with each other.

Whether you separate yourself as better than or less than makes no difference. It does not feel good to be judged by someone else as better than or less than. What doesn't feel good is the separation in a human being that is built for connection.

It feels good to be categorized as human, and we are all human. Our experience is uniquely our own, but being human is categorically the same. Let's not separate "us" from "them." Let us show up in good faith to this life and try to understand rather than judge.

No human is better than or less than another. This is why Jesus Christ, our Lord and Savior, doesn't work for me. If Jesus was a human that walked this earth, he is not better than me, and I am not less than him. Categorically, we are the same.

Humans are not qualified to make judgments on other people. Humans do not possess all the analytical data necessary to assess accurately. Additionally, when incorporating the arbitrary data of "right and wrong," the analysis becomes exponentially impossible. Finally, judgment is inherently a "better than / less than" determination. Who is qualified for that kind of determination?

Because I don't look like your prototypical mess that might occur from a lifetime of abuse, it does not mean I don't struggle. Because I look like I have my shit together does not mean I always feel like I have my shit together. Because I manage my addictions well so that my rock bottom is much higher than someone else's rock bottom, it does not mean my rock bottom feels any better or worse. Rock bottom is rock bottom.

Another part of this equation is that my abuser made restitution—not willingly but voluntarily and in good faith once his feet were held to the fire. I was compensated significantly and went on to build a beautiful life with that compensation.

What I did with that compensation was educate myself through the school of hard knocks. I studied and I researched. I learned through trial and error. My life has been an ongoing scientific experiment. Now, thirty years later, I have my self-accredited PhD in life and a self-accredited master's in high-conflict personalities.

I use my education to improve the lives of those around me. I am a constructive person. I build. I don't destroy. I grow. I change. I improve. I repair. I contribute.

I am not a mess. I have my shit together. To some extent, gaining weight is my way of saying to people, "I am one of you. I don't have my shit together." Then I lose that construct when I lose the weight. "You're right. I'm not one of you. I do have my shit together."

I Am God—God Is Me

Being heavy or being fit are different sides of the same coin, and that coin is not "worthiness." The coin is "physical and mental health." I kept flipping the coin to get the side that proved my worthiness. I was flipping the wrong coin.

Where I found my worthiness was right where I lost it. I was searching outside of myself, where the light was better. Instead, I needed to search inside myself, where the darkness obscured the search but was the actual location where my worthiness got lost. I needed to search in the deep dark corners of my identity. My search and rescue mission is complete now that my worthiness has been recovered.

Shame had my worthiness locked up in a cell. My worthiness was being starved of fuel and attention. Instead, shame stole that fuel and attention and hid the ruse from my awareness.

Once heavy and looking in the mirror caused the shame to flood me, I was able to recognize it. I was able to identify it. Once my worthiness was recovered, shame was out of place. The dissonance became about "why is shame here?" Shame does not belong here.

Remember how I begged God to take the pain away when Jeff left? Remember how the pain eventually went away? Not because God did the work, but because I did. The concept of God was just there to support me in the monumental efforts necessary to restore my worthiness after Jeff left.

That work paid off. Once shame was flooding me when I looked in the mirror at my heavy body, I called shame in for questioning. I interrogated shame as the sneaky grinch that stole my worthiness. Shame apologized and left.

Obviously, that didn't really happen, but that is how I picture it. I had a dream the other night that had my stepdad in it. I walked into a bathroom, and he was on the floor mangled and a mess. He stood up and said, slurring, "Were you worried about me?"

I was not worried about him. I was going in to use the bathroom for something shameful. I remember feeling ashamed in the dream. When I woke up, I realized that shame was his, not mine. He was a disaster. His delusional question about being worried about him was strangely cathartic.

No, I was not worried about you, Bill. I was coming in to use the bathroom. I stumbled across your mess of a mind and body. I wasn't looking for you, but I found you. You're welcome.

It was his shame killing him, not me. I'm not worried about him, but I am worried about me. I am letting his shame kill me. That is what I am worried about.

My body is not healthy. When I am this overweight, I am less concerned about how it looks and hugely concerned about my health. It is the same kind of anxiety I had when I was pregnant. My anxiety is off the charts that I am going to die because I am overweight.

I believe this is a survival mechanism. While I have spent my entire life fluctuating heavy and fit, my focus has been on how my body looks. My anxiety gets triggered when I'm heavy, which employs shame to do the dirty work. When my body is fit, my shame keeps the bustling factory manufacturing worthiness.

The thing is, worthiness is not something that can be manufactured. It is organic and sustainable all on its own. However, a sense of a higher order of things is necessary for that worthiness to be produced organically and sustainably.

I know that I do not get control over whether I live or die. I only have control over how I live. In my heavy body, I constantly find myself praying to God to not take my life from me, to not leave my children motherless. I'm constantly praying that I don't develop cancer, an aneurysm, or a blood clot of any kind.

In my mind, being overweight is like playing Russian roulette. I have spun that barrel too many times. One of these times, I am going to get the bullet.

However, I know that praying is not going to help me in and of itself. Praying is a passive way to not take responsibility. I know that the praying needs to be followed up with focused hard work and dedication. What will help me is getting to work.

Now that I discovered that shame was sabotaging my efforts, I suspect I will crave taking better care of myself. Shame was forcing me to listen to other people's judgments of me. Now others can think what they want; it doesn't affect me.

Now people can't tell me I'm not an alcoholic just because I have my shit together. I can regulate my drinking, and I'm smart enough to outsmart the alcohol. I'm not letting it ruin my life or be a cause for suffering. I am an alcoholic, and no one can take that away from me.

I've gotten to acceptance of the catastrophic losses I've had. My catastrophic losses don't look like losing someone to actual death. Instead, my catastrophic losses were of things I never had. I never had a mother or father that took compassionate care of me. I had to accept these losses even though I never had them to begin with.

I had a stepdad that gave me unwanted sexual attention. While the sexual attention was unwanted, I desperately needed the attention of a caring adult. This was not a one-size-fits-all or a one-size-fits-most kind of caring. This was a custom-fit any-caring-will-do kind of caring.

This was the kind of caring that pointed my compass north. The way a compass works is that opposite poles attract, and every magnet has both a north and south pole. A compass detects the Earth's natural magnetic fields. Magnets are amazing science. Again, there must be a higher order to this universe.

At any rate, the kind of adult caring I was receiving was a frigid north pole. Eventually, I figured that out. It was not the direction I wanted to go. All I knew was that if my compass was pointing north, I needed to walk in a different direction. So I did.

Now I have ended up here, where I have recognized that I have been carrying the shame of another. Where I have recognized that there must be a higher order to this universe that I am trying to understand. Where I have found God, and God is me.

Who else made all this happen? I didn't ask to be born into this life. This is the life I got. What I have done with it is make it work for me and make it work for the people I serve. I serve my children, my clients, and the people I care about.

The shame that I used to identify as "profound loneliness" was not wrong. It was profound loneliness because I didn't have my authentic self. I didn't have me, so I was in search of fulfilling that profound loneliness with someone else. I have come to find out the only piece that fit was finding me.

It took determining that I'm an alcoholic and that doesn't make me a bad person. Alcoholism is a part of my authenticity. How I manage my alcoholism is also part of my authenticity. Being a high achiever is another part of my authenticity. It was born of stress, but look at what stress does to coal. It makes diamonds.

Being heavy and being fit are both parts of my authenticity. Being heavy is my way of fitting in. Being fit is my way of standing out. I will settle on my authentic body type when it is no longer about what it looks like and becomes aligned with who I am. When my body weight is no longer a reflection of my internal struggle and is instead a genuine reflection of how I feel about myself. When my internal struggle is no longer a struggle—it is a snuggling up of me to who I am.

I am in recovery, and I will always be recovering my authenticity from the rubble of these losses. This is my first step into the arena in a significantly meaningful way. I have found my authenticity, and I have shared it with you. Thank you for allowing me into your life, and thank you for listening.

What an amazing gift I have been given in this lifetime. I don't understand it, and I am trying to. I am grateful all the same.

About the Author

Amy Hart is a fifty-one-year-old single mother of many. She raised or contributed to raising many of the adults in her life along with their children, her own biological children, and many dogs. Being a mother is her native genius, and she has a self-accredited PhD in life along with self-accredited master's degrees in conflict resolution and personality disorders.

She also accredits herself with being a professional therapy client. Teasing apart the conflict and sources of conflict in her life required twenty years of therapy two to three times a week. She continues to participate regularly in group therapy and individual therapy as needed to continue her recovery work. Through therapy, she has become a professional problem solver in her own life.

Amy discovered that conflict resolution is her passion when she became a professional mediator. Assisting others in resolving conflict has led to meaningful connections and satisfying resolutions. Amy provides mediation in many small-claims courts and has a private practice focused on divorce and parenting plans.

Writing became a passion for Amy early in her recovery process. She discovered that writing was extraordinarily therapeutic and cathartic. She then spent eight years writing to the men in her life in an effort to help them get their shit together. In 2020, she wrote *Recovery Sucks* to reach a broader audience that may actually want to hear what she has to say.

Printed in the USA
CPSIA information can be obtained
at www.ICGtesting.com
LVHW040617290723
753521LV00019B/60